FUNDAMENTALISM
in
American Religion
1880 - 1950

A forty-five-volume facsimile series
reproducing often extremely rare material
documenting the development of one of the
major religious movements of our time

■ *Edited by*
Joel A. Carpenter
Billy Graham Center, Wheaton College
■ *Advisory Editors*
Donald W. Dayton,
Northern Baptist Theological Seminary
George M. Marsden,
Duke University
Mark A. Noll,
Wheaton College
Grant Wacker,
University of North Carolina

A GARLAND SERIES

■ Fundamentalist versus Modernist
The Debates between John Roach Straton and Charles Francis Potter

Edited by
Joel A. Carpenter

Garland Publishing, Inc.
New York & London 1988

For a list of the titles in this series, see the final pages of this volume.
The facsimile of *The Battle Over the Bible* is from a copy in the library
of the Yale Divinity School, and that of *Was Christ both God and Man*
is from a copy in the Denver Conservatory; those of *Evolution versus
Creation*, and *The Virgin Birth, Fact or Fiction?* are from
copies in the Moody Bible Institute.

Library of Congress Cataloging-in-Pubication Data

Straton, John Roach, 1875-1929.
  Fundamentalist versus modernist : the debates between John Roach
  Stratton and Charles Franis Potter ; edited by Joel A. Carpenter.
    p. cm. — (Fundamentalism in American religion, 1880-1950)
  The Battle over the Bible — Evolution versus creation — The
  Virgin birth—fact or fiction? — Was Christ both God and man.
  ISBN 0-8240-5028-2 (alk. paper)
  1. Modernist-fundamentalist controversy. I. Potter, Charles
  Francis, 1885-1962. II. Carpenter, Joel A. III. Title.
  IV. Series.
  BT82.3.S76 1988
  273'.9—dc19   88-11231
                                                           CIP

BT
82.3
.S76
1988

Design by Valerie Mergentime
Printed on acid-free, 250-year-life paper
Manufactured in the United States of America

CONTENTS

- *The Battle Over the Bible*

- *Evolution versus Creation*

- *The Virgin Birth
  — Fact or Fiction ?*

- *Was Christ Both God and Man*

EDITOR'S NOTE

■ These debates, which took place in 1923–1924, were the most highly publicized events of the fundamentalist-modernist controversy before the Scopes Trial. John Roach Straton (1875–1929) was the pastor of Calvary Baptist Church in New York City and a fundamentalist spokesman of national reputation. A series of fundamentalist rallies held at Straton's church so annoyed Charles Francis Potter (1885–1962), a distinguished New York Unitarian pastor, that he challenged Straton to debate. Held before capacity audiences (three of them at Carnegie Hall), broadcast live on radio, and receiving major coverage in the press, these contests put the issues dividing modernists and fundamentalists squarely before the American public.

J.A.C.

THE BATTLE OVER
THE BIBLE

First in the Series of
Fundamentalist-Modernist Debates

between

Rev. JOHN ROACH STRATON, D.D.
PASTOR, CALVARY BAPTIST CHURCH
NEW YORK

and

Rev. CHARLES FRANCIS POTTER, M.A., S.T.M.
MINISTER, WEST SIDE UNITARIAN CHURCH
NEW YORK

NEW GDH YORK
GEORGE H. DORAN COMPANY

THE BATTLE OVER THE BIBLE
—C—
PRINTED IN THE UNITED STATES OF AMERICA

INTRODUCTION

By Rev. John Roach Straton, D.D.

When Rev. Charles F. Potter, Pastor of the West Side Unitarian Church, New York, challenged me to this series of debates on the great fundamental questions of religion, I promptly accepted his challenge. As to the desirability and value of religious debates there can scarcely be any division of opinion. The Bible enjoins us to "be ready always to give an answer to every man that asketh you a reason of the hope that is in you." (I Peter 3:15); and we are further exhorted to "contend earnestly for the faith which was once for all delivered unto the saints" (Jude 3). The ancient prophets were constantly debating and contending against error, as witness Elijah on Mount Carmel against the prophets of Baal. The New Testament is full of accounts of debates over the great truths of revealed religion, and periods of discussion and debate of such issues have always been periods of growth in the church. We may well be hopeful, therefore, that great good will finally come out of the widespread religious agitations of today. And certainly it is undeniable that if the great truths of religion cannot stand discussion and vindicate themselves on their merits, then they have no right to claim the allegiance and support of the human race.

The New York newspapers have naturally given much space, for years now, to the revolutionary religious views of the radicals, or "Modernists," as they call themselves. I felt that the debates would give an opportunity to get the other side—the conservative,

v

orthodox, believing side—before the public, and so it is proving.

At the time that Dr. Harry Emerson Fosdick, a Baptist, preached his radical sermon against the Fundamentalists, in which he took the side of the "Liberals" or "Modernists" against the true inspiration and authority of the Bible as God's word, against the Virgin Birth of our Lord, His substitutionary atonement, and His second coming, he also really caricatured the orthodox belief on some of these great questions. I felt, therefore, that he ought to be willing to face in the open a representative of those whose views he had misstated and distorted in the interest of his radical propaganda; and so, as President of our Baptist Fundamentalist League of New York, I challenged him to a series of joint debates on these questions. He declined and excused himself, under circumstances that made me feel that he was really running to cover.

Again, when Dr. W. H. P. Faunce, President of Brown University, a Baptist institution, came out with books and articles in magazines having a world-wide circulation, in which he also expressed views that it seemed to me amounted not only to a repudiation of our age-long Baptist beliefs, but to a denial of the very essentials of evangelical Christianity, I expressed the desire to meet him in debate for a frank public discussion of these vital issues. Nothing came of this either, however, as Dr. Faunce declined even to give the newspaper men an interview over these matters.

When Mr. Potter, therefore, challenged me to debates on these very questions at issue, and said that Drs. Fosdick and Faunce were friends of his, I felt moved to accept his challenge. I am really glad to debate with Mr. Potter because he is an out-and-out Modernist, who is not afraid to show his colors and who does not, like the Modernists within the orthodox ranks, resort to verbal ambiguities and the use of religious language with a double meaning. He calls a spade a spade, and is honest in his beliefs, or, perhaps I should say, his unbeliefs. I think, too, that it will be most useful for the public to read just what Mr. Potter says in these debates, because it will demonstrate to all people just what Modernism is and just how radical and revolutionary are its views.

I am frank to say that I have no respect for the radicals in the Protestant denomination who insist on staying inside and tearing down the faith of the church while they still eat the bread of the church! I cannot regard them as either consistent, courageous or honest men. Robert Ingersoll was, in the beginning, a son of the church; but when he lost his faith he had the fairness and courage to step out of the ranks and carry on his propaganda on a self-supporting platform of his own making. Therefore, while deploring and even execrating his views one could, nevertheless, respect the man for his consistency and honesty.

I, therefore, though pained by his views, nevertheless respect Mr. Potter because when he lost his faith in Baptist and evangelical views of religion he left the Baptist church and joined the Unitarians. He did exactly the right thing, and while, therefore, there can be absolutely no religious fellowship between us, I can still strike hands with him as an honest human being and debate with him the great religious issues that divide us today.

I feel, too, as a Baptist, some sense of responsibility for Mr. Potter, since he is a product of one of our oldest Baptist universities and one of our most famous Baptist theological seminaries. But Mr. Potter was honest enough to step out when he could no longer conscientiously walk with the Baptists.

Because of this honesty and other lovable traits, I have hopes that through these discussions Mr. Potter may be led to see his errors and come back to the faith.

In the meantime, I am happy to be able to say that there were several conversions during the first debate, the printed form of which follows in this little book. I have had the great joy of baptizing and welcoming into Calvary Church some of those who were won at the debate. This encouraging fact makes me the more willing to do the extra work necessary in connection with these discussions. It also proves again that God's word will not return unto Him void, but that it will accomplish that whereunto He has sent it, even as His blessed promise is.

JOHN ROACH STRATON

Study of Calvary Baptist Church,
  New York City.

INTRODUCTION

By Rev. Charles Francis Potter, M.A., S.T.M.

The first of these debates has vindicated debating as the proper vehicle for conveying religious messages to the people. The church was crowded and many were turned away. The newspapers of the English speaking world 'front-paged" the debate the next day in a very fair and complete fashion. Thousands of people at home "listened in" on the radio.

Dr. Straton claims "conversions" on his side. On mine I have had adequate evidence of a most convincing nature that people are eager to hear the modern interpretation of religion, which has not always been made accessible to them. They want to hear both sides and then judge for themselves, and these debates make that possible.

Charles Francis Potter

*Study of West Side Unitarian Church,
New York City.*

CONTENTS

I

FOR THE AFFIRMATIVE*

Question.

RESOLVED THAT THE BIBLE IS THE INFALLIBLE WORD OF GOD

"Bring me the book!" exclaimed Sir Walter Scott on his death-bed. "What book?" asked Lockhart, his son-in-law. And the greatest literary genius of the Scottish people turned his eyes upon him and answered gently "There is but one book! Bring that!" Lockhart understood and handed him the Bible.

We are to deal with that book in this debate.

I come to this discussion with a certain degree of pleasure, because it gives me an opportunity to say a good word for the Bible. I am much indebted to it, as it has been the greatest formative influence in my life. My father was a Scotchman before he became an American, and he had the old-time devotion of the Scotch for the Scriptures. I was reared, therefore, on a mixed but well-balanced diet of oatmeal, Bible precepts, and hickory switch. It is not a bad combination as a developer of youth.

I think that the earliest memory of my life is the picture in my father's home where, every morning and every evening, he gathered the family around the wide-mouthed fireplace for the family worship. Father sat at one end of the circle and mother at the other, and the children and the servants in between, and father read to us from the Bible, and then sent up to the Throne of Heaven a fervent prayer, either of thanksgiving for blessings received or petitions for the needs of the new day. The last words

*First speech for the affirmative by Rev. John Roach Straton, DD., Pastor of Calvary Baptist Church.

13

that my sainted mother uttered were a quotation from the Bible, and in a time of recent bereavement that fell into our present home, when my wife and I had to say the long good-bye to our only daughter—a precious child of twelve and a half years—the teachings of the Bible were our only comfort and stay.

In this day, therefore, when so many preachers even are criticising the Bible and tearing it to pieces, I am glad of an opportunity to say a good word for the old Book. It has proved itself a true and tried friend. I have often put it to the test, and it has never failed me. To me it is God's word, and it has proved itself infallible. So it has one honest vote to begin with.

The way in which the subject for debate is stated, "RESOLVED THAT THE BIBLE IS THE IN-FALLIBLE WORD OF GOD," assumes the existence of a living God, capable of revealing Himself to men through a book. In championing the affirmative of this question, I do not, therefore, have to argue the existence of God.

I begin merely by pointing out a reasonable presupposition, namely, that God would necessarily reveal Himself to men. Can you conceive of a king undertaking to rule an earthly country without prescribing laws for his subjects? If such a thing would be unreasonable in an earthly king, then how completely absurd is the thought that the King of Heaven would not provide an adequate code of laws and directing principles for His subjects in this wonderful world of ours?

The thought of God leaving either His vast material or moral universe to drift without law and without intelligent direction is a thought which, upon its face, is so impossible that it is unthinkable to an intelligent mind. It is not remarkable, therefore, that we have a revelation from God. It would be far more remarkable if we did not have such a revelation.

Consequently, the only real issue before us is the question whether the Bible is that revelation. If the Bible is the final and complete revelation from a wise, powerful, holy and loving God, then it must be infallible and authoritative, and with that established, the affirmative has won.

I ask you, now, in the beginning of our thought together, to consider with me a group of facts, entirely outside the Bible's claims about itself, which seem to indicate that it is a book so absolutely unique that it cannot be accounted for on any ground other than that it is an infallible revelation from the living God. The first of these facts is:

I—THE FACT OF THE BIBLE'S MIRACULOUS PRESERVATION AND INCREASE

Now no one can deny that the Bible is here. It is an objective reality and not a subjective idea. Here it is! I hold a copy of it in my hand. It has not only existed for thousands of years, but it has existed in the face of efforts of all sorts to destroy it. Not only has it been subjected to the vicissitudes of fortune and the catastrophes of history that have utterly destroyed other valuable books, which were former treasures of the human race, but calculated and definite steps have been taken from time to time to wipe it utterly from the earth. Toustal bought and burned the whole of Tyndal's first edition, but he utterly failed to destroy the Book or to prevent its circulation. Tyndal took the money from this first edition and with it printed a far larger edition, and the Bibles were shipped into Old England wrapped up in bales of cloth, in barrels and kegs, and even in coffins used as packing cases! It is said that in one century 150,000 people were butchered for reading the Bible. The jailer's key, the headman's ax, the rope of the gallows, the fagot of the bigot, the powder of the poisoner, the dagger of the assassin have all combined in the effort to annihilate it.

Intellectual pride, too, has often rejected it because of the vanity of man's mind; and infidelity has battled against it with a relentlessness worthy of a better cause and a malignity unmatched elsewhere in the dark realm of prejudice, hatred and spite. What has the result been? Always victory for this venerable and noble old Book! It has successfully resisted the sophistries of Hume, the misguided eloquence of Gibbon, the rationalism of Rousseau, the ignorant blasphemies of Thomas Paine, the satirical mockery of Voltaire, the idle quibbling of Strauss, the shallow witticisms of Renan, the cheap buffoonery of Bob Ingersoll, the audacious assaults of the Communists of France, and the insidious duplicity of the rationalistic theologians of Prussianized Germany. As with Moses's bush, the Bible has burned, but it has not been consumed. Phoenix-like, it has risen from its ashes to new heights of usefulness and power.

500,000,000 BIBLES

In the 18th century the great French infidel, Voltaire, prophesied that, within a hundred years from the time when he wrote, the Bible would be an obsolete book. He declared that it would go entirely out of circulation and that it would be found only as a curio on the shelves of antiquarians. As a striking comment on this prophecy stands the fact that the house where Voltaire wrote it is now owned and used as a storehouse by the French Bible Society, and the very walls that looked down on the

sneering sceptic as he penned his prophecy are now literally lined with hundreds of Bibles!

One of the most remarkable facts of modern times is
that the Bible is still the world's "best seller." In some
quarters there is a tendency to discount the Bible in favor
of science, but I would point out the significant fact that
while there is scarcely a scientific text-book that is ten
years old that is not already out of date, the Bible after
all these thousands of years is still doing business at the
old stand! Yes, while a decade usually sees the death
and burial without hope of resurrection of the average
text-book or popular "best seller," and while even the
masterpieces of antiquity line the shores of time like
pathetic wrecks, this marvelous old Book lives on from
generation to generation, conquering and to conquer!

How do you account for it?

The rate at which Bibles are now being printed by the
American and British Bible Societies alone represents
an average of one every five seconds, twelve every minute,
720 an hour, 17,280 every day in the year. At the cen-
tennial celebration of these societies in Washington during President Roosevelt's administration—a meeting that
was attended by the President, the British ambassador
and other dignitaries representing the great civilized nations of mankind—facts were given showing that those
two societies had printed and circulated 250,000,000
Bibles in that one hundred years. Let your minds, my
friends, dwell upon that tremendous truth for a moment.
Supposing all of these Bibles should be brought together
at one spot upon the earth's surface. With them you
could construct a skyscraper beside which the Woolworth
Building would dwindle into insignificance. I have estimated that the weight of that number of Bibles was at
least 47,000 tons. To transport them would require a

train 25 miles long drawn by 225 locomotive engines, and if the pages of that number of Bibles were spread out upon the ground they would afford standing room for three times the present population of the earth!

Nor is that all. It is said that there are now at least 500,000,000 Bibles in the world. Averaging them at eight inches high each, it means that if they were laid end to end they would reach almost three times around the earth, and if you piled them up one on top of the other they would reach up 63,131 miles into the air!

Why, now, this marvelous record? What is it that has caused the Bible to live on in perennial youth and ever-increasing power until it has now been translated into over 700 languages and dialects of the earth, and seven-tenths of the children of men can read it in their mother tongue? What is the reason and the secret of it all? Jesus Christ said, "Thy word is truth!" Must that not be the secret of it? It is in the very nature of an error, delusion or lie to destroy itself. The lie carries in its bosom the seed of its own destruction. The poet has well said:

"Truth crushed to earth will rise again,
The eternal years of God are her's;
But error wounded, writhes in pain
And dies among her worshippers."

This old Book has not died, but has lived on and on in ever greater vigor.

Must this not be true because the Bible is the divine and infallible revelation from a wise and loving God? Have not men clung to this old Book because they have found in it the very bread and water of life? And is it not monstrous to suppose that a maze of myths or a cunningly-devised tissue of errors, superstitions and lies could so have gripped the human race?

II—THE FACT OF THE BIBLE'S UNIQUE UNIVERSALITY

Closely akin to what I have just been saying, I wish to call attention next to the fact that the Bible has a quality of universality which stamps it as infallible and divine. The Bible is not for one age, but for all time. Neither is it for one nation, but for every tribe and tongue. It speaks to the man of the twentieth century with the same appealing and compelling power as it did to the man of the first century. It speaks to the universal human heart, and that heart responds to its utterances as it does always instinctively to the voice of truth. Its truths convert the Chinaman or the Hottentot in exactly the same way that they convert the Englishman or the American. This cannot be said of any other of the world's so-called sacred books. The Koran or the Vedas, for example, have no appeal to the universal human mind and heart, but the Bible has, and this fact in itself stamps it as a book apart.

The very difficulties of the Bible constitute a part of this element of universality, and were doubtless, therefore, included deliberately in God's wise and loving plan for revealing Himself to man. The mystery element of the Bible troubles some minds, but mystery is a necessary part of any permanent religion. We are greater than anything which we can fully understand. We have mastered it, and, therefore, we will not worship the thing that we can understand completely, but will pass on and leave it, in the search for something higher. If we could fully explain all the mysteries contained in the Bible we would soon lay it aside. There are problems in nature that constantly challenge scientific faith and effort, and we know that we will never fathom all of the mysteries in this infinite universe. The Bible is a revelation of an infinite God, and so we will never fathom all of its mysteries.

The mystery element is a designed and essential part of the divine revelation. The difficulties, the seeming contradictions about which my opponent will probably speak, the accounts of the miracles, etc., which the Bible contains constitute a constant challenge to interest and faith. It is said that a writer once undertook a compilation of a list of the numerous works written about the Bible, and, having collected the titles of 60,000, he gave up in despair and quit. What other book ever existed about which a hundredth part of this could be said? And today the interest in the Bible is deeper and wider than ever before. The presence of this great crowd of people here at this debate is in itself proof of it. Yes, the best thought of the race is being given to the study of this old Book. It holds the center of interest even for many who do not follow its teachings. But few men study the Vedas or the Koran, but the best scholarship of the human race centers in the study of the Bible. The keenest intellects of all civilized nations, the men of profoundest patience in research, men of supreme genius in the fields of literature, archaeology, language and history are digging down for new treasures of truth in this inexhaustible gold mine. They cross-examine and exhaustively analyze every important word in each Book, and they weigh the meaning and setting of every phrase uttered by prophet or priest or spoken by the Man of Nazareth amid the hills of Judea or beside the limpid waves of Gallilee!

The age-long discussions which have raged about this venerable old volume constitute in themselves a source of its perennial life, and we are seeing already that God is overruling the efforts of modern rationalism and of destructive criticism for His glory and to bring new strength to the Bible. Even the efforts of sceptical critics have but served as the furnace which has purified the gold.

MODERN CRITICISM

Concerning the modern critical difficulties connected with the Bible, a word should be said. We are not to underestimate the part that scholarship plays in our religious interests. Those who love the Bible owe a debt to reverent scholarship which they can never pay. We may be sure, too, that down the ages new light is to break from the sacred page, as the Holy Spirit leads us into all the truth. But it has also become now perfectly evident that much of the criticism of the age has been born of vanity instead of humility, and that its work has been carried forward in the spirit of doubt rather than that of devotion.

In opposing the destructive criticism those who love the Bible are not opposing the search after truth. All should desire the truth from whatever quarter it may come. But the sober second thought of the world is coming to see that the methods of the destructive critics are, for the most part, unfair, vain and presumptuous to an astounding degree. These men complain of "dogma," and yet they themselves are the greatest dogmatists that the world has ever seen. And they dogmatize, too, not on the authority of a Divine revelation that has justified its claim for centuries, but only on their own hypotheses, theories and beliefs of what they think ought to be right. They are working on the assumption that the theories of evolution are true, and that they apply to the Bible, and they strain every point and even manufacture evidence when necessary to try to prove their theories. The book of Dr. Reginald Campbell of London on "The New Theology" is a conspicuous example of this truth.

One other illustration will suffice. Wellhausen asserted flatly that Moses could not have written the Pentateuch, because in the age of Moses society was very crude and writing, if known at all, was known only by a few! Therefore, he concluded that the idea of a carefully elaborated code of written laws coming under such circumstances and at such a time was unthinkable. On this dogmatic assumption Wellhausen proceeded to erect a mighty fort from which to bombard the battlements of revealed truth. A few years after he wrote, however, the "Code of Hammurabi" was discovered. Here we have an elaborate code of written laws, coming from the same part of the world in which Moses lived, and antedating the time of the Hebrew lawgiver by hundreds of years.

Thus, position after position of the critics has been overthrown and destroyed, and they are everywhere on the defensive today. In Germany, the home of scepticism and criticism, as well as in England and America, we see the plain signs of a conservative reaction, which is to usher in a new era of faith and devotion to the Bible.

The difficulties of the Bible, as a part of its quality of permanence and universality, also form an inexhaustible storehouse of food for faith. We said before that difficulties and mysteries are an essential part of any true and permanent religion, because if we could see all the way and fully understand everything connected with the religion we would leave it. The highest reach of moral grandeur in the entire Old Testament is that where the servant of God, though suffering in body and sorely bereaved and perplexed, nevertheless exclaims, "Though He slay me, yet will I believe in Him." It is easy to remain loyal when the sailing is clear and smooth, but moral grandeur is developed when we remain loyal even though the way is rough, uncertain and dark. This noble element in human character God has sought to develop, seemingly, by leaving some things dark in His Revelation.

The mere fact that we cannot fully understand all that is in the Bible or fathom its mysteries has kept it as the center of interest and devotion generation after generation. If, therefore, at this hour I had it in my power to clear up every mystery connected with it, and reconcile every alleged contradiction in it, I would leave it absolutely untouched, for the wisdom of God has planned it as it is, and it is sufficient.

III—THE FACT OF THE BIBLE'S REMARKABLE UNITY IN DIVERSITY

The next concrete and understandable fact to which I would invite your attention is the remarkable unity in diversity which characterizes the Bible. This fact, as I shall show, argues that there is but one author of the Book and, of necessity, that this author is God.

We hear from many sides today this assertion: "The Bible is just like any other book." And following this is the assertion that we need to regard it merely as "literature," and to give it its place in the other literatures of the world. But the Bible is not "just like any other book." As well say that a telescope is "just like any other brass!" It is not. True it is brass, but brass in a peculiar relation and shaped for a specific and unusual purpose. The man who uses up his time analyzing it, that he may determine its chemical composition, or who spends his energies in speculations concerning the half-effaced name of its maker, would fail to get any benefit from the telescope, even if he did not completely ruin the instrument. The telescope is not like any other brass, and a man who uses it in the wrong way really abuses it, at the same time that he denies himself a most uplifting and inspiring experience. He might be gazing with rapt vision and leaping heart upon the before unseen glories of the midnight heavens. The critical attitude toward the Bible prevents many a soul from catching through it the visions of eternal glory.

Yes, the Bible is perfectly unique. There is not another book on earth like it, nor is it like any other book. Indeed, it is not one book, but a library of 66 books composed by 40 different writers from all ranks of society, and requiring at least 1,500 years in its composition. It took 20 years to give the world Gibbon's Rome; Clark's Commentary required in its composition 26 years; Webster's Dictionary, 36 years, but it required 1,500 years to produce the Bible; and its authors came from every walk of life. Shepherds, fishermen, priests, warriors, statesmen, husbandmen, kings contributed to it. Amos was a vine dresser; Solomon was an illustrious king; David was a shepherd; Moses was a great statesman; Peter was an unlettered fisherman: Paul was a ripe scholar. Yet throughout this Book there is a marvelous unity. Though it was written by these different men from almost every walk of life, and, though it was 1,500 years in the making, it is, nevertheless, a harmonious whole. One spirit breathes through it all; one great ideal and purpose shines with ever-increasing brightness from its beginning to its end.

Though in 66 divisions, the Bible is one Book. Why? There is but one answer to the question. The answer is because the Holy Spirit of the Living God was the real Author! Suppose that forty-eight men should walk into this church tonight. One man we will say comes from Maine, another from California, another from

Georgia, and so on from each state, each bearing a block of marble of peculiar shape. Suppose I pile up these blocks in order, until I have a beautiful marble statue here, perfectly symmeetrical and faultless in its grace. If then I should ask: "How did these men, whoe have never seen each other before, chisel out that beautiful statue?" You would say: "That is easily explained. One man planned the whole statue, made the patterns, gave the directions, and distributed them around; and so, because each man worked by the pattern, the work fits accurately when completed." Very well. Here is a Book coming from all quarters, written by men of all classes, scattered through a period of fifteen hundred years, and yet this Book is fitted together as a wondrous and harmonious whole. How was it done? "Holy men of God spake as they were moved by the Holy Ghost." One mind inspired the whole Book! One voice speaks in it all! Behind each of the writers, though making use in each case of their individual temperament and style, the Holy Spirit stood down the ages speaking God's message to the needy hearts of sinful and lost men.

"Whence but from heaven could men unskilled in arts,
In several ages, born in several parts,
Weave such agreeing truths? Or how or why
Should all conspire to cheat us with a lie?
Unasked their pains, ungrateful their advice,
Starving their gains, and martyrdom their price."

The Bible is a glorious temple of truth, with its broad foundations in Genesis, its majestic columns rising in the record of patriarch prophet and priest, its roof-tree in the Gospels of Jesus Christ, and its majestic dome in the Revelation of a New Heaven and New Earth wherein will dwell righteousness. The miraculous unity in diversity of this Book argues conclusively to the thoughtful mind the oneness and divinity of its origin and, therefore, its infallibility.

IV—THE STRIKING FACT OF THE BIBLE'S FULFILLED
PROPHECIES

There is another most conclusive proof of the divine origin and infallibility of the Bible, and that is fulfilled prophecy. Prophecy is the foretelling of events before they happen, and only God can do that as it requires omniscience, and God speaks, therefore, through the prophets. Amos said: "Surely the Lord Jehovah will do nothing except He reveal His secret unto His servants the prophets." (Amos 3:7.) And in the Acts of the Apostles it is written: "God hath spoken by the mouth of all His holy prophets since the world began." (Acts 3:21.)

God Himself, through the Book, challenges us to faith in it because of fulfilled prophecy. He says: "I am God, and there is none like Me; declaring the end from the beginning, and from ancient times the things that are not yet done." (Isaiah 46:9-10.)

And even Christ based His claims to faith and obedience upon the correctness of His prophecies. He said: "I tell you before it come to pass, that, when it is come to pass, ye may believe that I am He." (John 13:19.)

These Bible prophecies are not like the prophecies of the Delphic oracle, for example, where either one of two events would prove the prophecy, as in the answer the oracle made to one of the old kings that if he crossed a certain river with his army "it would bring about the destruction of a great nation." But either his nation or that of his foes might have been meant. The Bible prophecies are not like that. They are specific. They are so explicit and definite that they all but take one's breath away, and their fulfillment has been so remarkable that one thoughtful mind has said that "prophecy is the mold of history." Listen to just a few of them, by way of illustration:

Assyria, with its proud city of Nineveh, flourished in Zephaniah's day, yet he prophesied its utter destruction by God. This prophecy was literally fulfilled, and Nineveh has lain in desolation for ages, her very site forgotten for centuries. (Zeph. 2:13-15.)

Again, God speaking through Ezekiel prophesied not only destruction for ancient Tyre, but certain peculiar things about it that are most striking in their literal fulfillment. Listen to God's prophecy spoken through Ezekiel. He said:

"Behold, I am against thee, O Tyrus, and will cause many nations to come up against thee, as the sea causeth his waves to come up. And they shall destroy the walls of Tyrus, and break down her towers: I will also scrape her dust from her, and make her like the top of a rock. . . . And they shall make a spoil of thy riches, and make a prey of thy merchandise: and they shall break down thy walls, and destroy thy pleasant houses; and they shall lay thy stones and thy timber and thy dust in the midst of the water. . . . And I will make thee like the top of a rock: thou salt be a place to spread nets upon; thou shalt be built no more; for I the Lord have spoken it, saith the Lord God" (Ezek. 26:3, 4, 12, 14).

Here was the prophecy. Was it fulfilled? Yes, literally, in every detail. First came Nebuchadnezzar and took the city and spoiled it. The old city lay in ruins. The remaining inhabitants moved away to an island half a mile from shore, and there built a new city. Then came Alexander the Great, who besieged the new Tyre built on the island. He planned to attack the city by building a causeway from the mainland through the half mile of sea to the island.   To build this causeway, Alexander took the walls and towers, and timbers and the ruins of ancient Tyre's palaces and literally laid them "in the midst of the water."   So great was the demand for material that the mounds of ruins from the ancient city and even the "dust" was craped from the rocks and laid in the sea!   So it became literally "like the top of a rock . . . a place to spread nets upon."   And Tyre's history stands today as a dramatic monument to the infallible truthfulness of the Bible.

Take, again, the case of Babylon.   Jeremiah and Isaiah alike prophesied that that mighty empire, then in the heyday of its glory, would be utterly destroyed.   It would cease to exist, be forgotten, mould into dust, and be desolate forever.   God said through Isaiah:

"And Babylon, the glory of kingdoms, the beauty of the Chaldeans' pride, shall be as when God overthrew Sodom and Gomorrah.   It shall never be inhabited, neither shall it be dwelt in from generation to generation; neither shall the Arabian pitch tent there; neither shall shepherds make their flocks to lie down there.   But wild beasts of the desert shall lie there; and their houses shall be full of doleful creatures; and ostriches shall dwell there, and wild goats shall dance there.   And wolves shall cry in their castles, and jackals in the pleasant palaces.   I will also make it a possession for the porcupine, and pools of water, and I will sweep it with the besom of destruction, saith Jehovah of hosts."   (Isaiah 13:19-22, 14-21.)

These prophecies have been marvelously fulfilled. Jeremiah prophesied about Babylon that its destruction would be so complete that "they shall not take of thee a stone for a corner, nor a stone for foundations." (Jeremiah 51.)   Mr. Rassam remarks upon the fact that the natives living near the site of ancient Babylon use the *bricks* for building purposes, but always burn the *stone* thus discovered for lime, which fact wonderfully fulfills the divine words of Jeremiah. And as to the literal fulfillment of Isaiah's prophecy, it is worthy of note that he knew thousands of years before our days that the Arabs would survive even down to modern times as a nomadic people, still living in tents. Furthermore, observers have commented again and again on the number of wild beasts, reptiles and insect pests that abound among the ruins of ancient Babylon; and Rawlinson, in his well-known book on "EGYPT AND BABYLON" (page 206), says:

"On the actual ruins of Babylon the Arabian neither pitches his tent nor pastures his flocks, in the first place, because the nitrous soil produces no pasture to tempt him; secondly, because an evil reputation attaches to the entire site, which is thought to be the haunt of evil spirits."

I would like to ask why have not the Rationalists and the infidels, whether in the church or out, who are so eager to disprove God's word, gone and inhabited Babylon? God's fulfilled prophecies on multiplied millions of Bible pages stand a challenge to them to prove that the verdict passed on Babylon is untrue!

So I might go on for hours tracing out before you the prophecies of the Bible and their amazing, literal fulfillments. I might cite the case of Egypt, about which Ezekiel prophesied, not that it would become desolate and uninhabited as in the case of Tyre, Nineveh, Babylon, etc., but that it would become forever a subject nation, and so it has been. I might cite the marvelous prophecies of Daniel about the world empires that followed his day.

I might cite to you the prophecies concerning Israel, or, as we call them, the Jews. Quite wonderfully, every part of their history was foretold: their prosperity and greatness when they obeyed God, their decline and expulsion from their own land, when they disobeyed Him, their tragic and unparalleled sufferings, persecutions and sorrows, and yet their miraculous preservation, their multiplication in numbers, wealth and power, and finally their restoration to their own land, and glory to them and all mankind through their final obedience to God when Christ comes back again. Already in the "Zionist movement" we are seeing enacted before our very eyes the beginning of the fulfillment of the prophecies concerning their return to Palestine.

Listen to but one of these ancient prophecies: In Deuteronomy, the 28th chapter, it is written:

"And Jehovah will scatter thee among all peoples, from the one end of the earth even unto the other end of the earth. . . . And among these nations shalt thou find no ease, and there shall be no rest for the sole of thy foot. . . . And thy life shall hang in doubt before thee; and thou shalt fear night and day and shalt have no assurance of thy life." (Deut. 28:64-66.)

This has been literally and tragically fulfilled. There is nothing in all history so pathetic and so terrible as the history of the Jews. Two millions were killed or starved to death or sold into slavery worse than death in A.D. 70. Over half a million more were slaughtered by the Romans sixty years later. Other millions have tragically perished in Poland, Italy, Russia and other lands. Even here in free, democratic America thoughtful Jews have had to express their apprehension for the future, in the light of Henry Ford's propaganda and such movements as the Ku Klux Klan. No wonder that Milman says, in his "History of the Jews":

"Massacred by thousands, yet, springing up again from their undying stock, the Jews appear at all times and in all regions. Their perpetuity, their national immortality, is at once the most curious problem to the political inquirer; to the religious man a subject of profound and awful admiration." (Page 398, Vol. 2.)

Frederick the Great once said to his Chaplain that if his religion was true he ought to be able to prove it in one word. He demanded that he so prove it, and his Chaplain said: "Yes, sire, it is provable in one word— *Israel!*" If there were no other proof of the divine origin and infallibility of the Bible would stand proved forever by its fulfilled prophecies about the Jews!

And what shall we say about the prophecies connected with Jesus Christ Himself? Think, first, of the many prophecies about His coming to this earth, even including details as to place and miraculous manner of birth, as to His mother, the deeds of His life, the peculiar and most unusual incidents of His death and burial and resurrection, all of which were literally and exactly fulfilled. And think of the prophecies that Christ Himself uttered, and how they have been fulfilled. Though its golden beauty was still sparkling before their eyes, He prophesied to the men of His own day that the Temple would be utterly destroyed, and that not one stone of it would be left upon another. Amazing, yet it was literally fulfilled! At a time when Rome was mistress of the world, He foresaw the break-up of her power and prophesied not that nations would rise against Rome, but that "nation shall rise against nation, and kingdom against Kingdom." The political history of the world, He said, was not to be one Kingdom ruling all, or nations rising against that empire, but numbers of nations and Kingdoms, all in strife and warfare against each other. In the light of those prophecies, we can but stand in awe and wonder as we read in the pages of history the unending movements of kingdom against kingdom and nation against nation for these two thousand years.

Christ prophesied the history of His church, its trials, sufferings and sorrows and yet its glories and its final victories. And all of this has been fulfilled and is being fulfilled before our very eyes.

Christ and the apostle John prophesied that near the end of the age, the Gospel would be preached "to every nation, and kindred, and tongue, and people" on the face of the globe. (Matt. 24:12; Rev. 14:6.) At the time the prophecy was uttered its fulfillment seemed an impossibility. Only the invention of printing and the consequent increase in the number of Bibles made it possible. Yet the prediction was made, and Paul and other apostles proceeded to act as if they believed that an impossibility would be accomplished. It has been accomplished, and we have seen it in our day. While there are many thousands of other books in the world, how does it happen that not one of them has been translated into one-twentieth as many languages as the Bible? And how did those ancient prophets know that this would be the case?

In the light of all this, may we not see the absolute infallibility of God's word? And may we not know that Jesus spoke only the truth when He said: "Heaven and earth shall pass away, but my words shall not pass away!"

V—THE FACT OF THE BIBLE'S OWN CLAIMS CONCERNING
ITSELF

This leads me now to point out the fact that the Bible claims to be the word of God, and, therefore, it claims infallibility. It boldly states its own right to instruct and lead the children of men. I designedly bring this argument late in the discussion. I did not argue in the beginning that the Bible was the revelation of God because it said it was. I have marshalled the facts from the outside first. But now, in the light of those facts, I make bold to introduce the Bible that it may speak for itself. What does it claim for itself? Almost on every page the claim of its divine origin and infallibility is either implied or asserted. To be sure, it does not elaborate any formal theory of inspiration or infallibility, and yet inspiration and infallibility are implied from one end of it to the other. All through the Bible run such expressions as "Thus saith the Lord," etc. This phrase, "Thus saith the Lord," or its equivalent, is used in the Old Testament fully two thousand times.

Allow me to give you now a few of such expressions, taken almost at random from among the many that might be quoted.

In the case of Moses we are told that,

"God spake these words" (Exod. 20:1).

"And Moses wrote all the words of the Lord" (Exod. 24:4); and in repeating them to the children of Israel he was able to say, "these are the words which the Lord hath commanded" (Ex. 35:1).

David said, "The Spirit of the Lord spake by me, and His word was in my tongue (2 Sam. 23:2).

Isaiah said, "Hear, O heavens, and give ear, O earth, for the Lord has spoken." And he refers to his writings as the words of the Lord "at least twenty times."

Isaiah said, again, "To the law and to the testimony: if they speak not according to this word, it is because there is no light in them." (Isa. 8:20.)

Jeremiah, over one hundred times in his writings, said, "The Word of the Lord came unto me." (Jer. 1:4.)

Ezekiel wrote: "The Word of the Lord came expressly unto Ezekiel." (Ezek. 1:3.) He used such expressions sixty times.

Daniel tells us he received his message in vision. (Dan. 7:1); and from the lips of Gabriel (Dan. 9:21.)

Amos says he wrote "the words . . . which he saw concerning Israel," etc. (Am. 1:1.)

John says what he writes is "the Revelation of Jesus Christ, which God gave unto him." (Rev. 1:1.)

When Jeremiah was first inspired he seemed for the moment quite unconscious of the fact, so that God had actually to tell Him—"Behold, I have put My words in thy mouth." (Jer. 1:9.)

Peter said, "For the prophecy came not in old time by the will of man; but holy men of God spake as they were moved by the Holy Ghost." (2 Pet. 1:21.)

Paul said, "For this cause also thank we God without ceasing, because, when ye received the word of God which ye heard of us, ye received it not as the word of men, but as it is in truth, the word of God, which effectually worketh also in you that believe." (1 Thes. 2:13.) And the great classical text still stands:

"All scripture is given by inspiration of God, and is profitable for doctrine for reproof, for correction, for instruction in righteousness." (2 Tim. 3:16.)

These new Testament utterances concerning the inspiration and infallibility of scripture refer, for the most part, to the old Testament, and thus declare its full inspiration and authority. But the New Testament makes for itself the same claim. The Gospels are full of internal claims to be the inspired record of the Son of God when He was in the flesh. The Book of Acts is avowedly the history of the Holy Spirits work in and through the early churches. The book of Revelation explicitly claims to be just what its name implies, a real revelation from God. That leaves, then, only the epistles to be accounted for. Fourteen of these epistles are from the pen of Paul. He declares explicitly and repeatedly that what he writes is not of man but of God, and that it is to be received "not as the word of man, but, as it is in truth, the Word of God." (1 Thes. 2:13.) To the Galatians he wrote: "But I certify you, brethren, that the gospel which was preached of me is not after man. For I neither received it of man, neither was I taught it, but by the revelation of Jesus Christ." (Galatians 1:11-12.) And so again and again he repeated.

What he testifies of his own writings, Paul equally affirms of the writings of the other apostles. In his letter to the Ephesians he says truth not heretofore known has now been revealed to the "holy apostles and prophets by the Spirit." (Eph. 3:5.) In this he is in accord with the Son of God, who assured these very apostles that when they should speak (and therefore when they should write) it would not be themselves, but, as he said, "the Spirit of your Father which speaketh in you." (Matt. 10:20.)

Without hesitation it may be said the Apostle Paul claims full inspiration for the writings of Peter, James, John and Jude as made by the Spirit in and to them. The Apostle Peter, speaking not only for himself, but in the name of the other apostles, gives an added testimony to the inspiration of Paul's epistles. He says: "Even as our beloved brother Paul also according to the wisdom given unto him, hath written unto you; as also in all his epistles, speaking in them of these things; in which are some things hard to be understood, which they that are unlearned and unstable wrest, as they do also *the other scriptures,* unto their own destruction." (2 Pet. 3:15, 16.)

This is an unequivocal declaration by Peter that the writings of Paul are to be received upon the same authority as "the other Scriptures" of Israel; and it is this same Apostle Peter who, speaking of the inspiration of the Old Testament, says the men who wrote it "spake as they were moved by the Holy Ghost." (2 Pet. 1:21.) It is he who also declares that the spirit of Christ was in them as the source and inspiration of their testimony, leading them to write "beforehand the sufferings of

Christ, and the glory that should follow." (1 Pet. 1:11.)

Thus, it is plain that the entire New Testament claims to be the inspired and infallible Word of God.

Jesus Christ has left His record as to His faith in the Bible as the infallible Word of God. He prayed the Father and said: "Sanctify them through thy truth; thy Word is truth." He was constantly speaking of "the scriptures," and He said "the Scriptures cannot be broken." Indeed He proclaimed Himself to be the theme of all scriptures. On the walk to Emmaus and in the upper room at Jerusalem He announces that He Himself is the unique key to the understanding of the Bible, and there we may well let the matter rest. We can only exclaim, like that distressed disciple of old, "Lord, to whom shall we go? Thou hast the words of eternal life." (Compare Luke 24:13-35 and 36-49.)

Here, then, is the Bible's testimony concerning itself. The old Book comes into court with a good reputation as it makes these claims for itself. In the light of the wonderful record of its influence and its power, which I have tried to bring to your attention, I wish to ask who will dare to impeach it? Who will dare rise up in the face of this noble record and say that this old Book is a liar?

VI—THE FACT OF THE BIBLE'S SELF-AUTHENTICATING
AUTHORITY

If, now, the Bible is truly the Word of God, then it is infallible and should be received as a final self-authenticating authority. There must be in every field of human activity and interest some court of last appeal. It is true in the scientific world. Though the human consciousness continues to play a great part, and the activity of the human mind in the discovery, analysis and classification of new facts goes forward constantly in the science of

FOR THE AFFIRMATIVE   37

mathematics and in every other science, there are, nevertheless, final and axiomatic principles and truths which
can never be transcended and which stand, therefore, as
ultimate authority. A straight line is forever the shortest distance between two points and twice two will make
four to the end of time.

In medicine the need of authority exists. While the
different schools of medicine vary among themselves and
are constantly developing and perfecting their science,
there are, nevtrtheless, great general principles of healing and established facts underlying them all. While the
individual consciousness and skill of a given doctor has
a large room for play, his talents are, nevertheless, cir-
cumscribed by the things that are established, and that
are true forever. Let every doctor begin practicing
medicine according to his own whim and impulse, and
the undertaker and manufacturer of tombstones would
become speedily the most prosperous citizens in the community!

In the law there must be a seat of final authority and
a court of last appeal. While the law is a science that
is progressing, still, there are, nevertheless, a group of
principles and truths that are established and that are
absolutely final.

The fundamental axioms of the law—the axioms of
justice, equity and righteousness in the relationships between man and his fellows—are irrefutable and unchangeable. The consciousness of the individual does
not create these authoritative standards and principles.
The individual consciousness merely recognizes them as
true when the yare presented, and must act upon them
in obedience unless disaster is to follow.

Upon this truth of authority, therefore, the whole vast
structure of modern civilization is builded.

RELIGIOUS AUTHORITY.

Dare anyone say, then, that in the field of religion, where man's most vital interests for both time and eternity lie, there is no dependable authority, no infallible guide? Shall the highest interests of our natures to be left to caprice and chance? Are we to grope forever in darkness and uncertainty? Are there no fixed standards? No solid and enduring ground on which we can build our individual lives, establish our homes, order our society and found our hopes of Heaven? Is each one of us to be left to believe one thing one day—and that thing perhaps different from everything our neighbors are believing,—and another thing tomorrow, and another thing the next day, and so on and on?

The modernists and the rationalists exalt the individual consciousnes s as the seat of final authority. But this only means that God has been dethroned and man put in His place.

Now, my friends, let us look at it frankly and honestly. We do not wish to be offensive, but we must be loyal to the truth, and the truth is that this whole modern philosophy, when it is logically followed out, leads inevitably not only to atheism but also to anarchy!

A man who becomes a law unto himself and declares that he will do only what he thinks is right and what he wishes to do we call an anarchist. With sober hearts and earnest minds we need to face the question whether this truth does not apply also to the man in the religious world who says the same thing. If the consciousness of the individual is the seat of authority and the court of final appeal, then we have anarchy in the religious world. Every man will be a law unto himself. Conflicting authorities mean that there is no authority.

If it is argued that the Bible is fallible in part, then the question arises: "What part is fallible and what part is infallible? What part is true and what part is false? And who is to be the judge?" Is it not evident that such a contention leads to absolute religious anarchy?—that it makes every man a law unto himself? If we do not accept the Bible as authority, then we have to accept our own individual judgment as the final authority, or the judgment of some other man, expressed in a book or otherwise, and we are still utterly at sea; we still have no real authority: For, look you, one man may accept his own judgment as authoritative or the judgment of some other man or book, but you and I may not accept his conclusions or the conclusions of the other man or book at all. And so it comes down to it that we have no binding authority: that is to say, we have anarchy.

Is it not perfectly evident, my friends, that we must have some authority outside of ourselves, some absolute and unchanging standard, some court of final appeal to which all must submit, or there can only be confusion worse confounded in all matters of religion?

The whole matter of religious authority reduces itself to the question whether the infinitely holy and wise God has a right to rule His own world and His finite children. We must believe that He has. God's righteous will, then, is the ultimate source of authority in the religious world, and that will is revealed in the Bible. In this Book, either explicitly stated or clearly implied, there is every truth, precept and principle that the individual or the race can ever need.

"But," it is asked, "is there then to be no new truth? No progress in thought?" And we answer: Yes, there is to be constant progress in thought, but this is to come because the individual will learn better to think God's thoughts after Him! There is to be more and more new truth, but it is to be new truth that breaks out of the old Word. That Word is "forever established in Heaven," and we are not to add to it or take from it one jot or tittle. The heart of it is One "in whom there is no variableness nor shadow cast by the turning." One who is "the same yesterday, today, and forever." Man's chief glory is in learning of Him, and not in trying to surpass Him nor supplant Him with our feeble finite thoughts. New truth will come, but it will come bursting out of the eternal and infallible Word. The improvement must be in man and not in the Word. The Holy Spirit has been given us to lead us into all the truth, and He will not fail us if in prayer and humility we look to Him for guidance. The enlightening of the individual mind and the deepening of its power of perception merely enables the mind to enter into the deeper treasures that lie forever at the golden heart of Truth. The supreme need of this age is that we shall reestablish respect for authority everywhere, and that can come only through reestablishing respect for the Bible as God's Word.

INFLUENCE ON THE INDIVIDUAL

Now the striking thing is that the Bible actually exerts a vital and authoritative influence over men. It has a mystical power through which God speaks to men in a way that is mentally illuminating, inspiring, and to the individual, final and infallible. Let me quote to you, in this connection, no less a man than *Hon. Winston Churchill*, the great English statesman. Beyond any question he is one of the most practical men and one of the most gigantic minds of today, but in his book on

the great war,—"The World Crisis of 1914-1918,"—
which I have just been reading with profound interest,
and which many competent critics have declared the
greatest of the books on the war, I found Mr. Churchill
relating a striking incident.   In speaking of the tremendous sense of responsibility which came upon him when
he was selected to serve as the First Lord of the Ad-
miralty at the outbreak of the World War, and of his
uncertainty and apprehension about assuming such colossal responsibilities in the face of the known strength
of Germany and her vast preparations for war, Mr.
Churchill relates an experience he had with the Bible.
He says:

"That night when I went to bed, I saw a large Bible
lying on a table in my bedroom.   My mind was dom-
inated by the news I had received of the complete change
in my station, and of the task entrusted to me.   I thought
of the peril of Britain,—peace-loving, unthinking, little
prepared—of her power and virtue, and of her mission
of good sense and fair play.   I thought of mighty Germany, towering up in the splendor of her Imperial state
and delving down, in her profound, cold, patient, ruthless calculations.   I thought of the army corps I had
watched tramp past, wave after wave of valiant manhood, at the Breslau maneuvers in 1907; of the thousands of strong horses dragging cannon and great
howitzers up the ridges and along the roads around
Wurzburg in 1910.   I thought of German education
and thoroughness and all that their triumphs in science
and philosophy implied.   I thought of the sudden and
successful wars by which her power had been set up."

Then, with these thoughts in his mind he turned to
the Bible, without any plan of reading any particular
passage, and it opened to a passaage that greatly cheered

and strengthened his heart, and encouraged him to go forward with his new duties, and responsibilities.   He says:

"I opened the Book *at random,* and in the 9th chapter of Deutermony, I read:

"Hear O Israel; Thou art to pass over Jordan this day, to go in to possess nations greater and mightier than thyself, cities great and fenced up to heaven, A people great and tall, the children of the Anakim, whom thou knowest and of whom thou hast heard say, Who can stand before the children of Anak!   Understand therefore this day, that the Lord thy God is he which goeth over before thee; as a consuming fire, he shall destroy them, and he shall bring them down before they face; so shalt thou drive them out, and destroy them quickly, as the Lord hath said unto thee. Speak not thou in thine heart, after that the Lord thy God hath cast them out from before thee, saying: For my righteousness the Lord hath brought me in to possess this land; but for the wickedness of these nations the Lord doth drive them out from before thee.   Not for thy righteousness, nor for the uprightness of thine heart, dost thou go to possess their land, but for the wickedness of these nations the Lord thy God doth drive them out from before thee, and that he may perform the word which the Lord sware unto thy fathers."   (Deut. 9:1-5.)

This message from God's word did thus infallibly guide that great statesman in the hour of his supreme need.

THE BIBLE'S MORAL POWER

The Bible has also proved itself the infallible word of God to a great multitude of individuals in the field of morals and religion.   The *avowed purpose* of the Bible is to point the way to salvation, and the fact that it does this prove that it is infallible and divine.

We have in the membership of this church young

men whom I have baptized during this pastorate, some of whom have come from lives of crime and shame and have been made over into lives of purity, honesty, and noble service. They delight in nothing more than to quote from the Bible and tell how its truths saved them, and how its precepts guide and keep them in the way.

Some of you have doubtless seen that picture which sets forth the purifying and uplifting influence of the Bible on the individual character. The painting is entitled "The entrance of Thy Word Giveth Light." The artist had pictured the interior of a humble and poverty-stricken home. Upon the bed in the corner lay a young man. Evidently he had been a youth of right impulses and noble purpose, though his fine face was now marred sadly by the deep lines of sin. The young man lay upon the bed in the early morning after a night of drunkenness and debauchery. Beside him sat the venerable old mother of the wayward lad. A tear was upon her wrinkled cheek; the old family Bible was open upon her knee, and with her drawn, crooked finger she was tracing laboriously and reading the words of counsel and truth from the Book. And with marvelous spiritual insight and skill the artist had managed to suggest the dawn of hope upon the young man's face. Realizing his own weakness and his own inability to stand amidst the temptations of human life—convinced at last of his own moral impotence—there came to his penitent soul the revelation that there was another power, a Beneficent and Divine Power, that would strengthen his weak will and correct the sad abuses of his life, and so the entrance of God's word gave him light. That picture is true, and that experience has been repeated, in essence, many million times upon our earth. Because, therefore, of the fruit that this blessed old Book has borne we know that it is truth, and that it points the way to everlasting life.

Talk about the divine origin and infallibilitpy of the *Bible!* Are not such experiences final and conclusive as to this question? I submit that they are. So far as the question of infallibility is concerned, I bear my testimony that the Bible has been infallible for me, because it has been the greatest purifying, guiding, and inspiring power in my life. It has never failed me. Churchill found it so in his life, and a great multitude of others have found it so in their lives. Coleridge, the oet, said that he knew the Bible was true because "it found him at a deeper depth than any other book." Gladstone called the Bible "the impregnable Rock of Holy Scritupre," and acknowledged that he shaped his life by its teachings. Daniel Webster paid his tribute, to the influence of the Bible upon his life and character, and he admonished all men to accept it and follow it. He said:

"I believe that the Bible is to be understood and received in the plain and obvious meaning of its passages; for I cannot persuade myself that a book intended for the instruction and conversion of the whole world should cover its true meaning in any such mystery, and doubt none but critics and philosophers can discover it. If we abide by the principles taught in the Bible, our country will go on prospering and to prosper; but if we and our posterity neglect its instructions and authority no man can tell how sudden a catastrophe may overwhelm us and bury all our glory in profound obscurity."

I wish to add to these views of practical men of the world the following words from one of humanity's greatest scholars, the late Dr. James Orr, of the Free Church College of Glasgow. In speaking of the Bible, Dr. Orr says that it has a "saving and sanctifying power that wield the best proof of its divine origin." In his great book, on "The Problem of the Old Testament," he then says further:

"The Bible has a character and power of impression which belong to it as a living Book. Who, coming to this sacred Book with a sincere desire to know God's will for the direction of His life, will say that he cannot find it? Who desiring to be instructed in the way of salvation 'through faith which is in Christ Jesus' will consult its pages and say it is not made plain to him? Who, coming to it for equipment of his spiritual life, will say that there are still needs of that life which are still unprovided for? Who, seeking direction in the way of life everlasting, can doubt that, if he faithfully obeys its teachings he will reach that goal? The Scripture fulfills the ends for which it was given; no higher proof of its inspiration can be demanded."

These are nobple and significant words which I have quoted from some of the great minds and hearts of earth, and they all argue the divine origin and infallibility of the Bible as God's word.

AUTHORITATIVE PREACHING

A new understanding and a practical application of this old truth will bring renewed power to the modern pulpit and the church today. Why is it that with greater wealth, enlightenment and numbers than ever before in Christianity's history many of her churches, especially in our cities and centers of culture, are declining? The reason is not far to seek. A question mark concerning Christ and the Bible has gotten into many pulpits. Its poisonous roots reach down through the soil of uncertainty to the subsoil of doubt, and even into the dark, deadly mold of infidelity itself. Its fruits show in the preaching of the day. The trumpet is giving "an uncertain sound" and consequently few are "preparing themselves for the battle." The silly sensationalism, the "ragtime" religion that is seen in many of our churches, and the many little essays that are delivered from many of our ulpits, and dignified through courtesy with the name of "sermons," are pitiful in comparison with the grand preaching of the past, which gave forth a sure note of warning and promise by the very authority of God Himself, speaking through His Holy Word.

The rejection of authority in the civil state, in the home, in social life, and in the church, is the greatest and most menacing danger of today. Half of the world has been already plunged into anarchy, and the other half seems trembling upon the brink of that dreadful precipice, because the truth of authority has been rejected by the superficial thinking of the times. In the home, parental authority has waned, and the result is the wreck and ruin which is falling already upon the younger generations, which is the theme of magazine writers the world over, and the distress of thoughtful minds everywhere. In society the old-fashioned authority of decent standards of dress and conduct has been partly rejected, and the result is a reign of sensuality and the clogging of our divorce courts with the tragic tales of violated marriage vows, the setting adrift of little children with no hand to guide them upon the storm-tossed seas of human life, and the utter disruption of multitudes of American homes. And all of this has come about because of loss of faith in the Bible as God's infallible and authoritative Word.

I hope that my opponent realizes that a solemn responsibility rests upon him in this debate because, at last, these questions are the most important questions that are now engaging the attention of mankind. The supreme religious issue of this age is: do we believe God? Not do we believe about God. Every man who has any capacity for thought must believe something about some sort of God. The real issue of today is: do we believe God? A great multitude of devout and faithful souls the round world over hold that God has spoken to man in this venerable Book, and we believe God and what He says to us in the Book, and we believe, too, that the supreme strategy of the devil, whom Christ recognized as His arch enemy, centers today in his subtle attack upon the Bible. The devil's plan from the beginning has been to discount and discredit God's word. It is recorded here in Genesis that when the tempter came to our first mother, "he said unto the woman: yea, hath God said?" The very first step in the seductive sophistries of the devil, therefore, was to raise a question in the human mind concerning God's word. Then his next step was to deny God's word. When the woman told him that they were permitted to eat of the fruit of the trees of the garden except the fruit of the tree which was in the midst of the garden, for, said she "God hath said: ye shall not eat of it; neither shall ye touch it lest ye die," the devil made his master stroke. It is recorded here, "and the serpent said unto the woman: ye shall not surely die, for God doth know that in the day ye eat thereof, then your eyes shall be oenped an dye shall be as gods, knowing good and evil." (Gen. 3:1-5.)

First the devil raises a question as to whether God has really spoken—whether He has given us His word. and then he goes a step further and boldly denies God's word and declares God to be a liar. And that, my friends, is what he is still doing; and all of the sin and the sorrow, the suffering and the shame, that have come upon mankind have fallen upon the race because they have believed the devil's lies rather than God's word. Let us beware, those of us who lead the people, lest in these latter times we ourselves, allow ourselves to be deceived by the adversary and to fulfill what Paul said: "And for this cause God shall send them strong delusion, that they should believe a lie." (2 Thess. 2:11.)

FAITH AND SPIRITUAL VISION

There are but one or two other practical things that I need to say in this connection. In establishing the affirmative of this debate, I do not have to prove that the Bible is fully understandable down to its minutest detail. I have already pointed out that there are some difficulties, some mysteries and some seeming contradictions in the Book, but I showed that these difficulties have probably been left in the Bible purposely in the wisdom of God, as a perpetual stimulus to interest, and a constant challenge to faith! We should not allow these few minor difficulties, however, to decide our judgment about the Bible. In fairness, we must look at it as a whole. The question is: "Resolved that *the Bible* (the united whole) is the Infallible Word of God."

Again, in establishing the affirmative in this debate, I do not have to prove that the Bible is infallible to all men. I have shown that it is infallible to many—indeed, to all who will accept it; but, as with any other valuable gift, it must be accepted before it can be enjoyed. Now, as with any other gift, faith is the way by which we must accept the Bible, because of the undeniable and self-evident truth that spiritual things are spiritually discerned, just as physical things are physically discerned. I can discern the pulpit here only by looking at it with my physical eyes. I can determine that it is smooth only by running my physical hand over it. Likewise, it is true that there must be a spiritual eye in order to behold spiritual beauty and truth. Those who, through lack of faith, have no spiritual vision, and therefore do not accept the Bible, are like a blind man who at mid-day declares that the sun is not shining! The Bible "worketh effectually (only) in those that believe," but when there is the smallest degree of humility, of the spirit of teachableness, and of vital faith, it becomes the very word of God and an infallible guide to all who thus accept it!

Our first business, therefore, is to seek the leading of God's spirit that we may approach it in such a way as really to reach its beautiful and saving truth. It is not the proud and egotistical spirit of the critic, who comes to the Bible with an attitude of superior wisdom and condescension, but, rather, the humble and teachable soul who will find its richest treasures. Its message is to the heart and conscience as well as to the intellect of man, and faith is the open sesame by which we enter in.

The Bible is not an iron safe that can be opened only by some key which we are strong enough to forge or some combination that we are shrewd enough to figure out. The Bible is rather a beautiful flower which cannot be forced open, but which will open of itself in the sunlight of faith and love, and give forth a beauty and sweetness that are divine. We need, above all things else today, that warmth of appreciative atmosphere and of humble devotion which will cause its deeper spiritual beauties to unfold for us, and to exhale the rare perfume which so sweetened the lives of those in the generations that are gone.

GOOD FRUITS

And surely its fruitage has been blessed down all the years! Queen Victoria was once asked the secret of the greatness of the British Empire. She lifted a Bible from her table, opened it on her out-stretched hand and said: "Here it is!"

Whatever else anyone may think about Him, there is one principle that Jesus of Nazareth laid down which cannot be denied by any man. It is the principle that a good tree bringeth forth good fruit and an evil tree bringeth forth evil fruit. "Wherefore," said He, "by their fruits ye may judge them." Judged by this simple, safe, practical standard, what of the Bible? We know it is true and good because its fruits have been righteousness and truth and holiness down all the years.

Think what this old Book has done for our modern society. It has secured the acceptance of those principles and ideals which heathenism ignored and rejected, as, for example, the importance of the individual; the law of mutual love; the sacredness of human life, and the need for identity between belief and practice, or the doctrine of internal holiness. It has liberated womanhood and glorified childhood. It has taught the nations the value of monogamy, the sacredness of the marriage vow, the religious equality of the sexes and the sanctity of the home as the foundation unit in the organization of enlightened society. These and other forces of wisdom, purity and progress have their fountain-head in the Bible!

And particularly are these considerations applicable to our own country. The very foundations of the American Republic were laid down upon the open Bible. The most significant fact, at last, in the history of our country is the fact that the Plymouth Fathers, before ever they left the Mayflower and set foot upon these wild shores, opened the Bible in the cabin of the ship and drew up the first charter for their colony in the light of its teachings. The foundation stones in this country's greatness were not laid by men who doubted the Bible, who desecrated the Lord's day, and who neglected the church, or by women who were more regular in attendance on the playhouses than they were on the services of the sanctuary, who knew more about Ibsen than they did about God's word, who wore their complexions in the bureau drawer, who were past masters in the tango, the turkey-trot, and the grizzly-grapple, and who preferred to mother a mongrel puppy rather than a cooing baby! No, the greatness of our country was founded by men and women who held to the old faith, who lived lives of usefulness and service, who walked in the light of God's law, whose sorrows were comforted by the truths of His word, and whose hopes of Heaven were the main-stay and anchorage of their souls!

Wendell Phillips once eloquently exclaimed: "The answer to the Shasta is India; the answer to Confucianism is China; the answer to the Koran is Turkey; the answer to the Bible is Christian America!"

Because, therefore, of the fact of its miraculous preservation and its increase, the fact of its unique universality, the fact of its remarkable unity in diversity, the marvelous fact of its fulfilled prophesies, the fact of the overwhelming claims it makes for itself, and finally, the fact of its self-authenticating authority and its power over the individual and the race, I claim that it is demonstrated and proven, that this book is divine in its origin and infallible in its content.

II

IN THE NEGATIVE*

"RESOLVED, That the Bible is the Infallible Word of God." I want to call your attention to the exact wording of the subject under discussion. Notice that the resolution does not state, "Resolved, That the Bible is the *best* book in the world," nor, "Resolved, That we find God's Word in the Bible," neither of which resolutions would find me upholding the negative side.

When any one says that the Bible is the "infallible" word of God, we understand that person to mean that every part of the Bible is the word of God and therefore infallible. Indeed, the word "infallible" is somewhat unnecessary in the stating of this subject. If every verse and every word in the Bible is the word of God then it must be infallible. The question before us, which I submit to you, Mr. Chairman, Honorable Judges, Worthy Opponent, and Ladies and Gentlemen, is whether or not God is actually speaking in every verse, phrase and word in the Bible. I do not have to prove that it is all wrong. If any part of it is wrong, or untrue, the Book is not infallible, as that word is commonly understood by English-speaking people. Now, the Bible is a very precious book to me. I will not yield one whit to my worthy opponent either in the matter of attachment to the book or in the matter of the advantages of my early education. I was brought up in a Baptist home in New England, and compared to a New England Baptist home, Scotland has nothing to offer. My earliest memories are associated with the Bible. My mother entered me in a Baptist Sunday

*First speech for the negative by Rev. Charles Francis Potter, Minister West Side Unitarian Church, New York.

52

School when I was less than three years old, and I attended Sunday School regularly, except when I was sick in bed, from that time until I was 17 years old, and every Sunday in that Sunday School I recited about the Bible the things that I had studied in it during the week. When I was five years old a copy of the Bible was placed in my hands, and I began to read it, and I have been reading it ever since very carefully. I presume I have worn out a dozen copies. I read the New Testament through "out loud" to my mother, chapter by chapter, before I was 7 years old. By that time I was memorizing great sections of it. The Ten Commandments were, as the newspaper men say, "featured" in my early education. I remember distinctly reciting them with other boys and girls of my own age. I learned not only the abbreviated form, taught in most Sunday Schools, but as I was intensely interested, I learned the whole 20th Chapter of Exodus in which the Ten Commandments are contained.

Very distinctly I recall one afternoon when my mother caught me, as she thought, telling a lie. It was probably some childish exaggeration. My punishment was to stand in the parlor of our little home before the framed Ten Commandments, done in red worsted on perforated paper. I was to read these through a number of times. As I was doing so, there suddenly dawned upon my humiliated consciousness the startling fact that there was no "Thou shalt not lie." When I pointed out that fact to my mother, she seemed surprised, but rose to the occasion nobly by saying that "Thou shalt not bear false witness," was near enough for the purpose, and that I had better stand there awhile longer. But I could think of several kinds of lies which had nothing whatever to do with witnessing, and wondered why with "Thou shalt not steal," and "Thou shalt not kill," it didn't come straight out and say "Thou shalt not lie."

As I read the Old Testament, however, the answer gradually came to me. The reason why there wasn't any prohibition of lying was because lying wasn't a sin in the days of the Ten Commandments. Isaac and Jacob continually lied and the more they lied the better they seemed to get along. Jacob deceived his brother, then his father, and then his father-in-law, and the Lord blessed him and called him Israel (ruling with God) and his sons founded the 12 tribes of Israel. Thus early I learned by myself to question the doctrine of the sacred completeness of the Ten Commandments, and the infallibility of the Bible.

Naturally I looked at the Decalog closer and found other questionable statements. I asked my Sunday School teachers why we shouldn't keep Monday holy as well as Sunday, especially since what the fourth commandment really said was to keep Saturday holy.

I asked her if she thought it was right for God to be "a jealous God" when it was wrong for me to be a jealous boy, and if she thought it was altogether right for innocent children to have the "iniquities" of their dead and buried great grandfathers "visited" upon them.

Much to my surprise I found that these questions were either dodged or very unsatisfactorily answered by my religious instructors. They even seemed surprised that anybody should ask such questions. When I found that there was no help in that direction, I was left to my own resources and decided to make an original investigation of the infallibility of the Bible. As nearly as I can remember I was just about nine years old when I conducted a scientific laboratory test of this doctrine we are debating tonight. Mind you, I had never heard that there were such persons as higher critics.

I had found in my Bible two verses—

Matthew 21:22.

"And all things whatsoever ye ask in prayer believing, ye shall receive."

John 14:14.

"If ye shall ask anything in my name, that will I do."

There were many other verses along the same line and in all of them wa sthe promise that if I asked anything of God it would be given unto me. Consequently the test I proposed was fair enough. There seemed to be two conditions: First, I must ask in faith believing, and second, I must ask in Jesus' name. I remember distinctly phow I went down cellar and found an old wash bench and set up on it a wooden nine-pin. I knew that money was needed for my education and for things we lacked in the little home. It occurred to me that if once I could get hold of some money that things would be very much better. So I got down on my knees in the cellar and prayed earnestly to God that he would turn that wooden nine-pin into gold. I asked it in faith believing, for I had been repeatedly told that God could do anything. I asked it in Jesus' name. I prayed as hard as I knew how, and let me tell you that a more earnest prayer never was uttered. I had been told repeatedly that God could do anything, and I was giving him, as well as I could, a fair chance. When I arose from my knees and found that nine-pin was still wooden, something happened in my young mind and I questioned the infallibility of the Bible. Do you wonder? And remember that it was no German higher critic that put in my mind doubts as to the infallibility of the Bible.

Of course I was told that when prayer wasn't answered, it was because God knew that what we prayed for wasn't good for us to have. That seemed all right, too, but it didn't help the infallibility of the Bible any, because that wasn't what the verses had said. There were no reservations. Those verses had said "all things whatsoever ye ask" and "if ye shall ask anything."

But youth is elastic, and environment is powerful and I got over that blow. I feared I had been an atheist and I repented of my disloyalty. I was converted and joined the Baptist church at the age of eleven, by immersion. It was a very real conversion, too. I had conviction of sin and all the rest of the orthodox plan of salvation. Always I had wanted to be a minister and the idea grew stronger after I was baptized. I kept on in the Sunday School studying and thinking a great deal about the Bible and came to know it so well that at the age of fourteen I was taken from among the pupils of the Sunday School and made a teacher of a class of twelve 10-year-old boys. I found that some of them asked the same questions that I was still subconsciously asking.

An earnest church worker, a doctor's wife, formed a Bible study class which met on Tuesday evenings and which I joined at the age of sixteen. She suggested that we begin with Genesis, and inasmuch as I had been studying Genesis lately I was very glad to have her make this suggestion. The class lasted just three weeks. On the first night I presented her with a list of a dozen or more questions which had to do with the contradictions and inaccuracies which I, as a 16-year-old boy, unaided, mind you, by any books of higher criticism, had noticed as I read the Bible carefully. She glanced through the questions and said she could not answer them that night, but would try to the next meeting. I think that she visited the public library that week and I think she called on the minister. The next Tuesday night she said she would have to postpone those questions still another week. Although there was a good attendance at this class, it was announced on the third meeting night that that would be the last session of the class. I haven't had those questions answered yet.

When I was seventeen I went away to college. Almost the first week I was there we had a meeting of the Ministerial Union. This consisted of about forty young men studying for the Baptist ministry. In planning the monthly meetings of the Ministerial Union for that year it was decided to have debates. It was a very rash thing for a freshman to do, but I proposed that one of the subjects of the debates be the Virgin Birth. The upper class men asked me what there was to debate about the Virgin Birth. I told them I thought the matter was very debatable and the debate developed then and there. As I recall it, there were about twenty who maintained that the Virgin Birth was an historical fact and a necessary Christian doctrine. I was the only one who maintained the opposite, but when the afternoon was over my questions on the Virgin Birth had not been answered, and it had been decided not to have debates in the Ministerial Union.

From the first year of my college experience until I was graduated from the theological seminary I was known as "the Unitarian," a title which I indignantly repudiated because I had been taught that Unitarians did not believe in God. I was sure that I still believed in God, however, even if I did not believe every word of the Bible. I insisted that I was simply trying to find the truth and that there were some parts of the Bible

which did not seem to me to be true, and that the mere
statement by certain religious instructors that they must
be true because they were in the Bible did not seem to
me at all logical.

Now, these childhood and boyhood questions of mine,
I found, in later college years and in theological seminary years, are the very questions which are asked by the
so-called higher critics.   When I found that a number
of learned men, most of them Christians, were asking
the same questions which had bothered me about the
Bible, I began to read their books, but I thought them
very mild and tame.

The trouble with the higher critics appeared to me
to be that they were too much concerned with matters
of detail such as words in the text, minor discrepancies,
and things of that nature.   The things that troubled me
were not so much the fact that, for instance, there were
four different versions of the inscription on the Cross:

Matthew has it (Matt. 27:37). "This is Jesus, the King
of the Jews."
Mark has it (Mark 15:26). "The King of the Jews."
Luke has it (Luke 23:28). "This is the King of the Jews."
John has it (John 19:19). "Jesus of Nazareth, the King
of the Jews."

Of course I knew that this fact alone, which can easily
be verified by any one whether a higher critic or not,
proves that the Bible is not literally inspired and not the
infallible word of God.   But what concerned me more,
and really troubled me, were the direct contradictions
between various sections of the Bible and the things
which the Bible said God commanded and which seemed
to me wrong.

Let me direct your attention to several passages in the
Bible.   I hope you and the judges will make a note of

these references, and you can look them up in whatever version you think is the verbally inspired infallible word of God. I shall read them now from the commonly accepted version, the King James, used in Dr. Straton's pulpit. These passages I have grouped into three sections, *first,* those that are inaccurate, that is unscientific or unhistorical; *second,* those that are obvious contradictions, and *third,* those that represent God as doing or approving something which seems to me morally wrong.

INACCURACIES IN THE BIBLE

Unscientific

Lev. 11:6—"And the hare, because she cheweth the cud." It is well-known now, of course, that the hare and the rabbit are not cud-chewing animals, although they make motions with their lips and jaws which might easily be mistaken by an unscientific observer.

Gen. 3:14—The same sort of mistake is made when it was supposed that snakes eat dust.

Lev. 11:20-22—In this passage grasshoppers, crickets and locusts are spoken of as going upon all four. These insects all have six feet.

Joshua 10:12-14—Joshua making the sun stand still. Those who wrote that story had no idea of the astronomical havoc they were creating. If the sun had stood still "about a whole day," not only would the Amorites have perished, but Joshua and the Israelites as well.

Unhistoric

Luke 2—"Now it came to pass in those days, there went out a decree from Cesar Augustus that all the world should be taxed (*i. e.* enrolled). This was the first enrollment made when Quirinius was Governor of Syria."

Joseph and Mary went up to Bethlehem for enrollment and there Jesus was born (and Matthew says "in the days of Herod the King").

Three errors of history are to be noted in this passage:

1.   There is no record of a world census, not even a Roman world census, in the careful records of the Romans.

2.   A small enrollment in Palestine was made by Quirinius but it was ten years after the death of Herod.

3.   At the time of the birth of Jesus, the Governor of Syria was not Quirinius, but Quintus Sentius Saturninus.

CONTRADICTIONS IN THE BIBLE

2nd Sam'l. 6:23—"Michal, the daughter of Saul, had no child unto the day of her death."

2nd Sam'l. 21:8—"The five sons of Michal, the daughter of Saul."

Gen. 22:1—"And it came to pass after these things that God did tempt Abraham."

Jas. 1:13—"Let no man say when he is tempted, I am tempted of God for God cannot be tempted with evil, neither tempteth he any man."

1st Kings 8:46—"There is no man that sinneth not."

1st John 3:9—"Whosoever is born of God doth not commit sin; he cannot sin because he is born of God."

Matt. 5:33-34, Matt. 5:38-39, Matt. 5:43-44—(These passages flatly contradict the Mosaic law.)

If it be objected that the contradictions between the Old Testament and the New Testament are no proof of the infallibility of the Bible because we must interpret the Old Testament by the New Testament, how about the following contradictions within the New Testament, indeed, within the same book?

Rom. 2:11—"There is no respect of persons with God" (this means no partiality).

Rom. 9:13—"Jacob I loved, but Esau I hated."

Rom. 9:18—"So then he hath mercy on whom he will and whom he will he hardeneth."

Acts 9:7—"And the men who journeyed with him (Paul) stood speechless, *hearing* a *voice*, but seeing no man."

Acts 22:9—"They that were with me saw indeed the

light and were afraid; but *they heard not the voice* of him that spake to me."

In 1st Cor. 15:5 Paul says—"Christ was seen of the 12 apostles after his resurrection." But there were not 12. Judas hanged himself before the resurrection and Matthias was not elected until after the Ascension.

In Mark Jesus goes into the wilderness immediately after his baptism and stays 40 days in wilderness.

In John, the third day after baptism Jesus in Cana of Galilee at a wedding and the wilderness temptation is not mentioned.

My main contention, however, on which I would be willing to base my entire argument, is not the scientific inaccuracies, nor even the fully recognized contradictions in the text of the Bible. If the Bible is the word of God, the scientific mistakes prove him ignorant and the contradictions prove him inconsistent, and an inconsistent and ignorant God can hardly be called infallible. But my principal contention goes much deeper than that. It is based on morally degrading ideas of God which are contained in some parts of the Bible, where God is made by ignorant writers to sanction certain things which, if you and I did, we would be put behind steel bars.

MORALLY DEGRADING IDEAS OF GOD

Ex. 7:13, 11:10—God hardened Pharaoh's heart so that he would not let the children of Israel leave Egypt and then punished him severely for not letting them go.

Ex. 5:3—God told Moses to say to Pharaoh, "Let us go, we beseech thee, three days journey into the wilderness that we may sacrifice unto the Lord our God,' which was deceit, because they were planning to escape and not return. Then God told them (Ex. 11:2) to borrow all they could and carry it off with them; *i. e.* God is reported to have commanded them to lie and steal.

2nd Kings Chapter 9:10—Jehu was a hypocrite and wholesale murderer and yet the Bible says he did according to "all that was in God's heart," all that was "right in God's eyes," and received God's approval and reward.

Ex. 22:18—God said, "Thou shalt not suffer a witch to live." Very few in this audience would, if on a jury, sentence to death any woman charged with witchcraft no matter what the evidence, and yet on this supposed command of God, and because of the idea that the Bible is the infallible word of God, thousands of innocent women have been tortured and killed by religious fanatical literalists. This one verse alone proves my contention.

Deut. 21:18-21—"If a man have a stubborn and rebellious son, which will not obey the voice of his father, or the voice of his mother, and that, when they have chastened him, will not hearken unto them:

"Then shall his father and his mother lay hold on him, and bring him out unto the elders of his city, and unto the gate of his place;

"And they shall say unto the elders of his city, this, our son, is stubborn and rebellious, he will not obey our voice; he is a glutton and a drunkard.

"And all the men of his city shall stone him with stones, that he die; so shalt thou put evil away from among you; and all Israel shall hear, and fear."

Here is a command to stone to death disobedient children without trial, on the accusation of their parents. If the parents of New York obeyed this tomorrow, think of what it would mean. For one thing the parents would be arrested for murder, and rightly.

Deut. 14:21—And God said, "Ye shall not eat of anything which dieth of itself; thou shalt give it unto the stranger that is in the gates, that he may eat it; or thou mayest sell it to an alien."

No comment is necessary.

Any one of these inaccuracies, contradictions, or immoral sanctions, would, taken alone, prove my thesis that the Bible is not the infallible word of God. All of them, taken together, and many others which might be cited, constitute a body of evidence within the book itself which refutes my worthy opponent's contention. It is a wonder that there are not more inconsistencies in the volume, for it is a whole literature rather than a book by one author.

My worthy opponent is historically incorrect if he supposes that the Bible is a unity. The word "Bible" comes from two Greek words "ta biblia," which, being translated, mean "the books." There are 66 books in the Bible and they were written by very many different men over a long period of time, nearly a thousand years. If these books were arranged in the order in which they were written it would be possible to trace the changing and improving ideas about God which developed among the Hebrews.

They represent, in the Old Testament, the literature of the Hebrew race, and in the New Testament, the documents of early Christianity. Many of these books were written for special purposes, and I doubt if any one of them was written with the idea that it would be included in the Bible. Paul, for instance, writes a letter to the people of Thessolonica giving specific counsels for their peculiar situation. Take the Psalms alone, usually ascribed to David. It takes only a few hours' study to reveal that we have here, not a number of compositions by one man, but the final edition of the Hebrew hymn book, a compilation of many different hymns by many different authors. If you presume that they were all written by David, under the inspiration of God, and are the infallible word of God, how can you account for the imprecatory psalms? Will any one who believes in the God in whom Jesus believed, the loving Heavenly father, dare to say that it is God's infallible word which declares (Psalms 137:9) "Happy shall he be that taketh and dasheth thy little ones against the stones."

If the Bible is the infallible word of God, that means not only that what God was supposed to have originally said to inspired men is infallible, but it necessarily pre-supposes that there must have been infallible copyists during the period of hundreds of years before printing was invented. Thousands of early Christians and later monks, often-times wearied with long hours at the desk might easily have made errors in copying, as the existing manuscriptps show to even a superficial observer, that they did.

Remember that the Old Testament was written in Hebrew, which was translated into Greek, the Septuagint, and then into English. Remember that not all the Greek was translated. There was a part they left out, which was later put in between the Old and New Testaments and called the Apocrypha. In England, for many years, and it probably still obtains, if you swore in court on a Bible not containing the Apocrypha, your oath was valueless. In America the other kind will do. Which Bible is the infallible word of God?

Remember, too, that Jesus spoke in Aramaic which was translated into Greek and Latin and those in turn into English. This, you see, necessitates infallible translators, and if you think translators are infallible, you have only to compare the different versions of the Bible. Then, again, the printers must be infallible. They were not always. Take, for instance, the famous "Vinegar Bible" where a printer substituted, by mistake, the word "vinegar" for vineyard.

"There is many a slip twixt the cup and the lip," and it is a long way from the original words of the Bible to the copies which we have today, and if one link in the whole chain is weak, then my worthy opponent's contention that the Bible is the infallible word of God is a mistaken argument.

If he could show you one square inch of the original manuscripts, he might conceivably be entitled to say: "This God hath said." But the oldest manuscript of the New Testament we have is dated, at the very earliest, in the middle of the fourth century, over 300 years after Jesus died. Moreover, the oldest copy of the Hebrew Old Testament in existence dates somewhere around the 8th or 9th century A. D.

My main and final criticism of the assertion that the Bible is the infallible word of God is simply this: God is too great to be included between the covers of any printed book. Not the literature of a single race, nor even the literature of all races, is sufficient to comprehend the wonder and the glory and the goodness of God. We can read his message in the sunshine and the flowers. We can read the story of the making of the earth and of the life upon it carved deep in the eternal rocks. The aspirations toward goodness within the heart of man are a better evidence of God than all the books ever written.

III

REBUTTAL FOR THE AFFIRMATIVE*

I want to express my admiration for the adroit manner in which my opponent has handled his side of the question. I confess to a degree of distress, however, over the autobiographical parts of his address, particularly the portion where he referred to his early predilection for prevarication, and his disappointment as a lad in not finding a prohibition against lying among the Ten Commandments. It recalled to my mind the story of the pious old Quaker who had a worldly minded brother who greatly burdened and distressed him. This brother was given to such exaggeration that it got sometimes into gross prevarication. On one occasion he had exceeded all bounds. The older brother had caught him in glaring misstatements, and he said to him: "Jonathan, I do not desire to deal harshly with thee, but, Jonathan, if the Governor of Pennsylvania should say to me: 'Bring me hither the greatest liar in the State of Pennsylvania' I would come unto thee and say: 'Jonathan, the Governor hath need of thee!'" I will not say that my opponent has deliberately misstated the truth about the Bible in those alleged contradictions which he quoted. Nor did he actually call the Bible a liar. Like the old Quaker, he put it in a little more diplomatic language, but it amounts at last to about the same thing. I prefer to believe that he is just honestly mistaken about these things.

I confess to some personal disappointment over his presentation. I am loath to believe that my opponent is one who finds more enjoyment in the companionship of

*By Rev. John Roach Straton, D.D.

pale and sickly doubt than in that of strong faith and robust affirmation, or that he is one who is only happy when stumbling into some blind alley of alleged Scripture contradiction, or one who prefers to pick out the spots upon the sun rather than to see its full-orbed glory at noon-day.

SEEING ARIGHT

I am very sure that my opponent does not handle the other important matters of life as he handles the Bible. I am sure that he doesn't deal in that way, for example, with Mrs. Potter. At least I know that I cannot so deal with Mrs. Straton. If I should follow the policy of trying to find the flaws in the wife's character, if there are any, if I should come to her constantly and say: "Now this is wrong, and that is wrong with you," and "what on earth did you do that for?" etc., etc., I know that there would be trouble in my household. Nothing gives forth its best under the spirit of criticism and mere fault-finding, and so far as the wife is concerned, I see only the nobility of character and the wonderful charm and beauty which are an increasing joy and delight to me as the years come and go.

And is not that the proper attitude to take toward the Bible? Who in looking at a great impressionist picture would single out a particular lump of paint or a place where the weave of the canvas perhaps showed through the pigment, and judge the entire picture by that? The Bible, as already remarked, is a unity, and we need to look at it as a whole; and, viewed as a whole, my contention is that the claim is established that it is the infallible word of God. If not, then we have no guide and no fixed standards to which all must submit, that is to say, once more we have anarchy! If the Bible is true and infallible only in spots, then once more I ask who is to pick out the good spots? If one man has the right to tear from the Bible the pages telling of the Virgin Birth of our Lord, and if another has the right to tear out the pages teaching the transcendence and real personality of a living God, and if another has the right to tear out the pages containing the record of the bodily resurrection of Jesus, and if another has the hight to tear out the pages that teach the inspiration and authority of the Book, and if another has the right to reject baptism, and another has the right to throw overboard the teaching about divorce and the substitutionary atonement, and if another has the right to reject the miracles and the full deity of our Lord, then have not I the right, if I so desire, to tear out the pages carrying the ten commandments and satisfy the lusts of the flesh, and do otherwise according to my own sweet will?

If we are to say that the Bible is not infallible, then I ask again, who is to be the judge between the infallible and fallible parts of it?

I want to point out that my honorable opponent has not answered one single one of the tremendous facts that I presented in my opening argument. He has only regaled us with a lot of the old stock objections and arguments of scepticism and unbelief.

ALLEGED CONTRADICTIONS

If time permitted, it would be very easy to answer every alleged contradiction and every supposed error which my opponent has undertaken to point out. I will have to hope that all who are really interested will take the time after this meeting to look up these matters in any good Bible dictionary or commentary, or to consult some competent Bible student. In the meantime, I will have to content myself with calling attention to only a few of these alleged errors.

Take, for example, what he said about the supposed contradiction concerning the inscription on Christ's cross. There is no contradiction at all. The Scripture states that the inscription was written in three languages: Latin, Greek and Hebrew. It would be, therefore, far more accurate to speak of the "inscriptions" rather than the inscription.

Here they are:

Matthew says: "This is Jesus.....King of the Jews"
Mark says: ".................The King of the Jews"
Luke says: "This is..........the King of the Jews"
John says: "Jesus of Nazareth, the King of the Jews"

Total—"This is Jesus of Nazareth, the King of the Jews."

Evidently, then, the Holy Spirit, in inspiring the Gospel writers, was pleased to lead one evangelist to quote from the Latin, a second from the Greek, a third from the Hebrew, while a fourth was led by the same Spirit to give the substance of the whole; and this is exactly in line with what we find throughout the Gospels in other connections. A full view of Christ and His teachings can only be obtained by taking the four Gospel accounts together, as Matthew views Christ from the standpoint of a King, Mark from the standpoint of a servant, Luke from the standpoint of the Son of Man, and John from the standpoint of the Son of God.

So far from these alleged inconsistencies proving the untrustworthiness of the Bible, they prove the exact opposite. It is a well-known fact in all human testimony that different witnesses see different views of the same thing. In giving an account of an incident often statements seem to differ in surface detail, and yet they are in absolute accord *as to the essential fact.* If they agreed in minute detail, it would arouse suspicions of collusion and, therefore, possibly of designed deception.

Secular literature and history are full of illustrations of this truth. There is considerable difference among historians, for example, as to just when the battle of Waterloo began. The Duke of Wellington, the victor in the fight, declared that no man could tell when the battle commenced. One historian says that it started at eleven o'clock, and another declares that it began at twelve o'clock; but shall we decide because of these differences among witnesses that no battle was fought at all? I stood during the past Summer on the great mound of earth at the center of the Waterloo battlefield, which has been erected as a monument to commemorate the battle, and as the details of the tremendous contest were explained to me by a competent military man, I knew that a world-changing event had occurred on that spot, regardless of differences over minute details in it.

Let me give you another illustration of seeming contradiction from secular literature: In Winslow's "Journal of Plymouth Plantation" there is a statement about a ship which is alleged to have been sent out by "Master Thomas Weston"; but Bradford, in his narrative of the matter, mentions it as sent by "Mr. Weston *and another man.*" Both were right, and each narrator simply gave the account of the matter at the point where it made most emphasis on his own mind. John Adams, in his letters, tells the story of the daughter of Otis about her father's destruction of his own manuscripts. In one letter she says: "In one of his unhappy moments he committed them all to the flames," yet in the second letter she says: "He was several days in doing it." Now, this looks like a flat contradiction, and would be so regarded if we employed the methods adopted by the sceptics and destructive critics in connection with the narratives of the Bible. A clearer understanding, however, of the conditions will make plain her meaning. She meant that for several days her father was in a melancholy and pessimistic mood in regard to his literary work as set forth in his manuscripts, and finally, as a climax to this spirit of melancholy, "in one of his unhappy moments he committed them all to the flames."

So, if we had a full understanding of all the conditions of life and the circumstances under which the several narratives in the Bible were recorded, we would doubtless find that many of these difficulties would disappear. Those of us who hold to the infallibility of the Bible believe that the original manuscripts were absolutely accurate. No man would question the possibility of minor errors through copyists slipping in, however, and as I said in my opening speech, it seems evident that God may even have permitted some such difficulties to enter, to hold the interest of the world in the Book through all the ages, and in order to challenge and stimulate faith. If everything in the Bible was absolutely plain and simple we would have no faith in connection with it, but would walk by sight and not by faith. Many of the alleged contradictions and mistakes, however, are either misquotations by those who allege the mistakes, or are palpable strainings of interpretation.

My opponent thinks, for example, that Romans 2:11—"For there is no respect of persons with God"—contradicts Romans 9:13—"As it is written, Jacob have I loved, but Esau have I hated." This is due to a misunderstanding of the meaning of the words. When the Bible states that God is no respecter of persons it means that God does not "kotow" to any individual because of his wealth, position or eminence, but treats all men with equal justice and fairness.

Or, take again, what was said about the hare chewing the cud. It is almost laughably apparent that the Bible did not have in mind the American hare or jack-rabbit in this case, and it has been scientifically shown that the hare found in Palestine today uses his incisors in mastication, that he chews his food twice. But it is by no means certain exactly what animals are meant in the Levitical law by "hare" and "coney." In one connection in Hebrews the coney seems to be an animal with coarse and porsine-like hair which would explain the interdiction of his flesh for food purposes.

My opponent said that the same mistake is made in the Bible in connection with grasshoppers, locusts and crickets, which are spoken of as going on all fours, when they have six legs. But while it is true that the Palestinian locust has six legs, it walks on only the four forward legs, the hinder and longer legs being used only for springing. The passage to which my opponent refers guillotines his argument at a stroke. It is Leviticus 11:21, and reads as follows: "Every flying, creeping thing that goeth upon its fours, which has legs above its feet (or fours) *to leap withal upon the face of the ground.*"

It is well known also that the ancient Hebrews spoke of any animal that did not walk upright as going "on all fours." Think, too, of the utter incongruity of putting over against the moral grandeur of God as pictured in the Bible and the age-long influence of the old Book, a question about a grasshopper's legs!

And what shall be said of my opponent's confusion in the case of Michal, the daughter of Saul, and the sometime wife of David? He says that at one place the book of Samuel says that Michal never had children, but that at another it is stated she had borne five sons to Adriel, but this shows a lack of knowledge of the text of 2 Samuel 21:8 which says: "The five sons of Michal, the daughter of Saul, which she *brought up* for Adriel." (Authorized version.) Now, Michal was never the wife of Adriel, but her sister Merab was. The authorized version, therefore, shows her as foster-mother for her five nephews, the sons of her elder sister. The Chaldean version has this reading of the verse: "The five sons of Merab which she bore to Adriel and which Michal, the daughter of Saul, brought up." But it would seem that the Hebrew word means bore rather than trained, so such scholars as Dr. Hastings, and Dr. Schaff say that the name Michal in the passage is a scribal mis-entry by a copyist and should be Merab, which is perfectly consistent. The Syriac and the Arabic have Nedab which is the equivalent of Merab just as Uzziah is the equivalent of Azariah in the historical books of Israel.

And so of the references to the sun standing still. Some most interesting astronomical calculations have been made as to the possibility of just such an effect as that at the very time the incident occurred. But apart from that, who would say it was untrue if I declared that "I saw a beautiful sunrise this morning." Now I really saw no such thing. What I actually saw was an earth-roll, not a sun-rise. The sun doesn't "rise," yet we so say. The essential fact in the Joshua incident was that God miraculously prolonged the daylight, and to anyone who believes in miracles there is no difficulty whatever in accepting that as truth. I myself once saw such a wonderful after-glow, because of the peculiar atmospheric conditions and cloud effects, out in Cali-

fornia, that I read a newspaper out of doors after nine
o'clock at night!

A CONVERTED RATIONALIST

Let me take one more important and specific case in
which my opponent asserted positively that there was
an historical error. I refer to the matter of the taking
of the census at the time of the birth of Jesus, as recorded in the second chapter of Luke. My opponent
asserts that there are three errors of history in that
passage, and argues that no such census was taken.

Now I hold here in my hands one of the greatest and
most recent books dealing with the Bible times. This
book, "THE BEARING OF RECENT DISCOVERY
ON THE TRUSTWORTHINESS OF THE NEW
TESTAMENT," is from the pen of one of the greatest
men of our age, Sir William Ramsay, a recognized authority in his field. In the book he makes something of
a confession concerning his own early doubts about
some of the alleged historical errors, etc., in the New
Testament. He tells us how he refused to swallow the
theories of the German rationalists, however, and determined to go and see for himself. Thus he journeyed
over the New Testament lands and searched out the records on all disputed points, and he tells us *how he was
overwhelmed at last with the conviction of the accuracy
and the literal truthfulness of the New Testament in all
of these things.*

He deals with this matter of the census at length.
He says that the theories, implying that Luke invented
this story, "destroy themselves in the light of the facts."
He quotes from Roman records the edicts, "That all who
for any reason whatever are away from their own Nomos
should return to their home to enroll themselves," and

in connection with the return of Mary and Joseph to Bethlehem at the time of the birth of Jesus, he says: "From modern discovery it now appears that the order to return to the original home, though in a sense non-Roman in spirit, was the regular feature of the census *in the Eastern provinces.* * * * From a fair, unprejudiced and rational consideration of the evidence of Luke, Pliny, Tacitus, Clement and Tertullian, we conclude that the statements of Luke are all probable in themselves, and that the theory either of invention or of stupid error on his part is unreasonable and unjustifiable. * * * This theory is an astonishing example of modern European capacity for making false judgments." (Page 253.) And in speaking a little later of this same false scholarship, which presumptuously sets itself up as superior to God's word, Ramsay says:

"I confess that, when I see the self-satisfied and pretentious ignorance of the critical theologians miscalling and villifying this most wonderful little gem of historical insight and word painting, I find it difficult to restrain my indignation. These are the dull and blind savants whom the modern world has accepted as 'learned,' and to whom so many have humbly bowed down and done homage and worship."

So much, then, for my opponent's flat assertion that there are three errors of history in this one passage. There are no errors. The old Book is vindicated by facts, and it has been thus vindicated again and again over all such contested points. Dr. Sayce, another one of the world's leading archaeologists, has said truly: "Every turn of the spade has unearthed corroborative evidence of th eminute truthfulness of Scriptural history." And Professor Sayce said further in acknowledging a mistaken conclusion that he had reached on a point of Biblical history, "We must write our history of Elam all over again. We have been wrong and the tenth chapter of Genesis is right after all."

I can never forget the impression made upon my own mind as I stood before the inscriptions on the wall of the old temple at Karnak, Egypt, and saw there the account of Shishak's campaign in Israel, and the list of the names of the cities that he had conquered. The two accounts—one written upon the page of the Bible and the other carved in enduring stone—are in agreement! I can never forget, either, the thrill which I experienced in connection with the discoveries of Petrie at the treasure house of ancient Egypt, dating back to the time of the Israelitish bondage. He found there in those walls some brick made with straw and *other brick made without straw,* suggesting in a way that was dramatic and overwhelming the literal accuracy of the Bible account of how the ancient Israelites were so driven by their task masters. Some of the bricks that they made, of necessity, had to be made without straw.

THE MORAL CHARACTER OF GOD

Just a word, in closing, in reply to the aspersions which my opponent casts upon the moral character of God as He is pictured in the Old Testament record. Take, for example, his reference to the suggestion about giving defective things to strangers and aliens. How trivial and unfair was his interpretation! Apart entirely from considerations about the peculiar customs of the Hebrews, which differed radically from the customs of other ancient peoples, was it indeed not better to give to the poor that which was not of use to its owner than utterly to discard it without having it serve anyone? Does not my opponent know that thoughtful writers have commented again and again upon the nobility of the teaching of the Old Testament in connection with the "stranger"? We find the care with which God directed just treatment and consideration for strangers one of the most unique and noble elements in the Hebrew writings.

While, of course, it is well known that the Bible is a progressive revelation, and that the full-rounded view of the character of God can be obtained only in the light of both Old and New Testaments taken together, nevertheless, the aspersions cast upon God, as revealed in the Old Testament, are without warrant in fact or justification in ethics. It is certainly a strange paradox that faith in the God of the Bible, whom my opponent claims was an immoral Being, has produced the highest morality that the human race has ever known! While the foremost nations of antiquity were bowing down to dumb idols, while Egypt was worshipping the crocodile, while Athens was giving tens of thousands of women to the licentious rites of Venus, and Alexandria was rotting in sensuality through the worship of Aphrodite, while Rome was adoring the bloody god of war, and while even the Parsee could rise no higher than to turn his face eastward and adore the sun, the ancient Hebrews were worshipping a spiritual God—holy, just, righteous, and true.

The alleged immorality of God in directing the children of Israel to "borrow" from the Egyptians is entirely beside the mark. The revised version makes it perfectly plain that they "asked" gifts—not loans—and that the Egyptians "gave"—not "lent," as in the old version. God was the owner of all that silver and gold, and the children of Israel were His own chosen people, called out from among all others to bring God's truth and a

Savior for the whole world. If God, therefore, directed
that enough of the silver and gold which He owned in
Egypt be asked for to later adorn His Tabernacle and
Temple, He had the full right so to do. Further, it is
well known that ancient peoples were accustomed to
asking and receiving gifts from one another in connection with their religious rites,—and that there was an
abundance of gold in ancient Egypt—enough and to
spare for all—is proved by the recent discoveries in Tut-
ankh-amen's tomb! The Bible, too, says explicitly that
"the Lord gave the people favor in the sight of the
Egyptians, so that they gave unto them such things as
they required." (Ex. 12:36.) Evidently, God's spirit
moved the Egyptians to a sense of justice in remember-
ing the long years of labor which the Hebrews had
given them as slaves.

And now as to the alleged immorality of God in hardening the heart of Pharaoh, that also is beside the mark.
The Bible says in other places that Pharaoh hardened
his own heart. Every student of Scripture knows that
there is a difference between a case where God *permits*
men whose wills are already turned from Him, as was
the case with Pharaoh, to be hardened in heart, even
because of the fact that that very hardening opens the
way for possible redemption when judgment has fallen
upon them and they see the futility and sin of resisting
God, and a case where He plans and brings about the
hardening.

It is well known, too, to all fair minds who come to
the study of the Scriptures, that God had to deal with
ancient peoples and conditions as they were and not as
they should have been in some ideal state. Just as Jesus
said about divorce, that Moses permitted it because of
the "hardness of the hearts" of the people, so the stoning

of children and all of that has to be interpreted in the light of the age. There were no reformatories, etc., in that time, and the Hebrews were a nomadic people. Obedience to parents, therefore, was vitally necessary if any semblance of order was to be maintained in the families and the tribes. One such incorrigible and hopeless degenerate as is described in Deuteronomy 21:18-21 might not only pollute all the other children in a family, but spread ruin far and wide throughout the tribe. Those nomadic people would either have to take such a son, with his moral contagion and ruin to himself and others, along with them in their journeys, or else dispose of him in some other way. The influence of such a character would lead to things worse than death to other children, and so the parents were authorized to *bring him for trial* before the "elders of the city" (verse 20). The custom was for the elders to meet in "the gate" of the camp or city for the trial of all cases, and verse 19 here proves that parents were to bring any incorrigible, gluttonous drunken son to the elders for trial.

They were authorized to punish with death by stoning, the customary form of execution. The purpose of it all, however, was a *moral purpose from God's side*. The object was "so shalt thou put evil away from among you; and all Israel shall hear and fear" (verse 21). Evidently the purpose of the stern judgment was to prevent crimes among the young through a wholesome fear, and the fact that we have no record of any case of such stoning in the Bible shows that it worked out just as God planned that it should. Furthermore, the fact that Judaism and Christianity are the two religions that have protected and glorified childhood is a sufficient answer to the libel that God was cruel in His attitude to the young.

THE SUPREME NEED TODAY

And as regards the much trumpeted "imprecatory psalms," a discriminating student of Scripture can plainly see that such psalms, when rightly understood as a part of the divine revelation, cannot be said to be faulty in ethics. In some cases they were ebullitions of personal anger and the desire for vengeance which is a part of the weakness of universal humanity, and in other cases they are fore-tellers of God's righteous wrath against His foes and expressions of His judicial indignation against evil-doing.

The surgeon is not immoral when he amputates a putrid limb in order to save the life of the entire body, and God was not immoral when He ordered the cutting off of rotten individuals and groups to save the masses of the people from utter corruption and moral death. It would be well, too, for us, in this lax and easy-going age, if we had a little more of the moral stamina which separates sharply between God's friends and His foes and which would pronounce divine wrath against iniquity!

I come back once more, therefore, to re-emphasize the thought that the supreme need of this age is a reassertion of the authority of a wise, holy, and loving God. The youth of today are falling increasingly into moral decay and loose and silly ideals of life because parental authority has been relaxed and the right discipline of homes has been abandoned. An appalling wave of lawlessness is sweeping over America and the world because of disregard of constituted governmental authority. The blight of divorce and the ravages of sensuality are wasting our society because the authority of right social standards has been lightly and jauntily waved aside by the rebellious spirit of today. *The key to all these dangers is the fact that men have lost the fear of God and the reverence for His authoritative word, which characterized former generation; and we will see obedience to parents and respect for laws and the purification of social ideals brought about only when first of all men everywhere are willing again to bow their wills to the will of a heavenly Father and, in joy and strength, to walk in the way that He has laid out.*

The Bible has survived all of the foes of the past, and it will prove once more victorious against the foes of the present. The coat-of-arms of the French Bible and Tract Society is the picture of a Bible in the form of an anvil, around which numbers of broken hammers lie upon the ground, and the motto is: *"The hammers break; the anvil abides forever!"*

IV

REBUTTAL FOR THE NEGATIVE*

I almost feel like preaching a sermon, too, but I remember that this is a debate. The reason why I did not attempt to answer the statements in my opponent's first speech was the simple rule of debate understood by every debater, that the first speaker on the negative side does not attempt to answer the first speech on the affirmative side; he leaves that to the rebuttal. This is the rebuttal.

I maintain that the *first point* brought forward by my worthy opponent, namely, that the preservation of the Bible proves its infallibility, is valueless, because the preservation of any book for any period of time does not in any sense prove that what is said in it is true. I know of a number of old musty books in libraries carefully preserved from the bookworms and the dust, but what is in them is not therefore necessarily true.

Furthermore, under that point he maintained that because the Bible is the world's best seller, therefore it must be infallible. Have you been reading any of the best sellers lately? Do you think that they are all infallible? Is the number of volumes printed of a certain book any argument whatever as to the worth of what is in it?

The *second point* brought up by my opponent was the unique universality of the Bible, the fact that so many people have been helped by the Bible. My answer to that is that there are still in the world more Buddhists than there are Christians. Therefore, if universality is an argument, the Buddhists are right and not the Christians.

*By Rev. Charles Francis Potter.

82

The *third point* brought by my opponent was that we have unity in diversity in this Book, that it is a library of 66 books, and yet is unified into a "wondrous and harmonious whole." I showed you that the diversities, destroying the harmony, are often flat contradictions, and therefore answered that argument.

The *fourth point* brought forward was that the Bible's prophecies have been fulfilled, especially those about Jesus. It happens that I spent two solid years in the study of Hebrew, and took every passage in the Old Testament which was supposed to be a prophecy relating to Jesus, and a group of fifteen of us working together for two years decided that every one of the passages that were supposed to refer to Jesus were easily explained by their own particular circumstances and time, and did not necessarily refer to Jesus at all.

The other prophecies are very questionable. The ones about the destruction of Nineveh, Tyre and Babylon, recorded in Zephaniah, Ezekiel and Isaiah, which my worthy opponent quotes, are certainly accurate in many details, for the very simple reason that the "prophecies" were written after the destruction took place.

One was mentioned, Deuteronomy 28:64-66—"And Jehovah will scatter thee (the Jews) among all peoples, from one end of the earth even unto the other * * * Thou shalt fear night and day." Well, it may be that the Jews are scattered over the face of the earth, but I don't know, they seem to be coming together. I have met a million or more since I came to New York, and I take off my hat to a great many of them. I have been unable to discover that they are in fear night and day. If this passage refers to the Jews, that part of it has not been fulfilled. They are not in fear night and day.

Most of the rest of the people around here are in fear
lest they will not be able to meet the bills which the
Jews send to them at the first of the month.

(The passage referred to in the New Testament:
"Heaven and earth shall pass away, but my words shall
not pass away," you know was said before the New
Testament canon was completed. It was stated a great
many years before there was any New Testament. The
Bible itself had not been written, and therefore that cannot refer to the Bible. That applies to all so-called
"prophecies" of the New Testament quoted by my
worthy opponent.

As for the Bible itself, regarding itself as the infallible
word of God, my worthy opponent's *fifth point*, that is
no argument at all. It begs the question. You cannot prove that a book is infallible by the book itself.
That is plain for everybody to see. The only way you
can use the Book is to peruse the Book and examine it
and see if it squares up with facts. That is the only way
to see whether or not it is infallible. I leave the dis-
position of that to the judges.

The *sixth point* which was brought out by my worthy
opponent was that the Bible has a certain "self-authenticating authority." I did not get that. Did you? The
Bible has a self-authenticating authority! Now if I
should go out on the street and say, "I have a self-
authenticating authority, Mr. Policeman, get over there
out of the way," what would happen? If any book
claims to have a self-authenticating authority—what
does that mean anyhow—how can anything be *self*-
authenticating?

My opponent tried to explain it by saying that there
must be a court of last appeal, and this was it. The
proposition that a straight line is the shortest distance

between two points vindicates itself, he said. Yes, there is another thing that vindicates itself: that anything which has a greater specific gravity than water sinks. That is just as evident as that a straight line is the shortest distance between two points. But, this Book tells in the Old Testament of how miraculously an iron axehead was made to float. I maintain that the "self-authenticating authority" of the law of gravity proves to me that that axe-head—well, if it floated, it was not iron, and if it was iron, it did not float.

There is a court of last appeal, yes. It is neither in the church nor in the Book. A great deal of fun was cast by my worthy opponent upon those who think that consciousness of the individual is the court of last appeal. But I maintain that in matters religious there is only one connection, and that is between the conscience of a man and his God. And I maintain that the cultivated individual conscience is the court of last appeal, and that a man who says so is not a religious anarchist, he is merely a democrat.

I was glad that he referred to Winston Churchill in the war days at some length, about passing over Jordan and going in to the Promised Land, etc. That is just what the Kaiser thought he was doing. The German Emperor was an inveterate Bible reader, and everything he did in Belgium, I can find you a passage for in the Old Testament, where it states that the Lord told the children of Israel to do that very same thing.

In the *seventh point* brought forward by my worthy opponent, regarding the Bible's moral influence and power, he said, "it produced the goods." Well, it does, sometimes, just as the physician does. If he "produces the goods," that is, if he cures people three-fourths of the time, he is a good doctor. Many doctors have grateful patients, just as my worthy opponent has friends in this audience who could get up and testify of the curing power of the Bible. Many physicians have patients who can give testimony to the fact that they have been cured, but the physicians do not, therefore, claim infallibility, and infallibility is the point of this debate, don't forget that. I am not saying that the Bible is not a helpful book.

I was also very glad when my worthy opponent quoted Daniel Webster and said that Daniel Webster maintained that we should abide by the principles of the Bible. I myself am maintaining that we should abide by the principal truths of the Bible, but not by the very different statements that are made in certain parts of the Book by people who were ignorant men of their own time. I would like also to point out to my worthy opponent that this Daniel Webster who said, "Abide by the principles of the Bible," was a Unitarian.

The *final point* made by my worthy opponent was that this Book is a living thing. It is, but is that not rather an argument for fallibility rather than infallibility? It lives because it tells of how a certain group of people struggled toward God, and found Him, many of them, but the things that they said that God told them to do they sometimes made mistakes about. They said that God told them to do things that you and I know in our consciences were wrong to do. You know that you would not stone your boy if he were disobedient a hundred times. You are too good to do that, and if you are better than your God, then where is your God? You know that in the volume that we are referring to tonight there are many wonderful things. You know that in it there are many things which are helpful, but you can believe all that, as I do, and still maintain that this living thing, this book, like all living things is imperfect in parts and places.

In my worthy opponent's rebuttal he made some additional arguments which call for answer before I close.

He seemed greatly distressed, fearing that if the Bible has parts in it which we cannot accept as true, then we may be left without a moral guide. He implied plainly that he depends upon the Ten Commandments, and says that if those were deleted from the Bible, he would have the right, if he desired, to follow the lusts of the flesh. He asks who is to be the judge between the fallible and infallible parts. I reply that the enlightened conscience of man is, after all, the final and only guide.

He further misses the point in the matter of the inscriptions on the cross. If one evangelist quotes from a Latin translation, one from a Greek, and one from a Hebrew, then some very poor translating was done. If this is a sample of the translation of the whole Bible, then it is indeed a miracle that we have not more mistakes than the many I have pointed out.

As for the argument that "God may have even permitted some such difficulties to enter, to hold the interest of the world in the Book through all the ages, and in order to challenge and stimulate faith," that seems to me exceedingly unwise on God's part. To tell lies in order to seem interesting is a policy of very doubtful value. Honesty would seem a better policy. And as for stimulating faith, if a man's faith is to be measured by the size of his esophagus, then faith is synonymous with credulity, and the small boy was correct in defining faith as "believing what you know ain't so."

How can my opponent say God is no respecter of persons and "treats all men with equal justice and fairness," when the whole Old Testament is the record of how Jehovah protected, coddled and favored one small Semitic nation at the expense of the others?

There are four species of hare in the lands of the Bible. The Arabs call them all "arnabeh" so they are undoubtedly the same animal mentioned in Leviticus 11:6, for the Hebrew there is "arnebheth." These four species Lepus Syriacus, L. Synaiticus, L. Aegyptius and L. Isabellinus are all rodents and not ruminants; that is, they do *not* chew the cud.

The Leviticus 11:2 passage is ambiguous. Of course, grasshoppers "have legs above their feet." What good would their feet be if they didn't? The point of the whole matter is that even a Boy Scout reading the 11th chapter of Leviticus would laugh aloud at the ignorance of natural history therein imputed to Jehovah.

As for Michal, the childless woman with five sons, why doesn't this infallible book say "nephews" or "step-sons," or whatever they were? It says plainly, "sons." If you will turn to that verse, II Samuel 21:8, you will notice that in the King James version it says, "The five sons of Michal, the daughter of Saul, whom she brought up for Adriel." From that word "brought up" my opponent has inferred they were not her sons, but nephews. If you will look in the margin of your King James Bible, if it has marginal references, you will find that it says that the Hebrew of the passage is *"bare* to Adriel."

You will also find that the American Standard Revision Bible, which is always closer to the Hebrew, translates this passage, "whom she bare to Adriel." The very same Hebrew word, "yalad," is used here which is used in the first part of the same verse where it speaks of "the two sons of Rizpah, the daughter of Aiah, whom she *bare* unto Saul."

You see it is quite evident that the King James translators saw the difficulty of the contradiction between this verse and II Samuel 6:23 which says that Michal had no child, and so they took the rather dangerous liberty of translating the word "yalad," which every Hebrew scholar knows means "bare" in the sense of bringing forth in child-birth, to the word "brought up," in order to avoid the very obvious contradiction. To my mind, this was a cheat. Their conscience pricked them so that they put the correct translation in the margin, and the braver revisers put it back in the text.

If you will turn to I Samuel 18:19 you will see that the wife of Adriel was Merab, another of Saul's daughters. It is quite evident that the author of II Samuel 21:8 made a mistake and should have written "the five sons of Merab." This whole thing doubly proves my contention that there are mistakes in the Bible.

The fact that my opponent read a newspaper out-of-doors by after-glow after nine o'clock at night in California is no proof that Joshua made the sun stand still. I have read a newspaper out-of-doors at 10.30 p. m. in Edmonton, Alberta, Canada, and if you go north to the land of the midnight sun you can read one at midnight, but that does not prove that in Palestine "the sun stayed in the midst of heaven, and hasted not to go down about a whole day."

Sir William Ramsay's eulogy of Luke 2 proves nothing. Nearly every other scholar will admit that the confusing statements in that chapter are responsible for the fact that the birth of Jesus is variously set from B. C. 6 to A. D. 10. Even the conservative King James Version published by the Oxford University Press has Jesus Christ's birth dated in the year 5 *Before Christ*.

I still maintain that it is not right to give to a stranger

or sell to an alien meat from animals which have died of themselves. My worthy opponent says that it is better to give it to the poor than to let it be wasted. But the poor have scruples too, occasionally, and the Bible does not say that the strangers and aliens were poor. The strangers within the gates were guests and the aliens had money enough to buy the food. This supposed counsel of God advocated both a breach of hospitality and the practice of doubtful business ethics.

I resent also my worthy opponent's aspersions upon the other nations contemporary with the ancient Hebrews. Egypt, Athens, Alexandria and Rome were not all morally perfect, but their morals are at least favorably comparable with the earlier Israelites, whose own records show that they did not hesitate to sacrifice human beings to Jehovah.

It is hard to get my opponent's point of view about the "borrowing" of the jewels by the departing Israelites. He endorses it on two grounds, first, that the jewels were Jehovah's anyway, and second, that the Egyptians had plenty and didn't really need them. But Jehovah was not the god of the Egyptians. Even if he had been, the ethics of the case are certainly questionable. And as for saying that the rich Egyptians didn't need the jewels, that is what every thief robbing a rich man's house says today. My worthy opponent puts Jehovah in the same moral category with Robin Hood.

I still fail to see the fair play of a Jehovah who would harden a man's heart and then punish him for having a hard heart. If Jehovah did it to "open the way for redemption," then he was a theological politician with ways that were dark and tricks that were vain.

If, furthermore, "the stoning of children and all of that has to be interpreted in the light of the age," as my worthy opponent admits, then doesn't that place Jehovah in the same stage of moral development with his chosen people? A God who will command his worshippers to stone children to death for disobedience to parents is an immoral tribal deity whose words cannot by any casuistry be considered infallible for us today.

If the imprecatory Psalms are samples of "God's righteous wrath against his foes," if God is happy when the little children of his worst enemies are dashed against the stones, then I, for one, cannot worship such a God, or consider his word infallible.

If men today have lost the fear of God, as my opponent laments, let me tell him the reason. It is just because they cannot fear such an ignorant, malicious, grotesque God as the Jehovah of the Old Testament. Such a God inspires not fear, but hearty laughter today. The God of today is much different, more like the loving Father of whom Jesus the Carpenter spoke.

What we are contending tonight, my friends, is simply this: That the Bible is not the infallible word of God. We do find in it inspiration and help. We do find messages from God, but the contention which, I maintain, has been proved both in my first speech and in the rebuttal, is this: That the Bible is not the infallible word of God. (End of rebuttal.)

V

THE JUDGES' REPORT*

Judge Almet F. Jenks said: "Mr. President, ladies and gentlemen, I have been called by my associates to make the announcement of the decision of the judges. We unite somewhat in the regret that the first canon of Aristotle in logic, as I remember it, was not observed more strictly in a plain and clear and, if possible, accepted definition of the term of the question. It would have been better if the minds of the two speakers, both eloquent and able, could have agreed upon the full force and purport of the words in which the question is stated. The apt phrase of the question is the word 'infallible.'

We have agreed that no man shall attempt any speech, because perhaps it would be an anti-climax, and I have but to announce the decision of the judges. We are not united. The vote is two for Doctor Potter and one for his opponent."

*The Judges deliberated from 10:13 P. M. to 10:26 P. M., a period of thirteen minutes. The judges were former Justice Almet F. Jenks, Judge Ernest L. Conant and Mr. C. Neal Barney, former mayor of Lynn, Mass. Two of these men are Episcopalians and one a Universalist.

EVOLUTION VERSUS CREATION

Rev. JOHN ROACH STRATON, d. d.
and
Rev. CHARLES FRANCIS POTTER, m.a., s.t.m.

This book contains the only official text of the second of a series of five theological debates between Rev. Charles Francis Potter, challenger, and Dr. John Roach Straton, to be published under the following titles:

I: THE BATTLE OVER THE BIBLE
Question: The Bible is the Infallible Word of God

II: EVOLUTION VERSUS CREATION
Question: The Earth and Man Came by Evolution

III: THE VIRGIN BIRTH—FACT OR FICTION?
Question: The Miraculous Virgin Birth of Jesus Christ is a Fact and an Essential Christian Doctrine

IV: WAS CHRIST BOTH GOD AND MAN?
Question: Jesus Christ is the Only Divine Son of God

V: UTOPIA—BY MAN'S EFFORT OR CHRIST'S RETURN?
Question: Jesus Christ Will Return in Bodily Presence to this Earth and Establish the Reign of Universal Peace and Righteousness

Dr. Straton takes the affirmative in all but the second debate. The first debate was held in Calvary Baptist Church, New York on December 20, 1923, the second in Carnegie Hall, January 28, 1924, and the third and fourth also in Carnegie Hall, on March 22 and April 28, 1924. Copies of each debate will be published separately at 50 cents each and the entire series on completion will be reissued in one volume, cloth at $2.00.

These debates may be obtained from the Religious Literature Departments of the Calvary Baptist Church and the West Side Unitarian Church or at all booksellers.

NEW YORK : GEORGE H. DORAN COMPANY

EVOLUTION VERSUS CREATION:

Second in the Series of
Fundamentalist-Modernist Debates .

between

Rev. JOHN ROACH STRATON, D.D.
PASTOR, CALVARY BAPTIST CHURCH
NEW YORK

and

Rev. CHARLES FRANCIS POTTER, M.A., S.T.M.
MINISTER, WEST SIDE UNITARIAN CHURCH
NEW YORK

NEW YORK
GEORGE H. DORAN COMPANY

INTRODUCTION

By Rev. John Roach Straton, D.D.

The debate which follows aroused intense interest not only in New York but throughout the country and even in foreign lands.

In delivering my speeches during the debate, I had, on account of the time limit, to condense some of the paragraphs that are herein printed and also some of the quotations from authorities. In preparation for the debate, as I did not know, of course, just what particular aspect of the very wide question of evolution Mr. Potter might emphasize in his opening argument, I had to be prepared thoroughly on every side of the question. I had in my manuscript, therefore, a number of very valuable quotations, and much other matter that is really important in the full consideration of the question of evolution, which I could not use on account of the time limit, and which is not printed in this book.

I purpose, therefore, bringing out another volume on the subject: "The New Infidelity—Evolution Versus God," in which I shall hope to give a thoroughgoing discussion of the entire subject of evolution, with an adequate exposition of Bible teaching as related to these issues, and also with a frank consideration of the conflict between the great doctrines of revealed religion and the evolutionary theories, and the disastrous results of the evolutionary teachings upon individual morals and Christian consecration.

I acknowledge Mr. Potter's courtesy in agreeing to the fuller quoting herein of authorities, etc., than was possible in the spoken debate.

I need only add that this second debate once more, I feel, justifies my original willingness to go into these debates, because, as I remarked in the introduction to the printed form of the first debate—"The Battle Over the Bible,"—I foresaw that they would bring before the people a clear statement of what Modernism really is and what it inevitably leads to.

JOHN ROACH STRATON.

Study of Calvary Baptist Church,
New York City.

INTRODUCTION

By Rev. Charles Francis Potter, M.A., S.T.M.

I have agreed to the inclusion in Dr. Straton's speeches of more matter than he actually presented in the debate. As this extra matter is largely quotation from authorities, however, it does not change his line of argument, and makes the book more valuable.

There should be many debates on evolution in the coming years. Both evolutionists and creationists need to know more of each other's arguments, for there is much unscientific dogmatism on both sides.

Sometime I hope to participate in or listen to a debate phrased as follows:

"Resolved that evolution is a more reasonable theory for accounting for the origin of the earth and man than the Genesis creation story."

Charles Francis Potter.

Study of West Side Unitarian Church,
New York City.

vii

CONTENTS

I

FOR THE AFFIRMATIVE*

Question:
Resolved, That the Earth and Man Came by Evolution

Mr. Chairman, Honorable Judges, Worthy Opponent, Gentlemen of the Press, Ladies and Gentlemen of this audience and of the invisible audience of thousands of radio listeners:—

Ever since man has been on the earth he has been wondering how he got here, and how the earth got here.

The very earliest literature of our ancestors which we have yet discovered is largely concerned with these two great problems, and the first questions of the growing child of today are, "Who made me, and who made the earth?" Mankind, young and old, has always had an insatiable curiosity about these matters, and your presence here tonight indicates that the interest in these problems is not only as strong as in former times, but is even increasing. It will assist us in our approach to this question tonight if we examine some of the theories which savage and semi-civilized men have held.

LEGENDS OF CREATION

It is very fascinating to study the various legends of the different races of mankind, which tell about how they think the earth and man came into existence.

There is a tribe of Indians in Paraguay who believe that God originally existed in the shape of a beetle, liv-

---

* First speech for the affirmative by Rev. Charles Francis Potter, Minister of West Side Unitarian Church.

11

ing in a hole in the earth. This beetle, they think, formed man and woman out of the clay which he excavated from this hole. Man and woman, according to them, were at first one being, like Siamese twins. This was rather awkward, so they asked the beetle to separate them. He cut them apart and gave them the power of having children. Accordingly, this man and woman became the father and mother of all mankind. A tribe of Mexicans, the Michoacans, believed that a great god, named Tucapacha, made the first man and woman out of clay. When the couple went to bathe, they melted in the water, so Tucapacha tried again and made them out of ashes, with a similar result. Growing wiser because of these failures, he made them out of metal, and they were able to take their bath without falling to pieces. From their children came all the races of men.

In West Africa, some of the tribes of Togoland believe that God still makes men from clay. When he wants to make a good man, he takes good clay. For a bad man he uses poor clay. They believe that in the beginning God made a man in this fashion and put him on the earth. After that God made a woman. The two looked at each other and, according to the legend, they began to laugh. Thereupon God made them go forth into the world. We might add to this legend that they have been laughing at each other ever since.

A tribe of Australian blacks living near Melbourne used to think that the creator, Pund-Jel, cut out great sheets of bark with a big knife. Then he mixed some clay and worked it up like putty to the proper consistency. Upon the pieces of bark he then moulded the clay into human form. He was so pleased with his work, that is, he saw that it was so good, that he danced around the images for joy. He did not like the bald appearance of the heads of the images, so he took some stringy bark from the eucalyptus tree and made hair of it, which he put on the heads of the clay men. It was such an improvement that he danced around them again. Next, he lay down upon the images, and blew his breath forcibly into their mouths and their noses. Soon the images moved, spoke, and then stood up and were full-grown men.

This West African story will be recognized by those familiar with Greek mythology as resembling the one about Prometheus who, according to legend, moulded the earliest men from clay which he found at Penopeus at Phocis.

A Babylonian account of creation, preserved to us by Berosus, a Babylonian priest, says that the great god, Bel, cut off his own head. The blood was mixed with earth by the other gods. From the mixture the first men were made. The Babylonians said that that was why men were somewhat wise, because the mortal part, the clay, was mixed with the divine part, the blood.

Another tribe in that part of the earth had a legend which was quite similar to the Babylonian in many respects. The divine element in man was due, not to blood, as the Babylonians said, but to the divine breath which they believed was put into man in much the same fashion as the Australian blacks conceived of it, namely, by blowing it into man's mouth and nostrils.

The tribe of which I am speaking, which lived at the eastern end of the Mediterranean Sea many years ago, the Habiru, had other parts in their creation story which were very interesting. They were very inquisitive, these people, and asked a number of questions, and out of the answers to the questions grew their creation story.

The questions were very natural ones, such as, "How did the world get here?" "Where did man come from?" "Why is man different from the animals?" "Why is he conscious of sex and feels ashamed, while the beasts do not?" "Why is it that man, who seems to be above the beasts, has to toil and labor and get his bread by the sweat of his brow?" "Why is it that women, unlike the beasts, seem to suffer so in childbirth?"

These and other questions they answered in their Creation story. Some of the answers in the legend were rather original. Others were evidently copied from old Babylonian, Chaldean and other creation myths with which they were somewhat familiar.

The Creation story which they finally evolved ran something like this:

When God created the earth he also created the heavens above the flat earth. It was all dark. The earth was formless, but God moved in spirit form in the space between the earth and the heavens, and he said, "Let light come." And light did come. And he separated the light from the darkness and he called the light day and the darkness night. The next day he saw that he was in trouble unless he made some improvements, for there were evidently waters in the heavens as well as waters on the earth. In order to separate the waters below from the waters above he made what they call a "rakia," like a great inverted bowl above the flat earth. This kept the heavenly waters from descending upon the earth. That was his second day's work. (Later on in the story we find that God got angry and opened some trap doors, or windows, or skylights in this "rakia" or firmament and let the heavenly waters down upon the earth and caused a great deluge.)

The third day he separated the dry land from the waters and created grass, seed-bearing herbs, and fruit trees.

The fourth day he fastened lights on the underside of this inverted bowl, or "rakia"—two big ones—one for the day time called the sun, one for the night called the moon, and a lot of smaller ones called stars.

The fifth day he created fishes and birds.

The sixth day he created the animals and man and woman and gave man the charge of all the animals.

On the evening of the sixth day he looked the whole creation over and decided it was very good, so he took the seventh day for a rest.

There were other versions of this creation story which this Semitic tribe at the east end of the Mediterranean Sea believed. In one of them God did not create man and woman together as this first account says, but made man some little time before he created woman. He made man out of the dust of the ground and breathed into his nostrils the breath of life. After the man had lived in the company of the animals for a while, he wanted better company, and God made him go to sleep, took out a rib, and made a woman for him. This rib story is a very common one, by the way, among several of the tribes of the earth. It was found widely current in Polynesia when the first white men visited the islands.

There were many other interesting things in connection with this Semitic legend, but as most of you have heard it before I will not go into them.

Of course you see the inconsistencies in this story. Notice that this primitive tribe very naively said that God created light on the first day, but that he did not make the sun, moon and stars until the fourth day. How could there be day and night without the sun? Then again, the whole idea of all creation being completed in six days of 24 hours each is extremely primitive. It is no use to say that these days were ages, because the word used is "yom" which, in the language of this tribe, means a day of 24 hours; more precisely, the light part of the 24 hours.

All these inconsistencies in the legend would merely amuse us, just as the similar ones of other tribes amused you tonight, if it were not for the fact that the creation story of this primitive tribe, the "Habiru," was passed on to their descendants and became very influential in the thought of a great many other nations who have lived since, for the "Habiru" were the Hebrews, and this is the story which you find in the first part of Genesis, in the Bible.

When the Christian Church was founded, the Jewish legend of creation was taken along into the new religion, and made a part of it. Down through the centuries, since the beginnings of Christianity, this Hebrew legend has persisted and is accepted by many people today as an actual scientific account. Many people actually believe that this gives an adequate explanation of how the earth and how man came. What is more, the reason why I am debating here tonight is because the Fundamentalists of today want this primitive Hebrew legend taught as actual scientific truth in our public schools in America.

Only last week the North Carolina State Board of Education with the approval of the Governor is reported to have prohibited the teaching of evolution in the schools under its jurisdiction.

I do not know whether or not my worthy opponent will champion this ancient Hebrew version of creation here tonight. I presume that he will, because he has constantly done so for a good many years, and he can hardly go back on it now. What I am here for tonight is to set forth before you a considerably different explanation of how the earth and man came, the theory of evolution, championed by the scientists of the modern world. I shall not set it forth in scientific phraseology, as I am not a scientist, but I shall endeavor to speak in plain language the arguments for evolution which seem to me valid. I bespeak your sympathetic attention.

Our debate resolution is stated, "Resolved, That the Earth and Man Came by Evolution." In order that we may not dovetail our arguments, but may really clash on the central issue of the entire debate, Dr. Straton and I have agreed to take for our common definition of Evolution the one given by LeConte. This definition is found in the book, "Evolution and Its Relation to Religious Thought," written by Joseph LeConte, at one time Professor of Biology and Natural History in the University of California. In the edition of 1889 the definition is found on page 8, and reads as follows:

"Evolution is (1) continuous, *progressive change,* (2) *according to certain* (that is, fixed) *laws,* (3) and by means of *resident forces.*"

You have noticed that there are two sections to the question under discussion. Dr. Straton and I thought it would be well to include the evolution of both the earth and man, inasmuch as these two were so closely related and are, in popular thought at least, always connected. I shall therefore devote the first part of my thesis to three arguments for the evolution of the earth, and the second part to eight arguments for the evolution of man.

ARGUMENTS FOR THE EVOLUTION OF THE EARTH

1. *The Changes Now Going On*

Even a child can notice the changes that are now going on in the earth. When you go to your favorite seashore next summer, you will find that the coast-line is somewhat different from what it was last summer. There is a deeper indentation here and a larger sandbar there. If you go to Niagara this summer, you may notice that the Gorge is cut deeper than it was when you went there on your wedding trip. Scientists have been able to reckon the age of Niagara Falls by figuring the rate at which those hard rocks are worn away by the action of the falling water.

Not long since, some of our Fundamentalist friends

thought that the hand of the Lord had been laid in chastening on the wicked people of certain sections of Japan. It is quite evident, however, that this was not a supernatural phenomenon, but a very natural occurrence in the evolution of the earth's crust. What happened at Tokyo was a change according to certain laws, and by means of resident forces, and was not due to the peculiar wickedness of people who happened to occupy that particular area. These changes and many others that are now going on point to the evolution of the earth. The great forces of erosion and the settling of the earth's crust are all recent chapters in the change of the earth from its earlier forms to its present one.

2. *The Evidence of Past Changes*

It is when we examine deep cuts into the earth's crust that we are able to see more clearly the drama of evolution as it has affected the earth. It is impossible, of course, to give in a few minutes the entire story of how the earth has evolved, but any one who has been down far enough into the earth's crust to visit a coal mine, knows that there we find many evidences of the fact that the earth was once much different from what it is now. Once I went down into a coal mine, and the miners brought me fossils which they had found. When you see in the coal the natural fossil imprint of a great equatorial fern, you realize that at one time that which is now black coal was the vegetation of a hot climate, and you know that conditions on the earth in that far distant time were considerably different from what they are now. In other words, the evolution of the earth becomes a real fact to you. You believe the geologist when he tells you that it took longer to lay down one vein of coal than the six thousand years which some ignorant people think comprises the time from the day of creation until now.

3. *The Testimony of Astronomy*

With the perfection of various instruments used by astronomers we have brought before our very eyes the view of the worlds in the making. There are now available for every one who cares to look at them, actual photographs of great stars and suns which are now in the condition in which the earth was millions of years before it cooled off enough for life to appear on it. Great spiral nebulae, huge rolling masses of gaseous vapor, looking very much like enormous Fourth of July pin-wheels, can actually be seen. They are in different stages of condensation. Some are hardly more than great areas of vapor. Others have a well-defined nucleus at the center. Still others, like our own sun, seem to be fairly solid, and gases appear as streamers from their circumference.

Sometime in the distant past, our own earth went through these stages and gradually cooled. The vapors condensed into water, and the earth became gradually fit for life. The spectroscope has revealed that the stars are composed of the same elements as the earth and astronomy proves the earth a satellite of the sun, hence we have proof of the origin of the earth from nebulous gaseous material.

If we use our own eyes in coal mines and at the small end of a great telescope, and if we then do even a very little thinking, we will, I think, be more inclined to believe in the evolution of the earth through long ages of time, rather than think that some Jehovah-God created it in one short 24-hour day, as the Hebrew legend says.

ARGUMENTS FOR THE EVOLUTION OF MAN

1. *From Ancient Life on the Earth* (*Paleontology*)

All the arguments which we shall present for the evolution of man are deduced from facts which may be verified

by any one in this audience who will visit the various
places where this information is available.

One of the earliest clues to the evolution of animal life
on the earth was found in the various strata of the earth
itself.   In the processes of the evolution of the earth,
mountains have been worn down by erosion, and the re-
sultant sand and dirt, combined with the decaying animal
and vegetable matter, has been deposited in strata or
layers all over the surface of the earth.   Obviously, the
further down you dig the older are the layers which you
find.   In some places on the earth these layers have been
almost undisturbed since they were laid down.   In others,
they have been tilted and sometimes completely reversed,
but scientists are able to determine which are the older
strata by a careful study of the various sections where
rivers have cut deep gorges, or where cracks have occurred owing to volcanic action.   When I drive from my
home in Pelham to my church on 110th Street and ride
along Riverside Drive, I look across at the Palisades and
notice very distinct strata of different colored rocks on
the Jersey side, a daily demonstration of the evolution
of the earth.

Now when we examine these layers in places where
they have not been disturbed, we find evidences of animal
life in many of the layers, and the further down we go,
the simpler become the forms of life.   It is possible by
painstaking study to discover a genuine progression of
forms from ancient simpler forms to the modern highly
complex animal organisms.   In other words, we find a
gradual progression from lower types to higher types of
animal life as we proceed from the lower to the higher
strata.   We also find that the animals and plants of the
highest, that is the newest geologic strata, resemble most
the animals and plants of the present day.

Another law which appears from examination of these
strata is this: Very commonly we find a new group of

animals appearing near the end of some geologic age
during which changes of climate were taking place.
That new group, as a rule, became the dominant group
of the next period, evidently because it had become somewhat hardened to the changed conditions and was ready
to meet the trials of the new environment. (This is
well pointed out on page 70 in Dr. Newman's "Readings
in Evolution," published by the University of Chicago
Press, which is one of the most satisfactory books on the
whole subject of Evolution.)

From these readily observable facts it is evident to a
logical mind that the geologic strata furnish very worth-
while testimony of the evolution of animal life on the
earth. When we add to this the recently available ob-
servations of those who have discovered the buried
remains of man himself in these various strata we have
a strong argument for the evolution of man himself.

I presume you are more or less familiar with the fossil
remains of ancient man. In post-glacial time, about
25,000 years ago, lived an interesting people called the
Cro-Magnon race. Their skeletons have been found in
Europe. Twice as long ago lived the Neanderthal Man.
150,000 years ago, approximately, lived the Piltdown
Race. Approximately 375,000 years ago lived the
Heidelberg man, and the earliest human remains found
upon the earth are those of the Pithecanthropus or Ape-
man found in Java, and dated by scientists about half a
million years ago.

All these races that I have mentioned have left fossil
specimens. When we compare their anatomical structure
we find a steady growth away from the ape-like form
toward the present human skeleton. Doubtless many
more specimens will be found in the next few years. We
have only begun to discover the scattered remains of our
very ancient ancestors, but we have discovered enough

already to indicate a number of so-called "missing links" between the earlier types and the present.

2. *From Geographical Distribution (Geography)*

When Charles Darwin went "rolling down to Rio," and saw the armadillo "a-dilloing in his arma," he found that the peculiar group of archaic mammals known as edentates, or toothless ones, including the armadillos, sloths, and ant-eaters, was practically confined to South America. When he found that the *fossil* edentates are also found only in South America, he had a very powerful argument for evolution. These fossil edentates resemble the existing specimens, but differ from them by having less developed forms.

It was evident to him, as it is to us, that the present armadillos are changed descendants of the ancient ones. It is very doubtful if any of these armadillos were driven into the ark by Noah, because South America was absolutely unknown at that time, and under the then current modes of transportation it would have been very difficult to get them to the eastern end of the Mediterranean. It is quite evident then, that, to use the words of A. R. Wallace, "all the existing forms of life have been derived from other forms by a natural process of descent with modification, and that this same process has been in action during past geologic time."

3. *From the Similarity of Man to Other Animals (Comparative Anatomy)*

The third argument for the evolution of man is from the similarity of man's body to those of other animals. Comparative anatomy reveals that not only the higher mammals, but the lower ones, even the reptiles and fishes, have many striking similarities of structure to the skeleton of the human animal. The counterparts of our various organs can be found among practically all quadrupeds. Our arms correspond to their front legs, and so on all through the body. If God had created man to walk erect why did he give him a body so similar to the animals, a body which has many parts which are of no use to him, and often are dangerous to his life.

4. *From Pensioners or Relics in Man's Body (Anatomy)*

There are many vestigial remnants in man like the vermiform appendix, the rudimentary tail at the end of the backbone called by anatomists the coccyx, the wisdom teeth, the third eyelid, the muscles for moving the ear, and many others. These all are atavistic relics of animal ancestors. They had a use once but that use no longer remains. None of these things are of any possible use to us now, and they are frequently the seat of trouble. Prof. Osborne has called them "pensioners,"— that is, they are now supported by an organism to which they were once of service.

The coccyx or skeleton tail alone proves man's connection with the monkey family. If you were to take an X-ray photograph of the lower end of Mr. Bryan's backbone, you would have proof enough of the falsity of his arguments. There are even four muscles for wagging the tail, revealed by every dissection of a human body.

We never use our wisdom teeth, but our animal ancestors, who cracked bones, did have use for them. We certainly cannot deny our relation to our animal ancestors; it is only a false pride which leads us to disavow the connection.

5. *From the Disadvantages of the Upright Position (Physiology)*

Man is frequently uncomfortable because of the fact that he has to walk continually upon his hind legs. His body is not adapted for that position; particularly among women this causes great discomfort, especially in the abdominal region. This is well-known among doctors, who find that many of their cases are due to abdominal displacements consequent upon the upright position.

Any one who has observed the difficulty which children have in learning to walk, and who has noticed the ease with which other animals, which are quadrupeds, learn to walk within a few hours or days after birth, easily realizes that the upright position is not natural to man.

The fact that the arch of the foot so often breaks down is an indication that man was not originally intended to walk erect. The fact that man is forced by eye strain to wear spectacles, and that in sleep or after death the eye-balls tend to roll upward, is an indication that the eye has not yet accommodated itself to its comparatively new position. The form of rupture called "inguinal hernia" is due to pressure of the intestines on one of the veins in the abdomen. Quadrupeds do not have this derangement. It is entirely due to the upright position.

All these difficulties and others which might be mentioned are due to the fact that the upright position is still unnatural to us. This is one of the reasons why you seldom find a practicing physician who does not believe in evolution.

6. From Pre-Natal Life (Embryology)

The human embryo-foetus, the unborn child, passes through all stages of animal evolution from a primitive one-celled form, up through fishes, reptiles, and early mammals to man. Every doctor knows this fact, and many of them have in their possession preserved specimens of prematurely born human embryos which prove the theory of the evolution of the individual. At one stage the embryo has gill-slits; at another stage, a tail longer than its hind-legs, and at the sixth month, hair all over its body. Even after birth the human animal exhibits certain simian characteristics, like tenacity of grip and inturned foot-soles.

Many a proud father has told me how strong his newly born infant was, how the child would grip his father's outstretched fingers and remain suspended for a full minute or longer. And every mother knows how the baby's legs and feet look startlingly like a monkey's when the child first begins to sit erect.

The evolution of each individual from a tiny cell through more and more complex and specialized forms up at last to man certainly shows the possibility of the race having come that way. Scientists tell us that each individual lives over again, recapitulates, the life of the race, so that each one of us, in his own biological development is an argument for the evolutionary process. Certainly if the individual evolves from a tiny cell, one one-hundred and twentieth of an inch in diameter, hardly visible to the naked eye, there is no real physical difficulty in the race having thus evolved. The study of embryology, therefore, contributes to the belief that man came by evolution.

7. *From Creative Evolution As Practised by Scientists Today*

New species of insects and plants have been produced by such scientists as the Morgan School and Luther Burbank. The spineless cactus and the loganberry are really new species. Experimentation with the drosophila, or fruit-flies, has, by changing and controlling the environment and food, produced more than fifty new species. Here we have evolution of plant and animal life going on right before our eyes.

8. *From Blood Tests (Chemistry)*

The chemical researches of Dr. George H. F. Nuttall of the University of California, and Professors Reichert and Brown of the University of Pennsylvania have definitely proved man's blood relationship to the lower animals. Not only this, but the proportional relationship can be indicated almost to a mathematical exactness. Still further, the relation of the various types of animals to each other can be determined by the experiments with de-fibrinated human blood and the oxyhemoglobin crystals of the blood.

Because of all these scientific facts which we have deduced, for these eight reasons, we maintain that man's body has evolved from primitive life on the earth. Between the creation account in Genesis and the general theory of evolution, the probability is overwhelmingly on the side of the latter. Evolution best accounts for the known facts, especially recently ascertained ones. Furthermore, since Evolution gave the clue, there has been such a rapid growth of science that it has progressed and produced beneficial results more in the last few years than in the previous history of mankind. As President McMurrich, of the American Association for the Advancement of Science, said recently, "All through the almost overwhelming flood of new knowledge there runs the guiding clue supplied by the doctrine of evolution. That has been the stimulus and dominating idea in all these studies; without it many, very many of them would never have been conceived and knowledge would have lost thereby."

THE EVOLUTION OF MIND AND SOUL

You may have noticed that my arguments for the evolution of man have all been confined to proofs of the evolution of man's body, and you may be saying, "But how about his mind and soul?" May I remind you all, and call it especially to the attention of the judges, that inasmuch as man's mind and soul (whatever definitions we may give for mind and soul, and whether these be natural or supernatural phenomena), have never been

proved to exist apart from his body, it is not necessary
for me to prove that they have come by evolution. My
thesis, if you have agreed with me thus far, is therefore
already proved.

But both the mind and soul of man have evolved. It
is only necessary for me to call your attention to the
earlier primitive theory of the origin of life and the
present-day doctrine of Evolution to show the evolution
of man's mind itself.

The earliest historic records we have and the comparative studies made of primitive races now existing show
that man's mind was originally very simple and closely
allied in its general processes to the mind of the animals.
Indeed, it is hard to draw the line between an intelligent
animal and a lower type of man in respect to the power
of their minds.

As for man's soul, or his spiritual nature, we have only
to compare the primitive religions, full of myths and
queer fancies, with the developed religions of today, to
be assured that just as man's body has developed, so has
his mind and soul. The evolution of man's mind and
soul, which a study of the human race reveals, is paralleled in the development of the individual: At first, a
child has a very simple mental equipment which rapidly
grows until he reaches his maturity. The religion of a
child is very similar to the religion of the early races.
At first he believes in myths and magic, and then reaches
the Ten Commandment stage, from which, if his development be normal, he reaches the higher types of religious
faith.

THE SO-CALLED "GAPS" IN EVOLUTION

Now as we view the whole drama of evolution there
appear certain gaps which trouble some who otherwise
are inclined to believe in the evolutionary process. They
see evidences of the evolution of the earth once it got

started. They see evidences of the animal life on the earth once that got under way. They see evidences of the evolution of man, once he was separated from the animals, but just how the earth started and how animate life started on the inanimate planet, and how thinking reasoning man with a spiritual life developed from the animals, they cannot quite understand. Consequently there are many people who are semi-evolutionists and who believe that at these gaps or crises in the evolution of the earth and the life upon it, including man, some super-natural person must have stepped in. They think some creator made the earth in the first instance, that he intro-duced life upon the earth and that when that life evolved to a point where the animals might become man, then he inserted his hand in the machinery again and in some way put a soul into man. In other words, these people believe in a natural order of things except for certain appearances of the supernatural. But that is be-cause these people still retain a belief in a *transcendent* God, a sort of absentee Lord of the Universe, who was not quite great enough to make a universe that would run itself, so he was obliged occasionally to insert his hand or his power and by a miracle add something vital.

Now, my idea of God is that he is a supremely power-ful being—a personal force, not in personal form, who operates through natural laws. I believe that every event in nature occurs and has occurred by natural law.

I believe that at no time has a transcendent God inter-fered with the universe, but that God has been immanent in the evolutionary processes from the very beginning; that every upthrust of this life force has been a mani-festation of God; that you and I are manifestations of God, rather imperfect to be sure, but progressing toward better things.

God is, and always has been, immanent in the universe.

He was existent in the spiral nebulae from which this
earth was formed. He was existent in the matter which
gradually cooled and which formed until this earth became more like what it is now. He was immanent in the
dust and slime in the early stages. He was immanent in
the first forms of animate life which came directly from
the inanimate matter which existed before. He was
immanent in every reaching upward of the earlier forms
of life. He was immanent when our last animal ancestor
became gradually conscious of himself and of his difference from the beasts which had preceded him.

God has been present at every progressive development of mankind since that day. There is nothing supernatural about it. It is all natural. No miracles have
occurred unless all matter and life are miraculous.

I cannot believe in creation unless that creation is absolutely continuous, and if so, it becomes evolution. I
maintain that the earth and all life upon it, and man himself, have all come by constant, progressive change according to certain laws and by means of resident forces, and
I would include in these resident forces the life spirit,
God, himself.

Evolution is not only not against God: it is our best
evidence of Him. A wonderfully beautiful poem by
the Unitarian Dr. William Herbert Carruth expresses the
thought of God in Evolution:

> "A fire-mist and a planet,
> A crystal and a cell,
> A jelly-fish and a saurian,
> And caves where the cave-men dwell.
> Then a glimpse of law and beauty
> And a face turned *from* the sod:—
> Some call it Evolution
> And others call it God."

II

IN THE NEGATIVE*

There are but two notable theories concerning the origin of the earth and of man—one is creation by a living God; the other is evolution by dead force.

Evolution is not a fact of science, but a dogma of philosophy. Both its history and its essential nature prove that it belongs primarily to the realm of subjective speculation and not to the field of demonstrated fact. Even Professor Conklin, of Princeton, while declaring his acceptance of the theory of evolution, nevertheless says that "evolution must ever remain a theory." ("The Direction of Human Evolution"—preface.) Now a mere "theory" cannot be a science. Hence the term "the science of evolution" is a misnomer, and evolution should not seek to gain vogue by running on the prestige and popularity of the exact sciences.

Those of us who deny the theory of evolution, therefore, have no antagonism to true science. We only object to having that which is merely an hypothesis proclaimed dogmatically as though it were really fact. So far as I am personally concerned I am ready to accept evolution if it can really be proved true. Every man ought to be willing to accept truth from any quarter, however destructive it may be of former convictions. It is significant, however, that many who at first are fascinated by the plausible generalizations of evolution, turn from it after

* First speech for the negative by Rev. John Roach Straton, D.D., Pastor, Calvary Baptist Church, New York.

fuller examination of its alleged evidence and more
mature consideration of its claims.

The great scientist, Prof. George Romanes, of Oxford,
had such an experience. For a period in his life he was
an infidel and extreme evolutionist; and it is highly significant that during that time he wrote and spoke strongly
against the Bible teaching of Creation, and against super-
naturalism in all its forms. But later in life, through
the letters of a Japanese missionary friend, dealing with
experimental and practical religion, he changed his views
entirely, accepted the Bible, and died in 1894, confessing
his faith in God and in the full Diety of Jesus Christ.
("The Other Side of Evolution," p. 109.)

I, also, have had a similar experience. For quite a
period of my life—extending into a part of the time that
I have been a preacher—I was an evolutionist; or at
least I thought that I was, and accepted that view of the
universe and of man; but fuller study, both in the field
of science and philosophy, not only convinced me that
evolution is a colossal error, but that when logically followed out, it is utterly incompatible with the Christian
religion.

My honorable opponent, before the first debate of this
series, remarked that he had some advantage over me because before he became a Unitarian he was a Baptist, and
therefore he thought he knew about what my arguments
would be in the debate on the Bible.

I now profess the same advantage over him. I was
once an evolutionist and sceptic, but I have come back
to the truth of Creation by a living God rather than evolution by blind chance. Therefore, I can speak with a
deeper degree of conviction than if I had not passed
through such an experience. We have agreed to accept
LeConte's concise definition, namely that evolution is
"continuous progressive change, according to fixed laws,
and by resident forces." We have the privilege, however,

of turning the light of other and fuller definitions from authoritative sources upon the question, that we may see clearly just what evolution really is and what it leads to.

It is highly significant that the idea of evolution originated in pagan and heathen minds and was not a native product of the Christian intellect. The Greek philosophers speculated about the origin of the world in a fire mist, and Aristotle developed some of the main ideas of evolution long before Lamarck or Darwin or Spencer lived.

The Century Dictionary and Encyclopedia defines evolution in mechanical terms and as "opposed to creationism."

Huxley specifically declared: "It is clear that the doctrine of evolution is directly antagonistic to that of creation—as applied to the creation of the world as a whole, it is opposed to that of direct creative volition. Evolution, if consistently accepted, makes it impossible to believe the Bible."

Huxley's discussions with Gladstone and others were all based on the idea that the theory of evolution was incompatible with the Bible and the God of the Bible.

Sir Oliver Lodge says:

"Taught by science, we learn that there has been no fall of man; there has been a rise. Through an ape-like ancestry, back through a tadpole and fish-like ancestry, away to the early beginnings of life, the origin of man is being traced." ("Ideals of Science and Faith.")

In his article on evolution in the Encyclopedia Britannica, Professor James Sulley defines evolution as a "natural history of the cosmos, including organic beings, expressed in physical terms as a mechanical process." Lamarck, Darwin, Spencer and the more recent evolutionists, even those who try to hold on to faith in some sort of God while still holding to these theories, all define evolution in purely mechanical terms which really, of necessity, exclude God. And Darwin lost his faith in a living God through these evolutionary ideas.

Ernst Haeckel, the most logical, consistent and thoroughgoing of modern evolutionists, the only legitimate successor to Darwin's place and greatness, argued that evolution could completely dispense with the supernatural in any form and with any sort of personal interposition.

He explicitly denied the existence of a living God. He said:

"This notion [of a personal God or creator] is rendered quite untenable by the advancements of Monistic science. It is already antiquated and is destined before the present century is ended to drop out of currency." ("Christianity and Anti-Christianity," p. 189.)

Another frank evolutionist, Carl Vogt, says:

"Evolution turns the Creator out of doors."

PANTHEISM AND MAN-WORSHIP

My opponent, therefore, cannot claim God as the "resident force" under our definition, as he tried to do, unless, indeed, he is willing to admit himself a Pantheist, and say that God is wholly locked up in nature. If we admit any god outside of nature, then we must say with Genesis: "In the beginning, God." A living God, therefore, must be before the material world which He made. Hence, He cannot be wholly in that material world. A living God must be transcendent as well as immanent. He is before and above the world, and yet in it through His providential control and directing care. The engineer cannot be in his engine. He is the maker and driver of the engine, and his skill and controlling power are in it, but the engineer himself cannot be in the fire and the steam that drive the engine. The idea of any sort of "spirit" or living God locked up in the earth as it passed through stages of gaseous nebulosity and then of molten fire, etc., is simply unthinkable. It is an absurdity. The only possible god of evolution is the god of Pantheism, not a *living* being at all, but merely the "principle" or "law" of nature.

Now since the only god possible to evolution is Pantheism—god in nature as a mere "principle" or "law" or "eternal energy," as Spencer put it—it is proper that we should point out that Pantheism always has and always will lead to ruinous moral and social results when it is accepted by men.

For one thing, it leads to the worship of nature—principally the sun. And the awful immorality and the social decay of ancient Egypt, and other countries through the worship of the sun and of nature, should be a sufficient warning to us. Another inevitable and immediate result of Pantheism is that it leads to the deification of man, and hence to self-worship, with all the vanity and moral and social decay that inevitably follow such colossal error.

Therefore, the issue in this debate is not only an issue between creation and evolution, but between God and no God.

NO "THEISTIC" OR "CHRISTIAN" EVOLUTION

Furthermore, it is evident that there is no possible compromise between these two systems of thought. There is no middle ground. Either creation is true and evolution is false, or else evolution is true and creation is false. Either we must accept the revelation of a living God, and His creative and redemptive activities as given in the Bible, or we must utterly reject this and turn to the infidel philosophy of chance and materialism.

In other words, there is no such thing as so-called "theistic" or "Christian" evolution. Such terms are misnomers. Christianity is a religion founded on definite

historical facts. These facts—including the creation of
the world, and the creation, fall and salvation of man—
are recorded in the Bible. If, therefore, the Bible is
rejected, Christianity itself is rejected. In the face of
the essential nature of evolution, and in the light of definitions of it already given, the terms "Christianity" and
"evolution" are mutually exclusive and self-contradictory.
If it is Christianity, then it is not evolution; and if it is
evolution, then it is not Christianity. The mixed teachings of such men as Henry Drummond, Lyman Abbott,
and others, prove that they did not think these evolutionary theories through to their logical and inevitable
conclusion in unbelief. Such men either do not know
what real Christianity is, or else they do not know what
real evolution is. They are manifestly self-deceived if
they try to hold on to both evolution and Christianity.

THE QUESTION FOR DEBATE

The question for debate is, "Resolved, That the Earth
and Man Came by Evolution." There are two parts in
this resolution. The first relates to the origin of the
earth and the second relates to the origin of man. The
subject, therefore, involves first a consideration of inorganic evolution, or the alleged evolution of matter until
it reached its present form in our earth; and the second,
the question of organic evolution, with its alleged origin
of life upon this planet, through materialistic natural
forces, culminating in the coming of man.

My opponent is championing the affirmative in this
debate, and because of the fact that he is seeking to
establish a theory which is exactly contrary to the Revelation upon which Christendom has founded its life and
institutions for thousands of years, the burden of proof
is upon him. He must prove two things: first, that the
earth originated or "came" by evolution; and, secondly,
that man originated or "came" by evolution. He must

establish these two propositions by *facts* that are intelligible and convincing to the reasonable mind, and these facts must come in the form of credible evidence, and not mere supposition, guesses or hypotheses. Unless he can establish both of these propositions by facts, then he has lost the debate. My task in the debate is merely to point out the impossibility of his so doing, and to show that there is a far clearer and simpler way to account for the origin of the earth and man than by so-called evolution.

The question for debate is not, therefore, primarily a question of method. It is primarily a question of origins. Method cannot begin to work until something has originated for the method to work in or on. Hence a beginning must precede any evolution. The very name of such a book as Darwin's "Origin of Species" shows that. The real issue in the debate is whether the earth and man originated, or came, by *design* through the creative power of God, or by *chance* through the haphazard operation of evolution. It is the issue between naturalism and supernaturalism; between calculated planning and mere fortuitous circumstance.

It is to be clearly noted that there is a difference between evolution and development. The principle of development in human life, social institutions, and even animals under man's selective skill, is freely admitted. It is in this sense that the word evolution is often used by newspaper editors, speakers, magazine writers, etc. But this is radically different from evolution in the technical and scientific sense in which we are to consider it in this debate. In the technical sense it must be restricted to the alleged origin of matter and life through mechanical forces and without divine creative power; and, after such origin, the descent of all inorganic matter and all organic life from their simple primitive origins.

I ask the careful attention, then, of the judges and

the audience to the *exact form* of the question for debate, and the full *content* of the definition of evolution upon which my opponent and I have agreed. The question is "Resolved, That the Earth and Man Came—that is, Originated—by Evolution." The definition is that of the geologist LeConte, that evolution is "continuous progressive change; according to fixed laws; by *resident* forces." This means that evolution is (1) *"continuous* progressive change"; that is to say, its operation must be going on progressively now just as it is alleged it has always gone on in the past; (2) "according to *fixed* laws"; that is, there can be *no change* in the controlling laws and principles; evolution cannot be one thing in a former age and another thing today; and (3) "by *resident forces";* that is, there can be no outside interference—all must come *from within,* however great the modifications and changes in outward forms may appear

And, since it is claimed that evolution is a universal law that accounts for all things, and that it is operative everywhere, there ought to be an abundance of facts· on all sides to prove it if it is really true. But when we turn to look for the facts, we find, strange to say, that they are simply not there.

PART ONE

How the Earth Came

Let us take up first, then, the question of the origin of the earth. Notice, to begin with, that the scientists frankly admit that they do not know and therefore cannot tell us how the earth originated. Darwin himself said, positively, "The beginning of the universe is an unsolvable mystery." Notice that he admitted that it was not only a mystery, but an unsolvable mystery. Tyndal declared: "Evolution does not profess to solve the ultimate mystery of the universe." Prof. Clifford states it still more bluntly. He says: "Of the beginning of the

universe, we know nothing at all." Prof. Edward Clodd
says: "Of the beginning, of what was before the present
state of things, we know nothing and speculation is futile; but since everything points to the finite duration of
the present creation, we must make a start somewhere"
("Story of Creation," p. 137).

But when we enter the so-called scientific field we are
plunged immediately into a morass of speculations, hypotheses and guesses about alleged facts, on which no
two of the scientists agree among themselves.

THE SLIPS OF SCIENTISTS VS. THE "MISTAKES OF MOSES"

My opponent, in our last debate, pointed out some
alleged contradictions and supposed mistakes in the Bible.
I wish now to point out some of the blunders of science.

For instance, the temperature of the interior of the
earth is stated to be 1,530 degrees by one scientist, and
350,000 degrees by another! Herschel calculated the
mountains on the moon to be half a mile high, but Fergu-
son said they were fifteen miles high. Lyell estimated
that it had required over 35,000 years for the Niagara
River to eat back to the present position of the falls, but
he was later cut down to some 7,000 years. Lyell also
calculated that the delta at the mouth of the Mississippi
River had been 100,000 years in forming, but General
Humphrey, of the U. S. Survey, estimated it at only
4,000 years.

Glance now at the startling variations in scientific
guesses concerning the probable age of man. Myers says
that the Old Stone Age of man is to be measured not by
thousands but by millions of years. M. Rutot says the
relics of man which have been found date back to 139,000
years ago. Osborn places the first real man 500,000
years ago; James Geikie, 200,000; Croll, 980,000;
Sturge, 700,000; Townsend, 6,000; while Prof. LeConte

says: "The time which elapsed since man first appeared is still doubtful; some estimate it at more than 100,000 years, and some say 10,000." All the way from "millions" to 6,000 years! Well! well!

And when it comes to the question of the age of the earth, there is a variety and liberality of estimates, and a prodigal waste of ciphers, that fairly stagger the mind. No two of the scientists agree, even in their guesses, and when their estimates are brought side by side there is such a wide difference that the comparison becomes positively laughable. Prof. Ramsay, for example, estimated the age of our earth at fully *10,000 million* years. Sir Charles Lyell estimated it at four hundred million years. Charles Darwin said that it was more than three hundred million years. Dr. Croll, in his book on "Stellar Evolution," said that "at most it was twenty millions of years," while Prof. Tait, in his "Recent Advances in Physical Science," said that the age of the earth is "at most ten million years." Now, my friends, here is a little discrepancy between the highest and lowest estimates of nine thousand nine hundred and ninety *millions of years!* Well, that is a right considerable slice of time, we must all admit.

When we hear people say, therefore: "I would believe the Bible if it agreed with science," we have to ask: "What science?" How can the Bible possibly agree with both Professor Ramsay and Professor Tait, or with both Darwin or Lyell, when they themselves are millenniums apart?

I quote these figures not in a spirit of levity nor because I am lacking in respect for true science, when it stays in its appointed field and remains on solid ground, but I merely give these figures to show that the scientists really know nothing about the origin of the world, its age, or how it came into existence.

SOME SCIENTIFIC GUESSES

But as Prof. Clodd says, the scientists and philosophers must make a start somewhere. Not having any real facts and no true knowledge, when they turn from revelation, they are driven to guesswork.

As I have anticipated my opponent's argument in its main points in preparation for the debate, I will take up in passing some of the points he made, reserving a consideration of other points for my rebuttal. This will be an economy of time, and as the main lines of alleged evidences for evolution are comparatively narrow, it is really necessary to handle the matter in this fashion.

I congratulate my opponent on the presentation he has made of his side of the question. To have such a weak case, he has done well.

Let us take up, then, some of the guesses which the scientists have made in their effort to account for the origin of the earth on a materialistic basis.

We will consider, first, the so-called "nebular hypothesis," which is the main effort that the mind of man has made to account for the beginning of the earth on naturalistic grounds. In this connection, my opponent referred to some of the spiral nebulæ which have been observed by astronomers. I only say in passing that astronomers differ widely among themselves as to just what these spiral nebulæ are, and as to their real significance. Certainly, they have no direct connection with the proposition that our earth originated in a mass of nebulous matter that threw off portions of itself which became the planets with their satellites, etc. All of this is not only a mere guess, as the very term "nebular *hypothesis*" proves, but it must be admitted when the simplest facts are known that it is a bad guess. It is founded upon a series of assumptions so gigantic that they stagger the rational mind of man and stretch human credulity to the very breaking point.

No two scientists agree about it. Tyndal says that the world began in a "fire mist" that contracted as it became cold; but Spencer says it was a *cold cloud* which became heated as it contracted! Which shall we believe? Well, we cannot believe either if we follow true scientific experience, for the gases (or fire mists) that we know anything about do not act in either of those ways today. Further, there are now facts sufficient to throw the "nebular hypothesis" entirely out of court.

The simple fact that some of the bodies in our solar system, as, for example, our own moon and the satellites of Jupiter and Saturn, revolve from west to east, while the moons of Uranus and Neptune revolve from east to west, explodes the theory that the bodies in our solar system were thrown off and set revolving by some central, revolving parent mass of matter, for in that event they would all of necessity have to revolve in the same direction.

Furthermore, it must be self-evident that if the bodies of matter in our solar system were all thrown off, revolving rapidly, from a revolving mass of "parent matter," they would all naturally revolve with at least something like the same approximate speed, due regard of course being had to size. But this reasonable expectation is not met. Two of the eight principal planets in our solar system—namely, Mercury and Venus—have almost no rotation at all. Both of them move around the sun with the same side practically always toward that central object, just in the same way that our moon moves around the earth. Mercury occupies 88 days in its orbit and Venus 224 days in its orbit. Mercury only turns upon its axis four times in a year, while Venus is slower still, and takes seven or eight months to make one complete rotation.

Yet, despite these facts, the evolutionists—and especially the popular writers of today who, through their

"Outlines of History," "Outlines of Science," "Stories of Mankind," "Stories of the Bible," etc., are so profoundly influencing our children with their skepticism— build their entire structure upon this impossible "nebular hypothesis" in some one of its numerous forms.

GUESSER USED DOGMATICALLY

Take, for example, Wells, in his book, "The Outline of History." Wells builds the entire framework of his book upon the nebular hypothesis as a beginning, and then he goes on, in the accepted fashion of evolutionists, to account for the origin of the earth, the beginning of life, etc., and then gives his sketchy outline of human history, and bases his skepticism and *also his dangerous socialism* on this foundation. On the very first page of his book, Wells speaks of the sun. He says that "it is a mass of flaming matter," and then on page three he gives his version of the nebular hypothesis and the origin of our earth. I call attention to the dogmatic tone of his assertions. Accepting the conclusion of the "scientists" to whom he refers, he says:

"Vast ages ago the sun was a spinning, flaring mass of matter, not yet concentrated into a compact center of heat and light, considerably larger than it is now, and spinning very much faster, and that as it whirled a series of fragments detached themselves from it and became the planets. Our earth is one of the planets."

So there we have it. One is moved to inquire, but how does Mr. Wells know all this? He speaks with such cocksureness that we might well imagine that he was present and observed these remarkable gyrations of the sun, and the striking origin of our earth, which he so emphatically and dogmatically asserts. One is inclined to apply to Mr. Wells the questions the Almighty asked Job:

"Who is this that darkeneth counsel by words without knowledge? Gird up now thy loins like a man; for I will demand of thee, and answer thou me. Where wast thou when I laid the foundations of the earth? . . . When the morning stars sang together, and all the sons of God shouted for joy? Hast thou commanded the morning since thy days; and caused the dayspring to know his place? Knowest thou by what way is the light parted? Canst thou bind the sweet influences of Pleiades, or loose the bands of Orion? Hast thou an arm like God? or canst thou thunder with a voice like Him?"

And because of the intellectual pride and cock-sureness of some so-called "scholars" today, we greatly fear that Mr. Wells would not answer, as Job did, and say to God:
"I know that *Thou* canst do everything, and that no thought can be withholden from Thee. *Wherefore I abhor Myself, and repent in dust and ashes.*"
Now as to Mr. Wells' assertion, and the teaching of other evolutionists, that the sun is "a mass of flaming matter" and that our earth came from it, I wish to say that the latest scientific thought has reached the conclusion that the sun is not a mass of flaming matter at all. It is now believed that the sun is simply a gigantic center of electrical energy. Professor R. A. Milliken, winner of the Nobel prize, for example, late of the University of Chicago and now doing such a wonderful work in the West, is one of the greatest living authorities on radio activity. He asserts that real scientists long ago gave up the idea that the sun is a white-hot body engaged in cooling off. He says that the scientists have good evidence that the sun has existed much longer than such a process could possibly take. The assumption that heat waves could travel from any fire, however large, across 93 million miles of frozen space is impossible on the face of it. The new theory therefore, is that the sun is not "a mass of flaming matter" at all, but that it is simply *a center of electrical energy*—a great electro-magnetic field. The power of radio active matter, as these scientists point out, is indicated by the fact that, while radium is in the

process of disintegrating into lead it gives off 300,000 times as much heat as a piece of coal gives off in burning up. The scientists, therefore, are now arguing that the light and the heat that come to us from the sun are both electrical.

Therefore, the hypothesis that the sun, as the nebular, or parent mass of matter, threw off the earth and the other planets, breaks down completely.

THE PLANETESIMAL THEORY

Other hypotheses to account for the origin of the earth are just as unsatisfactory as the nebular hypothesis. My opponent did not touch upon the other theories, but as he may do so in his second speech, I anticipate him here. Perhaps the most popular theory, after the nebular hypothesis, is what is called "the planetesimal theory." Prof. Osborn seems to pin his faith to this particular theory. He says:

"According to the planetesimal theory as set forth by Chamberlain, the earth, instead of consisting of a primitive molten globe, as postulated by the old nebular hypothesis of Laplace, originated in a nebulous knot of solid matter as a nucleus of growth, which was fed by the infall or accretion of scattered nebulous matter (planetesimals) coming within the sphere of control of this knot." ("The Origin and Evolution of Life," p. 25.)

So, according to this, we started in a *knot* that had other matter dumped upon it, instead of a rotating ball of gas! We were created by a bombardment instead of a whirligig!

Well, we remark in passing, that the old earth is certainly tied up in a knot now, and all the gas—whether hot or cold, of statesmen, scientists, philosophers and debating preachers does not seem able to untie it!

But notice that this "planetesimal theory" is open to just as many fatal objections as the other nebular hypothesis. For one thing it is nothing but a guess.

For another thing, there is absolutely no explanation of *how this solid "knot of matter"* got there, and *that is the question in this debate.* Nor can this theory adequately account for the *spherical form of the earth,* or other vital phenomena—so we may just dismiss it as an incompetent witness, with the thanks of the court.

CHANCE VS. GOD

All of these theories try to substitute blind force or mere chance for the creative power of a living God, and I confidently submit that it is irrational so to do. It has been calculated, for example, that if the twenty-six letters of the alphabet were thrown about promiscuously by chance force, they might fall together in the present order of the alphabet—A-B-C-etc., once in five hundred million, million, million times that they were thus tossed up and allowed to fall by chance.

What then would be the probability of the countless combinations of nature coming together in the wonderful order of our earth if they had depended on the chance happenings to which evolution has to attribute them?

Not only is it true that scientific and philosophical speculation have not and cannot account for the origin of matter and force or energy, in our earth, but it is also true that there is no real knowledge concerning even the *nature* of matter and energy. The old "atomic theory," that matter is composed of minute indivisible particles, called "atoms" has had to be abandoned because the discovery of radio-activity and other facts about electricity seem to prove that the ultimate division of matter is not a solid particle, or "atom" at all, but rather a minute center of electrical energy, now called the "electron." The "electron" has simply crowded the "atom" off the stage! Therefore, the origin of the earth as a mass of matter is not only still an unsolved mystery, so far as science is concerned, but the origin and true nature of the *simplest component parts that make* up matter are now confessed to be a greater mystery than ever before.

Because of the established laws of the indestructibility of matter and the conservation of energy, it is now known that the quantity of both matter and energy in the world is fixed. No means are known to science by which either matter or energy can be either increased or diminished.

Now, since the accepted definition of evolution is that it is "continuous progressive change," we would have to expect the continued origination of both matter and energy by the "fixed law" of evolution today just as it is alleged to have produced them in the past. Since no such thing is going on, but, on the other hand, since it is known that the quantity of both matter and energy are not now being increased, therefore evolution with its "continuous progressive change," must be abandoned, and we are driven, of necessity, back to the truth that the matter and energy now in the world came in the beginning by creation.

Furthermore, since it is admitted that the earth had a beginning, unless, we accept the fact of God as the Creator in that beginning, then we are driven to the absurdity of thought that *nothing made something out of nothing.*

PART TWO

How Man Came

Coming, now, to the question of how man came, I remark merely that over against the evolutionary hypothesis is the plain statement of the Bible that "God created man in His own image."

That we may get a contrast between the two ideas of the origin and nature of man, I wish to give you first the picture of the Bible Adam and then the picture of the scientific Adam. I give you first the condensed Bible account as follows:

"And God said, let us make man in our image, after our likeness. . . . God created man in his own image, in the image of God created he him; male and female created He them. . . . The Lord God formed man of the dust of the ground and breathed into his nostrils the breath of life and man became a living soul. . . . God blessed them, and God said unto them, Be fruitful, and multiply, and replenish the earth, and subdue it; and have dominion. And the Lord God took the man, and put him into the garden of Eden to dress it and to keep it." (Gen. 1:26, 27; 11,7,15.) There it is,—all beautiful, inspiring and ennobling.

Here, now, is the evolutionists' account, as stated by Darwin:

"Man is descended from a hairy quadruped, furnished with a tail and pointed ears, probably arboreal in its habits and an inhabitant of the Old World. This creature, if its whole structure had been examined by a naturalist, would have been classed among the Quadrumana, as surely as would the common and still more ancient progenitor of the Old and New World monkeys. The Quadrumana and all the higher mammals are probably derived from an ancient marsupial animal, and this through a long line of diversified forms, either from some reptile-like, or some amphibion-like creature, and this again from some fish-like animal." (Darwin's "Descent of Man," ii, 372.)

Professor Edward Clodd, in his book, "The Making of a Man" (page 126), goes a step further than Darwin and tells us that this creature was changed from an ape into a man largely by learning to throw things with his front feet. I am not exaggerating it one whit, and Professor Clodd is not writing in any humorous vein. He is most serious when he speaks of our arboreal ancestor. Hear him:

"While some for awhile remained arboreal in their habits, never moving easily on the ground, although making some approach to upright motion, as seen in the shambling gait of the man like apes others developed a way of walking on their hind legs which entirely set free the fore limbs as organs of handling and throwing. Whatever were the conditions which permitted this, the advantage which it gives is obvious. *It was the making of a man*" (page 126).

So we were made, not by God as Genesis says, but by learning to throw things with our front feet.

A "CLOSE-UP" OF THE SCIENTIFIC "ADAM"

Let us see, now, a yet fuller description of this our illustrious first father; a "close-up" as the movie people would say. Professor Morris gives us a full detailed description of this unseen, yet seemingly well-known ancestor, in his book on "The Destiny of Man" (page 55). He says:

"It was probably much smaller than existing man, little if any more than four feet in height, and not more than half the weight of man. Its body was covered, though not profusely, with hair; the hair of the head being wooly or frizzly in texture and the face provided with a beard. The face was not jet black, like a typical African, but of a dull brown color; the hair being somewhat similar in color. The arms were long and lank, the back being much curved, the chest flat and narrow, the abdomen protruding, the legs rather short and bowed, the walk a waddling motion somewhat like that of the gibbon. It had deep-set eyes, greatly protruding mouth with gaping lips, huge ears and general 'ape-like' aspect."

Now, remember my friends this is not from "Puck" or "Judge" but from the pages of a supposedly serious book. Professor Morris speaks with such confidence, and gives us withal, such a detailed description of this Adam of science that we really ought, I suppose, to feel indebted to him. And yet, despite the fact that even the color of this creature's hair and the set of his eyes is given to us, strange to say, neither Professor Morris nor any other man was there to see him, for he was the father of us all!

And it was this beast that was "The image of God" and to which God imparted His spirit, if we are to believe the "theistic evolutionists." Yes this strange creature was the Adam of "theistic evolution." And this creature, described by Darwin, Morris, and others, is the one who, according to "theistic evolution," fell. But, let us inquire. from what did he fall? It is certainly difficult to conceive of such a monster falling. With his protruding abdomen, his bowed legs, and his thick sensuous lips, it would seem that he was about as low as any creature could get without any further fall. A thing has to be at some elevation before it can fall, but how did this awful creature, who had had no elevation, fall?

A SCIENTIFIC GENEALOGY

This, too, is the creature which, according to "theistic evolution," is a type of Christ, who is "the second Adam," and through whom Christ's lineage is traced back to God himself. Listen then to the genealogy of Christ, as given by the Bible, and then by evolution. The genealogy of Mary the mother of Jesus runs along in its close as follows:

"Which was the son of Noah, which was the son of Lamech, which was the son of Mathusala, which was the son of Enoch, which was the son of Jared, which was the son of Maleleel, which was the son of Enos, which was the son of Seth, which was the son of Adam, which was the son of God" (Luke 3:36-38).

But the "theistic evolutionists" genealogy would have to run along as follows:

"Which was the son of Enos, which was the son of Seth, which was the son of Adam, which was the son of an ape-like beast, which was the son of a reptile, which was the son of a fish, which was the son of a protoplasm, which was the son of a chemico-electrical reaction, which was the son of God."

Yes, that is about how the Adam of "theistic evolution" got here. And, as for Eve, why they say nothing at all about her. Will the women of today stand for that? Some women have complained about the "Eve" of the Bible, but evolution simply ignores woman all together; it does not dignify her by giving us any account of her origin whatsoever. It is always the "ape-man" who is pictured. Now a woman can stand a reasonable amount of criticism, but to be utterly ignored usually makes her furious. How will the women, then, vote in this matter of evolution?

THE ADMISSIONS OF SCIENTISTS

Unless the Bible account of the creation of man is true, then, as in the case of the origin of our earth, we *know* absolutely nothing about the way in which man appeared upon this planet. The gap between dead matter and sentient life has never been bridged except by guesses. Sir William Thompson argued that life came to this planet on a meteor. It just rode in on a free ticket. This, I suppose, we ought to call the "Shenandoah" or "Dixmude theory."

I wish to quote from the scientists and philosophers themselves explicit admissions that they really know nothing about the origin of life. The great philosopher Kant said:

"Give me matter, and I will explain the formation of the world; but give me matter *only* and I cannot explain the formation of even a caterpillar."

Huxley says: "Of the causes which led to the origin of living matter, it may be said that we know *absolutely nothing.*" Huxley, further, in his article on biology in the Encyclopedia Britannica, says: "The chasm between the not living and the living, the present state of knowledge cannot bridge." Herbert Spencer, in his work on biology (Vol. I, page 182), says: "The proximate chemical principles or chemical units—albumen, fibrine, gelatine, or the hypothetical protein substances—cannot possess the property of forming the endlessly varied structures of animal forms." And Charles Darwin himself admitted that "spontaneous generation" was an impossibility of thought.

And now, to bring these admissions of scientists that they really know nothing about the origin of life strictly up to date, I wish to quote from Professor Edward Clodd. Professor Clodd is an evolutionist of recognized standing, yet he says:

"The absence of *facts* forces us to confine ourselves largely to suggestions and probabilities" ("Making of a Man," page 188).

I wish also to quote from Prof. Henry Fairfield Osborn, one of the most aggressive and prominent proponents of the evolutionary idea in America today. As we all know, he is at the head of the American Museum of Natural History. His admissions, therefore, that the scientists really know nothing about the origin of life must be considered final and indisputable. Listen, now, to what he says in perhaps his greatest book, "The Origin and Evolution of Life." He says, on page 67:

"The mode of the origin of life is a matter of *pure speculation* in which we have as yet little observation or uniformitarian reasoning to guide us, for all the experiments of Butschli and others to imitate the original life process have proved fruitless."

He then puts forward what he himself calls "five hypotheses" in regard to the origin of life, but all of this, note, he himself admits is "a matter of pure speculation." In other words, it really proves nothing. It only proves, I submit, that evolution belongs, as I said in the beginning, to the realm of subjective speculation and not the field of established facts. Darwin, in his works, used such terms as "it may be supposed," etc., over eight hundred times; and to show you further how completely scientists are in the realm of what Osborn admitted is only "pure speculation," let me quote again from his book a typical sentence. He says, on page 132:

"The evolution of the articulates is *believed to be* as follows: From pre-Cambrian annelidan (wormlike) stock arose the trilobites with their chitinous armature and many jointed bodies. . . . Out of the eurypterid stock of Silurian times *may have come* the terrestrial scorpions . . . including the existing scorpions. It is *also possible* that the amphibious, terrestrial, and aërial Insecta were derived from the same . . . articulate. The true Crustacea also *have probably* developed out of the same pre-Cambrian stock."

Here, then, in this one brief quotation there are four may-have-beens, or mere possibilities, *suspended one from the other!* In this one quotation, Dr. Osborn dangles before us a hypothesis, on which he hangs a supposition, to which he attaches a guess, on which he pins a bare probability! It reminds one of the Scotchman's definition of scientific metaphysics. He said: "Imagine a fog bank. Now imagine a hole in the bank. Now imagine the bank gone, and the hole still there. That is metaphysics!"

SCIENTIFIC GUESSES ON THE ORIGIN OF MAN

There have been guesses many about the origin and development of life upon this planet. They have been even more varied, and, I say with respect, some of them more grotesque, than the theories about the origin of the earth. I wish to say here that I do not speak with any disrespect of science or scientists, nor am I prejudiced against the schools. I have been a student of science, to a limited extent, for many years, and rejoice in the great contribution which the exact sciences have made to the sum total of human knowledge and happiness. It was my privilege also to teach in two of our American universities for several years before I devoted my time entirely to the work of the ministry, and so I desire the prosperity of a true and righteous educational system. But no man, however friendly he may be to science, and to the schools, can blind his eyes to the fact that a little group of men in this country, especially, seem determined to put over the evolutionary hypothesis, and thus to make good on their own theories. Their training in German universities, some elements of commercialism through the printing of textbooks, etc., and other considerations enter into this determination, and we have a full right to turn the light on and to demand facts rather than these wild guesses and theories, which are being dogmatically given to our children in the schools today, as though they were established truth.

Now, what is the state of the case as to the origin of man? Briefly it is this: the scientists have failed completely in their attempt to bridge the chasm between dead matter and sentient, ethical life. They have failed signally to make out a case for the evolutionary hypothesis, so far as the origin of life is concerned. Dr. Alfred R. Wallace, who was really the co-discoverer with Darwin of the theories of evolution in their modern form, frankly admits that there are gaps in the evolutionary scheme which are not only unbridged but are unbridgable. He says:

"There must have been three interpositions of a Divine and Supernatural Power to account for things as they are. The agreement of science with Genesis is surely very striking. There is a gulf between matter and nothing; another between life and the non-living; and a third between man and the lower creation—and science cannot bridge any of them."

I submit now that my honorable opponent has scarcely touched upon the real issue in this debate in all of his opening address. The issue is how the earth and man came—that is, how they originated—and not what happened after they got here; but my opponent has done all that he could do in this connection, and he has done all that the scientists and the evolutionary philosophers of today have tried to do. Having failed to account for things in any rational way, or to produce any *facts* proving either the origin of the earth or the origin of man by natural forces, they have turned their attention to an effort to prove that evolution is a true process as applied to the development of life upon this planet, regardless of how it may have gotten here. They hope to make out a good case for the proposition that higher forms of life have evolved from lower, and then to urge that as *presumptive evidence* that the evolutionary process was continuous as regards the coming of life out of dead matter, even though that fact cannot be demonstrated.

I will meet my opponent, therefore, at this point, even though most of his arguments in these matters were not strictly upon the subject for debate.

There are at last but two great arguments for the evolutionary hypothesis as it relates to the development of life upon the planet. The first is the argument from biology and the second is the argument from geology. It is possible, therefore, to group my opponent's arguments under this broad and simple generalization. Let us take up first the arguments that lie in the field of biology.

THE ARGUMENT FROM BIOLOGY

Darwin's labors were largely in the field of biology.

Darwin's theory of the origin of species, which has been and still is, in its broad outlines, the main theory, was founded on two ideas: one was the doctrine of "natural selection" through the brute struggle for existence and the "survival of the fittest"; and the other was that of the inheritance of acquired characters. He held that the fittest survived in the life struggle because they had gained certain advantages over their weaker fellows, and that their naturally acquired characteristics passed down by heredity to their offspring. Thus, too, through the development and inheritance of many characteristics different from those in past generations, species originated in great varieties, and man finally emerged at the head of the procession.

But neither of these ideas of Darwin's has been proved true.

NO "NATURAL SELECTION"

Though admitting that there are over 2,000,000 species upon earth, Darwin himself had to say (*Life and Letters*, Vol. III, p. 25): "There are *two or three million of species* on earth—sufficient field, one might think, for observation. But it must be said today that, in spite of all the efforts of trained observers, *not one change of a species into another is on record.*" This statement can be made with even greater confidence now, after a lapse of over half a century since Mr. Darwin made the above admission.

Dr. N. S. Shaler, Department of Geology, Harvard, says:

"It begins to be evident that the Darwinian hypothesis is still essentially unverified. . . . It is not yet proven that a single species of the two or three million now inhabiting the earth has been established solely or mainly by the operation of natural selection."

And John Burroughs, although an evolutionist up to his recent death, said of Darwin, in the August, 1920, "Atlantic Monthly":

"He has already been as completely shorn of his selection doctrines as Sampson was shorn of his locks."

If these statements from scientific men mean anything at all, they mean, at least, that pure Darwinism is altogether unproven, if not that it is dead.

If now there is no "natural selection," then we are driven, of necessity, back to supernatural selection, but that violates the theory of evolution and is, therefore, contrary to the definition upon which we are going in this debate.

NO ACQUIRED CHARACTERS

Furthermore, the theory of acquired characters has not been proved by the scientists. The forms of vegetable and animal life that man succeeds in improving by human selection revert rapidly to type as soon as man's directing skill is withdrawn. This undeniable fact makes very reasonable the inference that there are certain established types and species which can be simply extended somewhat within the limits of the species, but that no change into a new species can come about either by natural or artificial selection. The scientist, Weismann, did some monumental work in this field, as did also Mendel. But no scientist has ever been able to bring forth a new species nor to demonstrate that acquired characters are hereditary.

My opponent referred to the work of Luther Burbank, but his assertion that Burbank has produced new species is not true. The loganberry, for example, is not a new species but simply a combination that comes from two berries belonging to the same species. Burbank and others have done wonderful things in producing varieties within species, and we rejoice in their work, but none of them have been able to leap over the bounds of species nor to prove that acquired characters are hereditary.

The very latest voice on this important subject was a statement during the recent sessions of the American Association for the Advancement of Science held in Cincinnati, Ohio. Dr. D. T. MacDougal, General Secretary of the Association, and Director of the Laboratory for Plant Physiology of the Carnegie Institution, declared during the meeting of the Association, as quoted in the "New York Times" of January 2, 1924, that the inheritance of acquired characters had not been established. Later in an article under his own signature in the "Times" of January 20, 1924, he repeated these statements. In referring to the claims of Dr. Kammer, the Austrian scientist, who asserts that he has proved that characteristics induced in salamanders, frogs, etc., by the action of temperatures, water and other agencies, are fixed and transmitted to the progeny, Dr. MacDougal said: "His proofs are not regarded as adequate." Not only do American scientists refuse to admit the claims of Dr. Kammer, but Dr. MacDougal says that the English scientists take the same position. He declares:

"He has presented his results to biologists in England and their attitude is in accordance with that held here."

So far, then, as facts for establishing "natural selection" and the inheritance of "acquired characters" are concerned, there are no such facts.

SIMILARITY OF STRUCTURE

Taking up morphology, it is found that there is a general similarity of plan between the lower animals and man. It is pointed out that the fin of the fish, the wing of the bird, the flipper of the whale, the leg of the animal and the arm of man are similar in structure. It is argued, therefore, that all of these forms of life have come from some remote common ancestor.

There are also certain other resemblances between man and the lower animals that, it is said, point to the same conclusion. This argument, put into simple language, may be stated as follows: That man and monkey are so much alike that man must have come from some sort of remote monkey ancestor. Thus, the argument from resemblance is to the effect that similarity argues oneness of original parentage, that similarity in structure and organic function is proof of common descent.

But in the name of all logic and all common sense and of sound reason, even granting for the sake of argument that such resemblances do exist, do they really prove the astounding conclusions that are founded upon them? I emphatically and without fear of successful contradiction declare that they do not. Resemblance proves nothing but resemblance. Similarity proves nothing but similarity.

For example, I myself have been often accused of resembling ex-President Woodrow Wilson. I do not know whether our honored ex-President has ever been given the affront of being told that he looks like me or not. If so, he possibly felt like one of the two friends who were given to joking each other because of their homeliness. They met on the street one day and one said to the other: "Jim, I met a man today who told me that I looked like you." Whereupon Jim doubled up his fist and said: "Where is the scoundrel? I want to maul him." "Oh," replied his friend, "you can't maul him. *I killed him!*" Seriously, my friends, I have been mistaken again and again for Woodrow Wilson, and once, while living in Baltimore, soon after Mr. Wilson married his present wife, Mrs. Straton and I together were mistaken for the President and Mrs. Wilson at a musical concert in the Lyric Theatre.

I submit that the argument of the evolutionists from resemblance proves only resemblance and not succession of descent. I have not descended from Woodrow Wilson, and I feel very sure that, staid Presbyterian that he is, he would emphatically disclaim any kinship whatever with a militant Baptist parson!

There are so many dissimilarities between man and the apes that the similarities are negligable— especially is this true in the realm of the mind, the moral and religious instincts, etc.

Virchow said: "The differences between man and monkey are so wide that almost any fragment is sufficient to diagnose them" ("Smithsonian Report," 1889, page 566).

RUDIMENTARY AND VESTIGIAL ORGANS

So, also, as to rudimentary or unused organs that are found in man and lower animals alike, and that my opponent discussed. They really prove nothing but resemblance, and no man can say that they are not really useful.

As we begin to push back the borders of our ignorance about these things light breaks in upon us. Professor Arthur Keith, in his address as President of the Anthropological Section of the British Association, meeting at Bournemouth ("Smithsonian Report," 1919, page 448), said:

"We have hitherto regarded the pineal gland, little bigger than a wheat grain and buried deeply in the brain, as a mere useless vestige of a median or parietal eye, derived from some distant human ancestor in whom that eye was functional, but on the clinical and experimental evidence now rapidly accumulating we must assign to it a place in the machinery which controls the growth of the body."

Of the thyroid gland, whose removal entails myxoedema, Huxley said: "The recent discovery of the important part played by the thyroid gland should be a warning to all speculators about useless organs."

And as for my opponent's references to Mr. Bryan's anatomy, I must express my surprise that he assailed our great commoner after that fashion when he is not here to defend his own tail!

Prof. A. Wilford Hall, in "The Problem of Human Life," so tersely refutes these false theories, that I must

quote him.   On page 374: "Now, as regards the 'little tail
of man,' about which Prof. Haeckel and Mr. Darwin have
so much to say, and which is regarded by all evolutionists
as such a powerful proof of man's descent from tailed
ancestors, I wish to remark that a more manifest and
inexcusable misconception was never harbored by men."
Then the author goes on to state that the spine in all
vertebrates develops first and the end protrudes until the
fleshy portion develops to cover it.   The fish, which
according to evolution, did not have a tailed animal for
an ancestor, also has this embryonic tail.   Thus, the whole
theory breaks down.

CLIMBING OUR OWN ANCESTRAL TREE

The same general arguments apply to embryology in
other respects also.   It has been found that embryos of
different forms of life are somewhat alike.   Therefore, it
is argued that they all came from some original common
ancestor.   Furthermore, it is known that the human
embryo passes through several distinct stages in its development, and it is claimed by some that these stages
*recapitulate the steps in the alleged evolutionary journey
of the race upward from the original protoplasm to man.*
Haeckel confidently asserted these claims.   He even named
this process the "biogenetic law."   He had us climbing
our own family tree while we were still embryos!

I pointed out, in the beginning, that this is all nothing
more than assumption and, as Osborn put it, lies in the
realm of "pure speculation" and not of demonstrated fact.
I now point out, further, that the idea that man has
evolved from lower forms of life because the human
embryo passes through a series of stages which are supposed to reflect the several stages in evolution, is not
consistent with the accepted principles of the evolutionary
hypothesis.   For one thing, as to the rate of development, evolution presupposes a slow and tedious process

covering, as Wells and Osborn and all of the others of them say, "millions and millions and millions of years." But the human embryo passes through its stages of development with tremendous rapidity, and in the case of the embryos of some other forms of life the progress is so rapid that it seems almost miraculous. The evolutionary hypothesis, therefore, which scorns miracles in other fields, cannot invoke a sustaining miracle in its own behalf and to prove its own claim. These ideas have long since been exploded.

An object lesson is sometimes most useful in bringing to our minds a conclusive demonstration of truth. I have brought down tonight and I hold here in my hands two victrola records. They are exactly alike. They are made of precisely the same material. They weigh the same. They are the same shape. Their circumference and diameter are identical, and even if you look at them through the microscope you see the same succession of little scratches and indentations upon both of them. And yet if I put one of these on a victrola it produces an inspiring solo from Caruso's glorious voice. If I put the other on the victrola it produces one of the disgusting pieces of ragtime jazz which libels the holy name of music today. What does it mean? It means, my friends, that the resemblances between the two victrola records are merely superficial resemblances at non-essential points. It means that the essential characters of the two records are vitally different, and the final result from them conclusively proves that. While they look alike and feel alike and are the same size, etc., nevertheless, they are in essential nature absolutely and radically unlike.

Now I submit that the argument is conclusive that the same thing is true as regards the similarity between the human embryo and the embryos of the lower animals. The two are absolutely different and distinct in *essential* nature. They are vitally different one from the other, despite surface resemblances, and, as with the victrola records, the final results from the two forms of embryo establish the fact that they are essentially different from each other even while still embryos. Professor Fairhurst, in his notable book *"Organic Evolution Considered,"* states the case clearly and conclusively. He says:

"Taking the embryos of man and fish the argument of the evolutionist is as follows: The embryos of man and fish, at a certain stage of development, are closely alike in appearance; therefore, man and fish had a common ancestral origin. The conclusion which the evolutionist draws is based upon a mere seeming and very transient resemblance, while the fact that the two embryos are essentially unlike is shown by the vast distance apart at which they arrive by development. . . . The egg which can be developed into a man is just as different in nature from the egg of a fish as the man is from the fish. The eggs are essentially unlike. The essential qualities of eggs are beyond the power of the miscroscope to reveal. The human embryo is produced by human beings only; and whatever may be its miscroscopic appearance, it is at every stage of its development strictly human. Embryology, as applied to evolution, fails in that it deals only with the surface of things."

I submit that there is no possible rational reply to his conclusion. Embryology has been considered one of the very strongest arguments for evolution, and yet in the face of the real facts, it breaks down completely.

Indeed some of the facts as already remarked in connection with the time element, are really the reverse of what the theory of evolution calls for. So far as the human embryo is concerned, it is now admitted that the entire first half of the supposed evolutionary progression is not repeated at all. In speaking upon this point, Professor Fairhurst says ("Organic Evolution Considered," page 147):

"There are radical differences between the embryos of

vertebrates and invertebrates. Worms and other articulates in embryo lie doubled backwards around the yolk, while all vertebrates are doubled in the opposite direction. According to the theory that the embryonic condition is a recapitulation of the stages of organic evolution, this fundamental fact of invertebrate embryology ought to have been preserved by the vertebrate. Evolution gives no account of this reversal of position by the vertebrates."

The author of the article on Embryology in the Encyclopedia Britannica, Oskar Heurtwig, Erich Wasmann, and other embryologists have completely shattered the "fish-like gill slits" of the human embryo, and other similar false inductions from embryology.

WHY GOD MADE ANIMALS LIKE MAN

Is there, then, any rational way to account for the resemblances between man and the lower animals? Yes there is. It is the fact of creation of all by one God. This resemblance of parts is just what we should expect in things originating from one intelligent operator, whether Creator or manufacturer. It is found in every factory. The wheel is the same in the wheelbarrow, the cart, the carriage and the locomotive. In fact, uniformity of plan proves unity in the cause, and not the diversity which chance evolution would necessitate. The Bible teaches that God made the lower animals before he made man. We may regard them, in a way, as understudies. Every sculptor makes models before he carves his final statue—so, perhaps, God made the lower animals. He found that a heart and circulatory system, lungs, brain, etc., all worked well. Looking with satisfaction upon these dumb creatures he had made, we may imagine Him saying: "*Now,* let us make man in our image, after our likeness!" The mere fact that all forms of animals have to breathe air and exist on the same sort of food largely necessitates more or less similarity between them.

THE ARGUMENT FROM GEOLOGY, THE ROCKS AND FOSSILS

The other great argument for evolution has been the argument from the rocks and fossils:—the argument from geology and paleontology. The argument here is that there has been a succession and ascent of life up to, and including man through lower forms of life, because of a succession of fossil life forms, which it is alleged are found in the rocks of the geological eras.

Dr. T. H. Morgan, of Columbia University, rests his faith in the theory of evolution on this geological foundation. He says:

"The direct evidence furnished by fossil remains is by all odds the strongest evidence we have in favor of organic evolution."

My opponent spoke with great confidence and assurance on this subject of the rocks, the "ancient life," in them, etc. But it is not true, as he asserts, that these matters are settled and proved. On the other hand, the methods and data on which the scientists ground the calculations behind their guesses and hypotheses are frequently so flimsy as to be utterly untrustworthy, especially as a foundation for sweeping aside the age-long faith of the race in the Bible as God's word, and in substituting for it the dogmas of speculative philosophy, and of what the Bible itself terms "science, falsely so called."

I wish to point out, in the beginning, that geologists and evolutionists who rely upon geology, convict themselves of begging the question or arguing in a circle. You ask the geologist, "how do you determine the age of the rocks and arrange your scheme of stratified rocks?" He answers: "Why, by the fossils that are in the rocks. We know that the simpler forms of life came first, and when we find these simpler forms in a given stratum of rock, we know, thereby, that that sort of stratum is the oldest." You ask the evolutionist upon what he founds his theory of the succession of life, beginning with simple forms, coming up to the more complex and culminating in man, and he answers: "Why I found my conclusion on the record of the rocks. The simplest forms of life are found as fossils in the oldest rocks, and the more complex forms of life in the more recent rock formations, etc." Here, then, I submit, you have a complete case of begging the question or arguing in a circle. On both sides they *assume* the very thing that is to be proved. The geologist says the oldest rocks are the oldest because the simplest forms of life are in them. The evolutionist says that evolution is true because the simplest forms of life are in the oldest rocks. There could not be a more complete case of arguing in a circle, and neither argument, therefore, can be of any force.

FRAGMENTARY AND INADEQUATE EVIDENCE

Not only is this true, but the scientists themselves admit that the fossil remains and the evidences of evolution from the rocks are really fragmentary and obscure in the extreme. So much so, that thoughtful observers are more and more having to reject such evidence. When confronted with the absurdity of their evidence, in fact the practically complete *absence of any evidence,* the evolutionists fall back upon the incompleteness of the geological record. They say that there is evidence to support evolution if they could only find it. Darwin, again and again, so pleaded on behalf of his theory. He said:

"Looking not to any one time, but to all time, if my theory be true, numberless intermediate varieties, linking closely together all the species of the same group, must assuredly have existed; but the very process of natural selection constantly tends, as has been so often remarked, to exterminate the parent-forms and the intermediate links. Consequently, evidence of their former existence could be found only among fossil remains, which are preserved, as we shall attempt to show in a future chapter, in an extremely imperfect and intermittent record" (page 184, "Origin of Species").

Darwin admits that there are some two or three million different species on the earth, and he tried bravely to get over the tremendous fact that no missing links between any of these species have been found. He says that the number of these *intermediate varieties* which have formerly existed must be "truly enormous," and then he appeals to the imperfection of the geological record to account for the overwhelming fact that *none* of them have been found. He says:

"Why then is not every geological formation and every stratum full of such intermediate links? Geology assuredly does not reveal any such finely-graduated organic chain; and this, perhaps, is the most obvious and serious objection which can be urged against the theory. The explanation lies, as I believe, in the extreme imperfection of the geological record" (page 334, "Origin of the Species").

The evolutionists, then, are like a litigant who comes into court with strong and positive evidence against him, but who says that while he has no evidence in his favor, nevertheless, such evidence ought to exist and no doubt does exist, but he has never been able to find it, despite diligent search; and yet, while he has no evidence, and while his opponent has strong evidence, nevertheless, he ought to be given the verdict because of his undiscovered evidence.

NO "MISSING LINKS"

Furthermore, the alleged "missing links" evidence is utterly inadequate and even laughably absurd. If the principle of evolution were true there would not only be missing links in the fossils, just as Darwin had to admit, but there ought to be living links on every side around us today. Instead of fixed species, with their several varieties, we would have a heterogeneous *mess* of living forms upon the earth, each grading into the other. We would have budding legs and developing eyes and sprouting wings and other transitional forms all around us. For if it is true, then upon its fundamental principle of conformity, evolution ought to be still in progress on every side. Herbert Spencer gives away the case, in fact, by admitting this. In his work on "Ethics," in speaking of further social evolution which may be anticipated, he lays down a principle which must apply to all phases of evolution, including organic evolution. He says:

"It seems not only rational to believe in some further evolution, but irrational to doubt it; irrational to suppose that the causes which have in the past worked such wonderful effects will in the future work no effects."

Precisely so, and if evolution were true we would see it in progress on every side. What we do see, however, is not the development of one species into another, but a fixity of species which is guarded by the universal law of sterility. Even branch varieties of the same species produce only hybrids when they are crossed.

THE APE-MEN

Now, we find the same striking limits to species when we turn to the fossils in the rocks. No "missing links" connecting one species with others have ever been discovered, and the scientists in their frantic efforts and deep desire to find such links, in order that they might prove the evolutionary hypothesis, have been at times pathetic and at times amusing.

Take, for example, the so-called ape-men, the alleged missing links, replicas of which we find in the humorous department of the American Museum of Natural History, namely, the "Hall of the Age of Man." As for the alleged ape-men or "missing links," they are few in numbers and far between. Even Prof. Osborn has to

admit this. He says in his little book on "The Hall of
the Age of Man":

"Five cases in the center hall are devoted to the story of
man, and that it can be compressed into so small a space is
an indication of the scarcity of his remains, for here are
displayed reproductions of all of the notable specimens that
have been discovered" (Leaflet No. 52, page 3).

Well, if evolution is a universal law, working in all
past time and everywhere, why is there such a scarcity?
And even in the case of the few so-called specimens they
have, only minute bits of bone were found in each instance, and from these small fragments, imaginary re-cre-
ations have been made, and even then the scientists did
not agree among themselves as to just how the restored
men should have looked.

These so-called "ape-men" are figments of the heated
and overly enthusiastic imagination of evolution's devotees. The "Piltdown man," for example, was no
"man" at all. All that they found in the gravel pit in
Sussex, England, near Piltdown Common, were two or
three bits of skull-bone, a piece of jaw-bone, and a
canine tooth. And these few fragments were not found
all together and at one time by the same person. They
were scattered widely in the gravel pit, some of them were
found by one person and others by another person, and
some of them were found in one year and others in another year. With these few little scraps, that a juggler
could conceal in the palm of one hand, and found under
these loose conditions, the scientists "reconstructed" the
"Piltdown man" and proclaimed it as a new genus, which
they called Eoanthropus or "Dawn-man," and they named
the species "Dawsoni" in honor of Mr. Dawson, the English scientist. But after the first reconstruction by Dawson
and Dr. A. Smith Woodward of the British Museum,
Prof. Arthur Keith, Curator of the Royal College of
Surgeons of London, took up these fragments of bone and

made a reconstructed man much higher than the ape-like creature that Drs. Dawson and Woodward had produced. Prof. Keith declared that the capacity of the Piltdown skull was nearer 1500 c.c. than 1070 as Dawson and Woodward had made it. And the climax was capped when Prof. Hrdlicka reached the conclusion that the Piltdown jaw and tooth did not belong with the fragments of skull at all but really "belonged to a fossil chimpanzee."

THE GREATEST HOAX OF ALL

And as for the "Java Ape-man," the case is even worse. Dr. Eugene Dubois, a Dutch physician, claimed to have found these bones in the Island of Java in 1891, but scientists have been suspicious about the genuineness of the find. There are only three fragments of this gentleman—the Java, or Trinil, Ape-man who, as mentioned by my opponent, has been given the overwhelming name "Pithecanthropus." There is a part of a skull, a part of a femur bone, and one molar tooth. The bones were not found at the same time or altogether in one place. The femur bone was found a year after the bit of skull was picked up. The bones were scattered far apart in a gravel pit on the bank of a rushing stream. The femur bone was fifty feet from where the skull was found. When Dr. Dubois discovered these pitiful bits of bones he announced his belief that they belonged to a being between the man apes and men.

Other scientists, however, who examined these bones asserted that the fragments did not belong to the same individual at all. The geologist, Dana, took the position that the bones, if they belonged to the same individual, belonged to a low-grade man or to an idiot. Virchow rejected them, and finally, another authority of the first rank, Prof. Klaatsch of Heidelberg University, declared that the creature was no missing link at all. And in a recent magazine article, to top the whole matter off, one of our American writers, as before intimated, throws a doubt upon the honesty and genuineness of the fragments.

And yet the authorities at the Museum have made up not only a cast of this imaginary creature, but a bronze bust, and he is shown to our school children as one of the links in the ascent of man!

And as for the few other alleged specimens in the "Hall of the Age of Man," a few words will suffice. As for the "Heidelberg man," nothing of him except a piece of jaw-bone was found. He is one-half of one per cent. original and 99½ per cent "restoration."

The case is as bad with the others. The Neanderthal skull has provoked from competent authorities a dozen or more opinions concerning itself. Here are a few: the skull belonged to a human idiot (Blake, Vogt, Hoelder, Zittel); to an old Celt; to an old Hollander; to an old Frieslander, and last, but not least, to a Mongolian Cossack of the year 1814. It was of these remains that Huxley said:

"In no sense can the Neanderthal bones be regarded as the remains of a human being intermediate between men and apes."

Dr. Thomas Dwight, Parkman professor of anatomy in Harvard University, says:

"The Neanderthal man is not a specimen of a race arrested in its upward climb, but rather of a race thrown down from a still higher position."

The "Cro-Magnon" man proves nothing, as it is admitted that he is not a "missing link," but is the equal of men of today.

Then there is the Talgai skull, still shown in the case at the museum, but about which little is said these days, and rightly so. For Mr. Archibald Meston, of Australia, former Chief Protector of Aborigines, has shown that it is the skull of one of the Australian black boys shot and buried on the spot in 1848.

I have been many times in the American Museum of Natural History. It is a great and wonderful institution, and there is much of first-rate interest and value to be seen there. But frankly, the "Hall of the Age of Man," as before suggested, ought to be labelled "Our Humorous Department."

I was up there a little while ago for a long period with Dr. William Gregory, Dr. Osborn's right-hand man, and a professor in Columbia University.

I asked Prof. Gregory, after we had gone over the data about the Java Ape-man, how old scientists estimated these fossils were, and he told me that the estimate was 500,000 years. I now ask the judges and this audience, as I asked Prof. Gregory, if any thoughtful mind can really believe that those old bones laid there undisturbed, right beside what is now a rushing stream, for 500,000 years? Is it not the most remote chance, in the face of earthquakes, fire, and flood, and the radical changes in climate and condition through which our earth has been known to pass, that for 500,000 years of time those old bones, which were *assumed* to belong to the *same individual* in the beginning, had really stayed in that one position?

This, then, is the "evidence," so far as "missing links" are concerned, of the evolution of man from the beasts. That idea is a libel on man, and an insult to Almighty God. So fragmentary and unreliable is this "evidence" that no judge or jury would convict even a horse-thief on such evidence, and certainly we ought not on it to convict man of a brute ancestry or convict the Bible of lying. I verily believe that if the little basketful of musty old bones and fossils, which have been found, after all these years of search in every part of the world, were brought together and presented as evidence for the evolution of man in any court of law, they would be thrown out of court with utmost scorn by judge and jury alike. They are simply not evidence according to any rules of evidence, either in law or true science.

ARTIFICIALITY OF THE GEOLOGICAL SCHEME

Not only is their alleged evidence utterly fragmentary and entirely inadequate, according to the admissions of Darwin, Osborn, and other scientists themselves, but it has now been demonstrated, as a result of recent research in the field of geology, that *the whole arrangement of the rocks in the old geological scheme is altogether artificial, contrary to now known facts, and, therefore, that it must be repudiated entirely.* I do not have to argue this matter, but will leave it to the most up-to-date voice of science itself. I have here the very latest book on geology. It is just off the press. It is called "The New Geology," and it is by Prof. George McCready Price, Professor of Geology in Union College, Nebraska. Prof. Price is a member of the American Association for the Advancement of Science, and other scientific societies. For over twenty years he has been engaged in gathering the data for this great and monumental book. The very name of the book is significant. It is "The New Geology," and Prof. Price argues that the time has come when the entire science of geology will have to be made over on a new and really scientific basis. He shows from facts gathered in every part of the world, accompanied by adequate diagrams, tables and beautiful illustrations, that the arrangement of the different sorts of rocks by the older geologists is not only a purely artificial and arbitrary scheme, but that the facts that have been discovered since that artificial arrangement of the rocks was worked out, utterly overthrow the whole scheme.

He shows that the stratified beds containing the fossils

are, as he puts it, "of quite limited extent, varying from a few square yards or a few acres, to a few hundred square miles in area," at most. He shows us from the facts, that the old "onion-coat" theory of the building up of the strata—the only logical theory, by the way, if evolution were really true—is not only utterly smashed to pieces and given up by scientists, but that their dependence upon these fragmentary beds has had to be given up because, as he says: "The various kinds of fossils, which were so long thought to be found only in the same relative order all over the globe wherever they occur, are now known to occur in practically every conceivable order" (Pages 17-18).

MAKING "FACTS" FIT

Instead of the older rocks being at the bottom, with the most primitive forms of fossils, and then the slightly less old on top of those, with the slightly higher fossil forms, and then the less old on top of that, and so on until the "younger" rocks, with the highly complex forms of life of recent times, on top, as was argued by my opponent, and as should be the case if there had been an orderly evolution, and if the different forms of life starting in remote ages had fallen down into the soil and been caught in the stratification as the deposits were made, and so on up to the age of man and his fossil remains, which should be right on the top of the whole series,—instead of all of this, Prof. Price shows that often the so-called oldest rocks are right on top of the strata and the so-called youngest are down at the bottom. He shows that some of the oldest rock stratas are up at the top of mountains, for example, and the youngest forms are down at the bottom of the mountains, and all in perfect order. He gives instances of this reverse order in stretches of territory in Europe and America, some of them as much as 1,800 miles long, containing as much as 20,000 square miles of territory, making the thought of an "over-thrust" impossible. He shows that these examples of reverse strata are found almost everywhere, a notable one beginning in our own state of New York, and running away up into Canada.

And upon these undeniable *facts,* written in the record of the rocks themselves, and now discovered by fuller research, he reaches his conclusion, namely, that the old order of the rocks, as classified, have been thus classified in a fanciful and unnatural manner, because of the dominating prejudices in favor of the evolutionary theory. He says:

"The dominant idea, of course, in the minds of those who arranged the geological series was the evolution theory regarding the development of life, and this theory is embalmed in the arrangement which was thus made."

He shows how the arrangement was rearranged from time to time, known facts being made to fit into the subjective scheme of evolution. Therefore, he reaches his conclusion and says:

"In many ways, the current system of geological classification seems absurd for those who realize the fanciful— we might almost say, the farcical—character of the reasons behind such an arrangement" (Page 283).

He further says:

"We could arrange all the books in a library according to their titles, from A, B, and C, down to X, Y, and Z; but it would be a purely artificial scheme, and to say that this arrangement proved that the books arranged under A, B, and C must have been written and published long before those arranged under X, Y, and Z, would be absurd" (Page 19).

GEOLOGICAL FACTS AGAINST EVOLUTION

Prof. Price, therefore, as a result of his investigations in the field of geology, as well as of embryology and the other sciences involved in the theory of evolution, reaches

in this great book the definite conclusion that the theory
of evolution is not only unproved but that it is demon-
strably false. He says, explicitly (Page 606) :

"The net results of all modern scientific investigation seem
to be that the plants and animals now alive could never have
originated by any such method of gradual development as
has been pictured to us in the name of natural science.
Certain it is that modern biology, and geology also, for
that matter, have simply developed a complete negative
demonstration against the easy assumptions of the earlier
scientists that plants and animals probably originated by a
gradual progression from the lower to the higher types by
processes similar to those which are now going on" (Page
606).

In the light of the undeniable geological facts which
have now been assembled, Prof. Price, therefore for-
mulates "The great law of conformable stratigraphic
sequence," which, he says, may be stated as follows :

"Any kind of fossiliferous bed whatever, 'young' or 'old,'
may be found occurring conformably on any other fossiliferous beds, 'older' or 'younger.' "

Then he adds :

"This law forever puts an end to all evolutionary speculations about the order in which the various plants and
animals have developed, in the minds of those who are
correctly informed regarding these facts. This law alone
is quite sufficient to relegate the whole theory of organic
evolution to the lumber room of science, there to become
the amusement of the future students of the history of
cosmological speculations" (Page 638).

These, then, are the conclusions of a thoroughly up-to-
date scientist, in the light of well-known and most recent
facts.

FALSIFYING "FACTS"

Indeed, so flimsy are the alleged "facts" which have
been assembled to bolster up the tottering theories of
evolution, that some of its zealots have resorted to actual

falsification in their efforts to make good on their theories.

Ernest Haeckel, for example, was caught falsifying, schematizing and forging certain diagrams by which he was endeavoring to prove his evolutionary theory. He was tried by the Jena University Court and the charge against him was *proved.* In reply, he said:

"I should feel utterly condemned and annihilated by the admission, were it not that hundreds of the best observers and most reputable biologists lie under the same charge. *The great majority of all morphological, anatomical, histological and embryological diagrams are not true to nature but are more or less doctored, schematized and reconstructed.*"

No wonder, therefore, that Professor Price, in speaking of the frantic way in which the evolutionists twist and stretch everywhere in their effort to make facts fit in with their fancies, says:

"The astonishment which I feel is due to the amazing power of a preconceived theory to blind the eyes and stultify the reasoning power of the shrewdest observer when confronted with a series of facts for which their theory has made no provision."

In reaching these conclusions, Dr. Price is merely moving in line with other great scientists and thinkers who have been forced finally to reject evolution. Sir J. William Dawson, the great geologist of Canada, utterly rejected it and says: "It is one of the strangest phenomena of humanity; it is *utterly destitute of proof"* (*Story of the Earth and Man,* page 317).

UNDERSTANDABLE SOLUTIONS

There are rational and easy ways of accounting for the phenomena of the fossils in the rocks and other such problems. The fossil remains of the lower and simpler forms of life found in some geological beds, is easily accounted for because of the well-known fact, that lower forms of life live for the most part in shallow water or at the edge of the sea, while the vertebrates, the fish and the great sea monsters, live in the deep water. Walk along the sea shore today and you will find the simple shell fish, the little fiddler crabs, and other simple forms of life there in the shallow water, and then you will look out and see the whales spouting several miles at sea. If, therefore, the animal life in one section of the sea, with its shore, were to be now changed into fossils, and these fossils should be discovered in some after age, the discoverers would find the remains of the simple forms of life in one place and the remains of higher forms—fish and other sea monsters—in another part.

Furthermore, just as we see around us today different forms of life, from the simplest one-cell animal up to and including all the other animals and human forms, *living side by side,* so the simplest forms of animals and human life lived side by side in the ages that are gone. There is absolutely not one scintilla of proof from real facts that the lower forms of life came first on this earth, or the higher forms evolved out of the lower.

It has been claimed that we can arrange the past races in an ascending order as they worked in stone, bronze or iron, in their successive history. This is a false theory. We have all these "ages" existing today. On the other hand Dr. Livingstone found no stone age in Africa. Dr. Schliemann found in the ruins of Troy the bronze age *below the stone age.* The early Egyptians used bronze, the later ones stone tools. In the Chaldean tombs all these are found together. Europe had the metal age while America had the stone age ("Creation and Evolution," by Prof. Townsend).

Professor Price, in his great book from which I have before quoted, because of the now known facts, therefore, reaches the conclusions which I gave from him. Not only so, but he goes further still and gives facts which demonstrate that there has been a great universal catastrophe, which overwhelmed most of the life whose fossil forms we now find. He gives, for example, the fact that mighty schools of fish are found today embedded in rock strata as fossils, and he shows that there is absolutely no evidence that these fish quietly sank down into the mud, and that sediment through long periods of time formed about them. On the other hand, he shows that the fossils of the fish are found with all their fins extended, which is always the case when they die suddenly. He, therefore, shows that the wild guesses about the time required for the formation of the rock stratifications, the fossils, etc., is absolutely exaggerated, and he takes his position with Dawson and other geologists upon this matter of the time. His argument is overwhelming, that the phenomena which we find in connection with the fossils in the earth, are all to be accounted for most rationally on the ground that there was a universal deluge, arising, as he points out, perhaps, because of the change in the inclination of the earth's axis to the plane of its orbit, which change sent great floods of water, tidal waves, sweeping in from the sea, overwhelming all forms of life and piling mud and sediment upon them, which in the course of time changed into coal and rock.

This great scientist, with many others, therefore, is led back to the account of the Bible teaching about the deluge and the other facts that go with the whole record of Bible truth.

POSITIVE FACTS PROVING THAT THE EARTH AND MAN
DID NOT COME BY EVOLUTION

Having shown from the admissions of the scientists themselves, and also from known facts, that the earth and man did not come by evolution, I wish now to present certain concrete facts which show that evolution is not only unproved but that it is unprovable and impossible as a theory to account for the origin of the earth and man.

1. If evolution is true, then we have two mutually self-contradictory and conflicting forces at work—one to preserve species without change, and the other to constantly change the species. Both of these things cannot be true.

2. There is no natural or "spontaneous generation."

Having no real knowledge about the origin of life, the scientists first tried to make out a case for "spontaneous generation"; but they utterly failed in this, and had themselves to disallow this theory. The very term "spontaneous generation" is a begging of the question by evolutionists. It assumes the very thing that is to be proved.

As we know the world now, matter and spirit, are two absolutely different things. They are as wide as the poles apart. Mud and mire and slime and stone are not only totally dissimilar from reason, and hope and faith and love, but they cannot in anyway be compared one with the other.

If, then, we are told they were originally one,—that the first life germ awoke out of dead matter, we naturally look for clear and overwhelming facts to prove such an incredible miracle. But no such facts are forthcoming from evolution, and it has to be reluctantly admitted by the evolutionists.

Since, then, spontaneous generation of life is confessedly impossible, and therefore did not occur, we are driven back to accept the only other alternative, namely, the creative agency of a Living God.

3. Furthermore, since "evolution" means an unfolding or unrolling, it is self-evident that whatever is evolved must first have been involved. Our accepted definition is that evolution is by "resident forces." No creative forces therefore, can be allowed anywhere along the

upward path of the alleged evolution. All must come
from within. That means that in the first life cell, germ,
or protoplasm which appeared on this planet, all the
phenomena, wonders, and glories of all after-life were
potentially contained. This is too much to believe.

REPRODUCTION BEFORE EVOLUTION

Not only that, but on this whole matter of the alleged
evolution of life, I wish to point out another most significant and really conclusive fact.

It is self-evident that there could be no evolution without the power of reproduction in living things. Since,
then, reproduction is a prior condition to evolution, it,
therefore, cannot be the product of evolution. Hence,
we face the logical necessity for direct creation as a
start for all developing life.

Furthermore, the power of reproduction is not in the
embryo but only in the mature parent. Therefore, a
parent form of life must have been created in the beginning to have produced the embryo from which offspring
alone can come.

An egg does not produce an egg. It produces a
chicken, and that produces another egg which produces
another chicken, and so on and on. Not only is it true,
however, that an embryo cannot produce an embryo, but
it is also true that an embryo is not improvable. Improvement can come only in the matured form, and not
in the germ or single life-cell, or embryo. The simplest
form of multiplying life is the amoeba. The amoeba
multiplies its kind, not through an embryo, but by dividing itself and thus forming into two amoebas, and they
in turn divide and form into others, and thus multiply.
But the two amoebas that came from the single amoeba
are each exactly like the first amoeba. They have no
resident force of self-improvement. The most serious
obstacle in the way of the theory of ascending life is the

impossibility of explaining how the so-called protozoa—minute animals composed of a single cell,—ever passed into the metazoa,—animals composed of many cells. Nothing but evasion and the most impossible guesses has ever bridged this chasm in life's alleged development.

Since, then, the power of reproduction is not in the embryo or single life cell, and since the embryo is not improvable but only the mature product, therefore, life could not have developed by evolution. The proposition that life started from a single cell, which in some unexplained way awoke out of dead matter, is utterly untenable and irrational. The first protoplasmic life cell would either have died because of the harsh and inhospitable conditions around it, or if it had lived it could have had no power of reproduction, as it was only a cell or embryo. And even if it is conceived of as having the power of increasing by division like the amoeba, it could only have produced other amoebas, and they in turn others, so that the only form of life on the earth would have been amoebas.

Since, then, these low forms of life have no resident power of self-improvement, therefore, we are again driven to the plan of outside forces operating upon them to produce higher and more complex forms of life. But that is a violation of evolution, according to our accepted definition, and therefore, we are driven again to accept creation, or the operation of a Power outside of the original life forms, to account for all living things.

4. The human mind is not simply greater in degree than that of the lower animals, but is generically different in kind. This cannot be harmonized with the theory of evolution, and points to direct creative power.

The distinctive characteristics and capacities of man, especially his moral and religious endowments, are so impossible of explanation by the theory of evolution,

that truth demands recognition of direct creative purpose
and power in explanation of man's origin and progress.

DEGENERATION VS. EVOLUTION

5. Many other positive facts could be cited disproving
evolution—I point out only one more, namely, degeneration rather than evolution. There are ample grounds for
the belief that both vegetable and animal life is in a process
of degeneration and decay on this planet, rather than a
process of evolution and improvement.

And this only goes to prove the teaching of the Bible
that man is a fallen being and that, therefore, the world
is moving toward judgment and the final re-creation of
all things in a "new heavens and a new earth, wherein
dwelleth righteousness."

There is such a thing as evolution of a kind in human
affairs, but this also only proves that man is a fallen
being who is frantically struggling to regain a lost estate.

A RATIONAL VIEW

Is there, then, any escape from these contradictions
and absurdities into which speculative philosophy and an
essentially godless materialism would plunge us? Is
there any solid ground on which we can build our lives
and found our hope of immortality?

Yes, I answer, with all confidence, there is ample
ground. There are ways very near at hand by which we
can solve the riddle of the universe and know the nature
and destiny of man.

I appeal first to a right view of the material world as
a whole. The Bible says: "Speak to the earth, and it
will teach you." When we view nature as a whole, and
not in little scraps and sections as the evolutionists try
to do, certain great overwhelming facts stand plainly out.
One of these is the fact of harmony.

As we observe the world around us, there is harmony

everywhere. Now there can never be harmony without design. The fact that the universe is a cosmos instead of a chaos proves this. But if there is design behind the universe, there must also be mind, for mind only can design. Dead matter cannot design. Blind force cannot design. The chair here cannot design to give an address; nor can the steam that operates the locomotive design to make the machine which it runs. Only mind can design; and when we see, therefore, design behind nature and the life of man, we must conclude that the Creator has, or is, Mind.

This leads us to another advance step, namely, that if *there is mind there must be personality,* for mind is always one of the characteristics of a person. Thus, as we contemplate the great Mind behind the world we know that God must be a living person. Not, indeed, a person such as you and I. We are finite and limited personalities. God is the infinite, unlimited and eternal personality.

> "We are broken lights of Thee—
> And Thou, O God, art more than we!"

Man is a living, loving, intelligent personality, and since it is inconceivable that the Creator should be less than His creation, we know that there is a God who is a living, loving, intelligent being!

But we can come home closer still in our thinking. We can turn to the very nature of our own minds and find the answer to the question of the origin of the world. The first dictum of the old Greek philosophy was "man, know thyself." I appeal to that. We have a sure foundation for rational appeal in the very nature of the human mind itself. Our minds are so constituted that we cannot separate between cause and effect. When we see a given effect we have at once to think of an adequate cause to produce this effect. We cannot avoid doing this.

It is written deep down in the very constitution of our beings so to do.

Here, in imagination, we may see a beautiful house standing in symmetry and majesty among its green trees —with its stately columns before it; its broad verandas and hospitable doors, and the inspiring symmetry of perfect walls and a noble roof. As we look upon such a scene as that we instinctively ask ourselves, "How did the house get there?" Now, we know that it did not come by chance. We might imagine all the materials of a house brought together in a great pile—all the braces and beams and boards and nails and shingles brought and dumped in together; and we might imagine, too, some unseen and mysterious force blindly stirring those materials, tossing them about, lifting them here, yonder and everywhere, but we know that a house would never result from any such process as that. No sleeper would find its position. No upright would reach its place. No weather-boarding would be nailed on, and no roof tree would rise above it all. Never can we have a house until there is a designing architect to plan it in his wisdom and execute it in his power. And so as we look out upon the great house we call the world, carpeted with the greenest grasses and the never-resting sea, walled in by the sweet air, domed by heaven's eternal blue and lighted by flaming sun and silvery moon, and the everlasting stars—as we see this great and beautiful home of man we must think of the Architect who designed it in His wisdom and who executed it in His love and power! And we have to violate the very constitution of our minds to do anything other than that. We cannot separate between cause and effect.

Notice, now, *we do not say there is no existence without a cause.* I have here a chair, and as I see that chair I instinctively ask what caused the chair. But the moment I see behind the chair the cabinetmaker, who designed and executed it, I am satisfied, and my mind goes no further. It rests content in the creative possibility of the cabinetmaker's personality as the cause of the chair. So when we see behind the phenomena of the material world an *existence who is all cause* for the reason that He is infinite, then we may pause for we have found the First Cause. But that is precisely what our Bibles have been saying to us for all these years. "In the beginning, God created the heavens and the earth," and God "created man in His own image."

III

REBUTTAL FOR THE AFFIRMATIVE*

Mr. Chairman, Honorable Judges, Worthy Opponent and Dear Friends All: May I say in the beginning that the only point that I can find out that my opponent made was, that evolution is only a theory. And may I answer that immediately by saying that the Genesis story is only a theory, and a much worse theory. I presented to you in my first speech the various reasons appealing to a logical mind whereby the hypothesis of evolution seems to be a more acceptable guess than the absurd, grotesque story which we find in the first chapters of Genesis. I am reminded of the story of Frederick the Great and his flute. It was said that Frederick the Great loved music, but to be strictly accurate, you should say that what Frederick the Great loved was flute music, and if you wanted to tell the actual truth, what he liked most was the music of his own flute when he played it himself. And when my worthy opponent says that the doctrine of evolution is incompatible with religion, remember that all that it means is, that it is incompatible with *his* religion. When he says that it is impossible to put God in nature, when he denies the possibility of an immanent God, remember that it is the transcendent God which is not there. It is impossible, of course, to put the transcendent God in nature, as I very deliberately proved.

As for the Century Dictionary's definition which he quoted, that evolution is antagonistic to creationism, it is one of the best arguments for my side which has been

---

* By Rev. Charles Francis Potter.

brought forward tonight. When he said that Huxley proved that evolution makes it impossible to believe in the Bible, I say, what of it? I thought we adequately disposed of that six weeks ago as far as this argument maintained. You cannot prove evolution by the Bible, but that is no argument on this platform against evolution. If Darwin lost faith in God, remember that it was the God of my worthy opponent that he lost faith in, and not in the immanent God of the Universe, for I am proud to say that the entire Darwin family were members of a Unitarian Church.

In the words of my opponent, quoting Haeckel, he said that Haeckel rejected God, and the actual words of the quotation were these: "Haeckel rejected a personal God, or Creator." Of course he did, but he did not reject an immanent God—the immanent God-life of the Universe. Others he quoted to prove that evolution turns the Creator out of doors, but what I am maintaining is, that the Creator concept of God ought to go out of doors. It is no longer of use. This is no argument whatever against the immanent God.

My worthy opponent pointed out, stating that I had not touched the question, that the question is, how the earth and man came, and not what happened after they got here. I wish to point out to you that he is still in bondage to the Genesis story, which presumes that the whole thing happened in six days long ago. I point out to you, as I did before, that the earth is still in the process of evolution. It has not yet fully come. We ourselves are still in a process of development, changing our form from quadrupeds to bipeds; we are still "evoluting." All the arguments that I brought forward proving the existence of evolution have to do with the earth and man as we find them today. What they were 4004 B. C. at nine o'clock of a Thursday morning, when Archbishop Usher thought the world was created, I do not know, because I was not there, and my opponent does not know because he was not there. You see, there are two different conceptions altogether. My opponent wants to make out that the Garden of Eden was a symphony orchestra; that this earth is supposed to be a Paradise, a beautiful place. He wants to make out that, when the world was created and the Lord looked upon it and "saw that it was good," that it was really good; that everything was all right; that it was Paradise; that Adam and Eve were perfect husband and wife; that everything went along all right. That is what he is trying to point out, but that is the wrong conception of this earth altogether. This earth is not and never has been yet a symphony orchestra recital. This earth is a piano factory, and there are a lot of shavings around, and we are trying to make better instruments, and bye-and-bye the harmony will come.

A great deal was made by my worthy opponent of the fact that scientists say that they know nothing or very little about the beginning of things. Now, the fact that Creationists think they know a lot about it is no argument whatever. To say "thus saith the Lord" does not make it so, you know. It is only what my worthy opponent and his predecessors way back to Moses think the Lord said, and we have got just as good a right to guess now. The fact that there are contradictions among scientists, paralleled by my worthy opponent to the facts which I pointed out in the first debate about the contradictions of the Bible, is utterly beside the case, because, while the advocates of the orthodox position about the Bible claim that it is infallible, scientists know enough to know that they do not know it all, and they do not claim to be infallible.

When LeConte, whose definition we are using, made the guess that the earth had existed from 10,000 to 100,000 years, may I point out to you that the book was published in 1889. He contrasted it with a statement made by Henry Fairfield Osborn in a book published in 1920, where the guess was 100,000 years. Scientists have learned something in 30 years, and they are willing to admit it. And may I point out that not even LeConte suggested as the date of the creation of the earth, 4004 B. C., which the Bible chronology would indicate. What I am arguing is, that the evolution of the earth took a long while and that it came by an evolutionary process, and that it was not done by Jehovah God some 6000 years ago.

My worthy opponent suggested, how does Wells know about the nebular hypothesis—was he there? Which is no argument whatever. What does my worthy opponent know about God making Adam and Eve? He was not there. If Prof. Milliken says that the sun is simply a great source of electrical energy, I do not see how that disproves evolution, do you? And if there is a planetesimal theory, all right; that does not disprove the evolution theory. These are only various experimental guesses that scientists are trying out. They are only sure that there is an evolutionary process. Whatever these other various branches of the theory may be, that does not disprove the central theory whatsoever.

Every bit of the evolutionary theory, so my opponent said, submits blind chance without God as the cause of things. I refer it to you as arbiters. Did I once refer the thing to blind chance, or did I leave God out? It is not so. The modern evolutionist, believing in God, does not talk of chance. He talks, as Bergson talks, of the vital impulse within all nature, which is the working of God Himself. Just because we cannot believe in a God with a long beard sitting upon a throne, to whom we must bow and kowtow as to an Oriental monarch, just because we cannot believe in that sort of God, the people who do not believe in evolution say that we do not believe in any God at all, and they have no right to say so. May

I point out to you that most of the evolutionists which were quoted by my worthy opponent are honored and respected members of churches today. Just because they happen not to belong to the Fundamentalist group is no argument whatever that they do not believe in God. When my friend said that not even the nature of matter is known, and dilated upon that subject, may I remind you that that is not the debate and has no connection with it whatsoever.

As for the arguments which he produced, I am rather puzzled, because, you see, contrary to the practice in debate, my opponent made his first speech a rebuttal. So I have got to rebut the rebuttal. He ridiculed the idea which I expressed as to how man came, and says that in the beginning God created the heavens and the earth and Adam and Eve. But that does not prove anything. He adduced no facts whatever to support his bare, bald statement. If he brings in the Bible as proof, that must be examined, and let me remind you that the statements made about the creation in Genesis were not made by people who were accustomed to stating facts in scientific language. They only gave what they thought happened, and a lot of things have been learned by the human race since first the Adam and Eve story gained circulation in popular literature among the Semitic tribes.

When he pictured to you the Bible Adam, such a glorified creature with such a glorified wife, he was drawing you a picture which no one can prove ever existed whatsoever. He did not produce the photograph, as I can produce the photograph of the spiral nebulæ in Andromeda. He quoted the Bible story, and told you that in the Bible account of creation you find dignity and beauty and law. And then he was so unwise as to bring in the question of the way woman was treated in that story. Just read it when you get home. And when he contrasted with admirable rhetoric the picture of Adam as given in the Old Testament with the probable ancestor of man, his description of an animal ancestor was not very attractive. But, friends, haven't we got to the point where we do not need to be flattered by being told that we came from some angelic creature? Aren't we men and women enough today, haven't we progressed far enough in this evolution, so that we may take credit to ourselves that we have come up from something like that, instead of being ashamed of having come down?

The 800 probables, which he quotes from Darwin, contrasting them with the 800 or 900 "thus saith the Lords" of the Old Testament, are no argument whatever, because not definitely connected with the subject of the evening.

I was much obliged to him for having pointed out that man has turned from ape to man by throwing things with his front feet. The development of the human hand is well known by every educator today. If you take a small child and try to educate him through his eyes and ears alone, you make a sad mistake; indeed, the very reason why we have manual training in the schools is because man learned by using his hands, just as our ancestors did. I thank him for the statement.

I was very sorry that the contrast was drawn between the genealogy of Christ according to the Bible and the genealogy of man according to theistic evolution, "which was the son of the ape, which was the son of the reptile," and so forth. Ridicule, of course, my friends, is no argument, as we all recognize. There is no point whatever in pointing out the genealogy of Christ in this connection, because that does not enter into this debate. We will treat of that amply in later debates. But, to come to the point where my opponent approached the subject of discussion, evolution, may I say that to say, as he did, that God made all species, and that none have come since, is to get into very hot water, because, if God made all the species of living things and none have been made since, remember that every species of animal parasite that inhabits man, every kind of "cootie," every germ of disease which we find on the earth, which is a living thing, as any doctor will tell you, must have been in Adam's body, and his 930 years must have been years of misery and suffering.   The whole argument about species is a specious argument, because species run into genera, and genera into families, and families into orders, orders into classes, classes into branches, and branches bring us right back to our own primitive ancestor. You cannot draw the line between species, as any botanist or other student of science will easily tell you. You cannot say where one species ends and another begins. You can take the 600 varieties of aster, and they run so off into the other members of that same family that even a botanist cannot tell the difference, and when you find that the line breaks down there, you find it also breaks down between the genera, between the families, and so it goes, and brings us all back to that same ancestor, whom we may not be proud of, but from whom we are all directly descended.

As to acquired characters being not transmitted, my worthy opponent does not understand.   Acquired characters are not transmitted to the direct offspring, but there is an influence upon the germ plasm which finds its effect in later generations.

As to his protest that Mr. Bryan was not here to defend himself: I simply used Mr. Bryan because I thought it was a little more polite than to say "my worthy opponent," but the same thing holds, and for the life of me I cannot see what my opponent's resemblance to Wilson has to do with this argument.

Let me say, in conclusion, answering his main argument, which really came at the very end, that this world is an effect, and that there must have been an adequate cause. I agree with him. When I disagree, it is only to maintain that this adequate cause has not got to be

the kind of God that he particularly believes in. The
reason why many a religious person refuses to accept
evolution is not because the proofs of it are not everywhere evident, but because he fears that by accepting it
he will lose God. Man's reason is largely convinced as
to evolution, almost persuaded, but his heart hesitates.
The acceptance of evolution and its religious conse-
quences, its influence on religion, does not mean aban-
doning God, but rather the acceptance of a different and
I think a better conception of God. I believed once in
my opponent's idea of God, but I do not now. The
Genesis idea postulates a transcendent, even an anthropomorphic God—that is, a God made in man's bodily
image, if you please. The evolution idea presents an
immanent God, closer than breathing and nearer than
hands and feet.

Just one question for my worthy opponent to answer:
If God was able to interfere at certain crises in the past,
this Hebrew anthropomorphic God, and do the things
that he was supposed to have done at certain times in the
past, why didn't he interfere between 1914 and 1918?
No, my friends, the World War absolutely dissipated
forever that idea of God. God is with us, but we have
got to change our idea of God, as every great epoch has
demanded a similar change. We must recognize that this
God that we are talking of is the God who sleeps in the
mineral, stirs in the vegetable, feels in the animal, and
thinks in man, and if another World War is to be pre-
vented, it must be done not by a transcendent God in the
skies, but by the God in you and me.

It seems to me that the facts in the case have been
presented to you, humbly, in the spirit of science—
for science never says "Thus saith the Lord"; it only
says, "I am trying to find the truth"—in that spirit, then,
which it seems to me is a better spirit than the older one,
we who believe in science and in evolution and in God

are finding that life takes on new meaning; that we have a great big job to do in this world, this piano factory that we are working in, and we are doing it with hope and joy and happiness in our hearts. We believe in evolution. We believe that the earth and man came by these resident forces according to fixed laws, which we cannot escape even by miracles when we want to; that it came by continuous, progressive change; that that is the hope of the world and not its despair, and that evolution reveals us God, rather than takes Him from us.

IV

REBUTTAL FOR THE NEGATIVE*

My friends, I will dispose of the humor first. I am glad that my honorable opponent was honorable enough at last to substitute me in Mr. Bryan's place. So I must now defend my own caudal appendage. My defense is this: My worthy opponent is free to believe that he has come along the route he has been arguing for tonight if he wants to, but he cannot make a monkey out of me! My opponent may admit these simian characters to his family tree if he so desires, but I confess I am a little more particular. I have a certain pride of ancestry. We have had five children in our home, and I have tried to instil into them the truth that, while they should not have a false pride, nevertheless it is true that blood counts and that they have something to live up to. I do not want to have to say to them, "While it is true that, on your mother's side you come from the Hillyers and Greens of Georgia, and on my mother's side, from the Carters and Lees of Virginia, and on my father's side, from the Douglasses and Stratons of Scotland, remember if you take a few more steps backward you will have to shake hands with a gorilla as your great, great, great grandfather!"

Now I know that when you go too far back you sometimes run into skeletons in the family closet. In my own family I have learned that more than one of those old fellows back there was strung up for loyalty to God and King. So I have to admit that some of my remote an-

* By Rev. John Roach Straton.

cestors hung by their necks, but I am willing to stake my life on the proposition that none of them ever hung by their tails!

Honorable judges, ladies and gentlemen, it is time to come back to the subject of this debate. The subject is, "Resolved, That the Earth and Man Came by Evolution"; and the definition is, that evolution is "continuous, progressive change, according to fixed laws, by resident forces." And I submit, in all fairness, that my opponent has not established the proposition that the earth and man came by these means. The burden of proof is upon him, because he is seeking to discount that theory and that belief, drawn from a definite Revelation, which has been the foundation of our society for thousands of years, and which will finally produce the highest and most glorious civilization that the world can ever know. Yes, the burden was upon him, and to overthrow the accepted belief of Christendom, it was necessary for him to produce facts that were acceptable to rational minds, and I submit that no such facts have been given.

No facts have been given, first of all, to bridge the gap between dead matter and sentient life; and then to bridge the gap between the alleged beginning of life in its low forms and its higher forms; and no argument and no facts have been given to bridge the tremendous gap between the crude instinct of the beast and the Godward aspirations of man.

Let me, therefore, just in rounding off our thought together, point out several things, meeting my opponent upon his own ground, that will answer, I think, satisfactorily the points he made, even though they were not directly on the subject for debate.

THE RELIABILITY OF THE BIBLE

He referred to the fact that the Bible ought not to be authority, and that we have no more grounds for believing what the Bible says than we have for believing these theories of evolution. Now, I submit that we have adequate grounds. We have the very facts of nature and life themselves, and we have also the long experience of the human race, verifying the teaching of the Bible!

My opponent harped much upon what he called the "absurd, grotesque story which we find in the first chapters of Genesis." But other thinkers do not share with my opponent his poor opinion of the Bible. Jean Paul said:

"The first leaf of the Mosaic record has more weight than all the folios of the men of science and philosophy combined."

This is true, and hair-splitting over differences about the alleged "errors" or the infallibility of the Bible does not at all change the fact that it is the greatest authority at last among the children of men. The Bible has been the great moral mentor and spiritual guide of the enlightened nations of the earth for thousands of years. Its influence is simply immeasurable, and its teachings have proved themselves to be truth because of the profound and uplifting power which they have exerted on the human race. It will take something more than the unsupported hypotheses of the materialists and the vague speculations of skeptics to overthrow it. The proposition that only a good tree can produce good fruit is undeniable, and the Bible comes to us with the credential of an age-long influence for righteousness and truth.

Whatever theory it sets forth, therefore, concerning the origin of the earth and man, has far stronger presuppositions in its favor than the wild and constantly changing theories of philosophers and the mutually contradictory ideas of scientists, because the Bible comes into court with a good reputation and a good influence, which could spring only from truth-telling and right character.

My opponent answered my remark that Wells really knows nothing about how the earth began because he was not there when God made the earth. He replied by saying that I do not know anything about it either, or about God making Adam and Eve, because I was not there. It is very true that I was not there, and Mr. Wells was not there, and Mr. Potter was not there, but there was One who was there! Jehovah—Christ was there, and He has told us through inspired men just what happened. Thank God, therefore, that He has not left us to grope in darkness, and to become doped with doubt, but has given us a Revelation that answers the eternal questions of human life and destiny, that satisfies the longing soul of man, and that is a "lamp to our feet and a light to our pathway"!

So far as my opponent's characterizations of the God of the Bible are concerned, and so far as his repeated thrusts at the teachings of the Bible are concerned, I have time only to say that the God of the Bible is not at all the one-sided and ridiculous being which my opponent pictured Him. The God of the Bible is both immanent in nature and transcendent to nature. Therefore, He is a real God, and has all power in both the material and spiritual worlds.

I would say, therefore, to all the vain and intellectually proud Modernists, just as Jesus said to the self-satisfied and skeptical Sadducees of His day: "Ye do err: not knowing the Scriptures nor the power of God."

And the point which my opponent made about the other creation myths and stories means merely that there was in the beginning a true understanding about the creation of the world, which was given, of necessity, by Revelation, but as the races scattered and became more and more sinful and degraded, the early purity of this tradition was perverted and corrupted and changed into many ridiculous forms. The mere fact that there are so many common elements, as, for example, the use of clay, etc.—in these distorted creation stories which, as my opponent admitted, come from all parts of the earth, shows that they all must have had a common origin,—that they were all true in the beginning but were then perverted, as before remarked, and changed with the passing years into their later foolish forms.

THE BLOOD PROOF

The Bible teaching has been vindicated at many points. My opponent, for example, referred to the blood. Now the Bible teaching about the blood is verified by the real facts of science, and it also completely disproves the theory of evolution.

The fact that there is a great variety of blood in the different species of animals negatives the theory of evolution, the foundation of which is uniformity. Science agrees with the Bible that the life is in the blood, and if all forms of animal life had come from a common ancestry, then the blood of all would have to be the same. But we find the blood of birds and reptiles and men so different that if the blood of one of these be injected into the veins of the other, death immediately follows. The blood also makes the type of flesh. Science again agrees with the Bible that "all flesh is not the same flesh; but there is one kind of flesh of men, another flesh of beasts, another of fishes, and another of birds" (I Cor. 15:39). But if all animal life had sprung from a common ancestor, then all flesh would have to be the same flesh. The Bible says, further, that "God hath made of one blood all nations of men for to dwell on all the face of the earth" (Acts 17:26). The distinction, therefore, which the Bible draws between man and beast at the point of blood and flesh is confirmed absolutely by science, and it completely disproves the theory of evolution. The

Bible is vindicated, by known facts whenever they are really discovered, and established.

THE FIXITY OF SPECIES

The teaching of the Bible stands vindicated and proved at another point, namely the fixity of species. Right here in Genesis the statement is made that when God created life—both vegetable and animal life—he ordained that all forms of life should bring forth only "after their kind" (Gen. 1:21), and according to their "seed" (Gen. 1:11). Now, so far as all human observation and experience go, that law of God, as recorded in the Bible, has been obeyed during all the ages of time! Every form of animal life that we know anything about brings forth only "after its kind." Baboons do not produce peacocks, and acorns do not bring forth apple trees. No! each produces after its kind, just as the Bible says; and when all the theories and sceptical speculations are done, I am here tonight to say that the fixity of species answers the evolutionary hypothesis completely, absolutely and forever! The species are fixed, and the life forms are fixed, and whatever varieties may have developed within the bounds of the God-made species, have come about through God's wisdom and power, and according to the potentialities which He implanted in vegetable and animal forms, and because He commanded them to increase and multiply and replenish the earth.

If evolution were true, let me repeat, we ought to find everywhere not only the fossils of endless intermediate forms in transitional stages, recording the change from one thing into another, as I showed you, but we ought now to see all around us, if evolution is really a "continuous" process, these intermediate forms of life. We ought to see horses developing into super-horses, and men sprouting wings with which to fly, and so on ad infinitum. Why is it that we have come up in each species, just so far and stopped, if evolution is really "continuous progressive change?" If it is that, it must go on! But it doesn't go on!

Thus we find in the deep truth of life itself—the closest and most obvious thing to us all—the reality of the Bible's teaching that each must increase "after its kind." There is a boundery which nature, or God, or whatever the power is, has fixed, and when that line is crossed, sterility is the result. Even when different branches of the same species are crossed, only hybrids result—and there is no offspring at all from crossing truly different species. The navel orange results from the grafting of two different types of orange, but the navel orange produces nothing from its seed. The mare and the donkey produce a mule, but the mule can produce nothing but a laugh! Bob Toombs, the Georgia statesman, said that "the mule is the most pathetic of all animals, in that he has neither the pride of ancestry nor the hope of posterity!" And that fixity of species, that fact of sterility when species are crossed, is a definite and everywhere present proof that the Bible is true and evolution is false!

I will admit that we have variation, and very wide variation, but because of this fixity, which is obvious and which science confirms, we know that it is variation only within the bounds of species. And this takes care of the question of "geographical distribution" that my opponent touched upon. The fact that the remains of elephants and other tropical animals have been found in North America, and that the remains of animals now found only in Australia have been found in England, goes to prove that the present continents were formerly all united, and this, with known changes of climate adequately accounts for the varieties of animals now found in different parts of the earth.

We not only see no changes in species now in progress, but there have been none, so far as men have been able to observe, for thousands of years. We have the mummies of apes which have come down from ancient Egypt, but those apes, living over three thousand years ago, are the same as the apes of today. Not only so, but we find this same survival of species over even "millions of years," if we accept the long-time estimates of the evolutionists. There are forms of life, called bacteria, living and acting today just as they lived and acted when they attacked the bodies of mastodons and other animals in remote past ages. The scientists have found evidences of the work of these bacteria in the bones of those ancient fossils, showing that the bacteria lived and acted then precisely as they do now. This proves that species do not evolve but stand still, and if there is any change, facts prove that they degenerate rather than evolve to higher forms.

CREATIVE DESIGN

Another point at which the teaching of the Bible is vindicated by what we see around us, and by which the theory of evolution is completely disproved, is the fact of design in the wonderful adaptations of instincts to organs in many forms of life. I touched upon design in my first speech but give it now a somewhat different application. The thought of a halfway beaver, for example, surviving in the midst of many foes, and doing the wonderful things that a beaver has to do to live at all, is an absurd thought! The individual could not have survived for a day, and thus the species must have perished!

The idea of transitional amendments is, therefore, contradictory to the fundamental principles of evolution. Darwin teaches that any evolution in nature, any new bodily organ or feature, must be *profitable* to the individuals of a species in order for the species to survive (See page 77, "Origin of Species"). But a half-formed wing or a budding leg or an incomplete eye would not be useful to the individual but an impediment. Only completed organs are useful to the individual. One principle of evolution is that nature abhors useless things and throws them off. Therefore, this other principle cannot be true that a useless half organ would be preserved by nature through long stretches of time, until it developed into a perfect organ through successive individuals!

Take again the water spider. Here is a creature so wonderful, and with habits of life so extraordinary, that it cannot possibly be conceived as coming from any process of evolution.

The water spider is a true spider, yet it lives much of the time and builds its nest under water, though it is an air-breathing animal like the other spiders. It first goes under the water and spins from its own body a waterproof silken envelope or bulb, which it attaches firmly to a rock or other object at the bottom of the water. The mouth of this bulb is downward, and of course in the beginning is filled with water, though it is waterproof on the outside. After making this home for itself, the water spider then goes to the surface and, because of the peculiar formation of the hairs on its legs, it can catch a bubble of air, which it carries down into the water and turns loose under its newly constructed home. The bubble of air rises until it strikes the top of the inside of the bulb, and there it stays, driving out a proportionate quantity of water. The spider then goes back and gets another bubble of air, and continues this operation until it has filled its house with air and driven out all the water. Then it lays its eggs, attaching them to the inside top wall of its house, and there rears its young in safety.

Now the spider could not possibly live and do these things unless it had a perfect instinct, and all of its organs were perfected for carrying out its instinct. The thought of a half water spider in the process of evolution is an absurdity! It would drown if it did not have all of the organs for spinning its waterproof house, on the one side, and all of the instincts through which it uses its organs and protects its young, on the other.

In Job God claims that He gives "the goodly wings unto the peacock," provides food for the ravens, causes the hawk to fly by His wisdom, to "stretch her wings toward the south," and the eagle to mount up at His command and "make her nest on high" (Job. 39). Thus the Bible teaches that God's designing wisdom and watchful care is over all things, and we see His handiwork in the wonders of nature on every hand.

EVOLUTION IMMORAL

There is another point at which the Bible is proved true and evolution false, and that is in the field of moral influence. Beyond any question, the evolutionary philosophy is a brutalizing and essentially immoral thing and it is utterly contrary to Bible teaching. Now I submit it as self-evident that nothing can be mentally true that is morally false. Truth is a unity, and nothing can be intellectually right that is ethically wrong. Now the theory of evolution is ethically wrong and it cannot, therefore, be intellectually right.

My opponent referred to God and the recent world War. He said that the war disproved the fact of a living transcendent God such as the Bible pictures. But his reference was not only untrue as to God, it was also most unfortunate for himself and the cause he is championing tonight.

A Living God was in the war. He saw to it that it was rightly won against overwhelming odds. He finally brought victory out of defeat for human liberty and eternal righteousness. Yes, through Christian America God triumphed in the war.

But I ask you to look at the really significant fact about the war, namely, the moral wreck and ruin which came to Germany, through the evolutionary philosophy, which really produced the war.   The old Germany of Goethe and Schiller and Luther—the Germany of the Christmas tree, of neighborly kindness, of music, and art, and true science—was miseducated and debauched by the importation, through the Prussians, of the godless and destructive evolutionary philosophy.   The military leaders of Prussia, encouraged by the Junkers, and the vain and ambitious Kaiser and his equally vain and ambitious forefathers, accepted and acted upon the teaching of Darwin as truth.

In one of the summaries of his "Origin of Species" Darwin speaks of evolution as the "one general law leading to the advancement of all organic beings—namely: multiply, vary, let the strongest live and the weakest die" (p. 297).

Here is "the survival of the fittest" with a vengeance! And this teaching bore its logical and inevitable fruit in Germany.

The half-crazed Nietzsche, who ended his days in the insane asylum, seized upon this teaching of Darwin with avidity, and from it he evolved his idea of the "superman"; and he taught the Germans that they were the supermen.   He referred to the German proudly as the "blond beast."   He glorified war and declared that it is a necessity.   He utterly repudiated and rejected the Christian religion.   He taught that Christ was a weakling, and that His religion was an enemy to the human race; that such things as love and sympathy and mercy are vices and not virtues, and that the strong ought to trample on and destroy the weak in order that "the fittest" may survive!

Trietschke and Von Bernhardi took this teaching of Darwin and Nietzsche as the basis of their philosophy, and they deliberately glorified war as Nietzsche had done. Their books were printed in cheap popular editions and spread by the Junkers and military masters of Germany throughout the empire, and thus the German nation was miseducated and misled.

Yes Germany took Darwinism literally. Darwin had taught the "survival of the fittest" in the brute struggle for supremacy, and Germany said: "That is true, and we propose to demonstrate that we are the fittest!" So she formulated her philosophy that "might makes right," which is simply a practical expression of Darwin's "survival of the fittest," and thus she sprung at the throat of an unsuspecting world!

Now, if Darwin taught truth, Germany was right, in 1914, and we cannot complain at the tearing up of treaties like "scraps of paper," at the wholesale raping of women, at the bombing of hospital ships, or the sending of the Lusitania to the bottom of the sea!

Nor is that all that is to be said of the moral ruin wrought by Darwinism and evolution in general. The wave of animalism, with its corrupting influence upon morals, has come through this philosophy of animalism, which is prostituting and destroying the human race. If we are merely highly developed beasts, then why should we not live like beasts? Monkey men make monkey morals!

The glorification of the flesh over the spirit, of animalism over idealism, through the brute philosophy of evolution, is the real key to the moral decay of the times!

That talented Englishman, who writes under the non de plume of the "Gentleman with a Duster" did not overstate the case when, in his book on "Painted Windows," he denounced Darwinism as the fountain-head of these modern ills. It is true, my friends, that all of these dangerous and disgusting wrongs of today can be traced back, so far as their rapid increase is concerned, to the time when the dark and sinister shadow of Darwinism fell across the fair fields of human life!

The truth of the creation as revealed in the Bible is an ennobling and inspiring truth. It links man to heaven and to God. The falsehood of evolution is a degrading and demoralizing one because it drags man down to beasthood and the mud.

THE TWO FUNDAMENTAL FALLACIES

In closing, I point out the two great fundamental fallacies of the evolutionary philosophy. The first is that nothing is fixed or final, but that all things are in a state of constant "flux and change." It is this false notion that is behind the mental weakness and the moral laxity of this philosophy. Because of this false idea, it is argued that there are no fixed and unchanging moral standards, and so the Ten Commnadments are jauntily thrown into the discard, and the youth of today are left to do as they please! The last sentence which is thrown on the screen in the film, "Evolution," which is being widely exhibited, is this: "The only unchanging thing is change."

It is as false as hell, and as ruinous as death! There are many things that are absolutely unchangeable. The proposition that twice two equals four is eternally true. The proposition that a straight line is the shortest distance between two points cannot "evolve" nor change nor alter forever. The true principles of physics and chemistry are unchangeable and eternal. The unchangeableness of "natural law" which the evolutionists invoke in their behalf negatives this other fundamental plea which they make of "continuous progressive change." The great ethical principles of justice, righteousness and truth are all unchanging. Likewise, the Word of God is "established forever in heaven." It cannot change, and the Christ that it pictures is "the same yesterday, today and forever!"

The philosophy which teaches that all things are changing is not a true philosophy, and there are great enduring realities upon which we can build our lives, establish our homes, and develop a sane and noble society.

The other fundamental falsehood of evolution is that strife and struggle are the way of life. It is not true that the brute struggle for existence and the "survival of the fittest" are the profoundest facts of nature and life. There is another higher and greater truth, a more universal principle than the principle of conflict, competition and war, and that is the fact of co-operation, helpfulness, and sacrifice in service. Despite our superficial prattle about the "survival of the fittest," the fact stands that the forces which make for union and harmony have always been greater than the forces which make for disunion and strife. The fundamental fact that the universe is a cosmos instead of a chaos proves that. The cohesive forces are stronger than the disruptive forces; the centripetal forces are greater than the centrifugal forces; the sunshine is superior to the storm, and the light has the power to drive darkness away. So the struggle for life is not the greatest factor, nor is it the factor that should be most stressed. The struggle for the life of others is of far greater prominence in nature, when we but see the truth deeply enough. The little bird will battle more fiercely for its young than for its own food or life, and everywhere self-sacrifice for others is seen. Nature is not prevailingly, therefore, "red in tooth and claw." Nutrition is accompanied by reproduction, in order that life may continue, and the sacrifices of fatherhood and motherhood throughout all of nature are, in themselves, eloquent of the truth that unselfishness and concern for others is infinitely greater, as well as more beautiful and more important, than the selfish struggle

for the "survival of the fittest."   All of which is but
proof of the cheering prophecy that "the meek shall
inherit the earth, and shall delight themselves in the
abundance of peace."

There is a great tenderness at the heart of the world,
and this expresses itself in the highest truth known to
man, namely, that "God is love."   The supreme expression of that love in human history was the cross that
stood on the place called Golgotha; and the One who was
nailed to the cross has taught us that God is not a heartless force, but a heavenly Father who, because of His
infinite love, gave His own son to die that we might be
saved from sin and enter into everlasting life.   It is the
philosophy of the cross, with its great teaching of
self-sacrifice in service, which is needed today, and not
the philosophy of the brute struggle for survival, the
philosophy of the shambles, which is the apotheosis of
self and the mother of all wars, immoralities, hatreds and
wrongs.

It is not true that we came up from the slime and the
beasts through the jungle, and that we pass out into a
night of oblivion unlighted by a single star.   It is true
that "in the beginning God created the heavens and the
earth" and that He made "man in His own image."   It
is true that we came from God through the Garden, and
that we are destined by obedience to Him to an eternity
of joy in a land that is "fairer than day," where we will
meet again our loved ones who went before, and upon
whose blissful shore there falls no shadow and rests no
stain!

The great need of the times is not self-assertiveness
and arrogant pride, but humility, gentleness and self-
sacrifice in service.

With the simple faith of a little child, therefore, we
can say with Cecil Frances Alexander, in his exquisite

poem, to which I have ventured to add a closing verse
of my own:

"All things bright and beautiful,
    All creatures great and small,
All things wise and wonderful,
    The Lord God made them all.
Each little flower that opens,
    Each little bird that sings,
He made their glowing colors,
    He made their tiny wings.

"The purple-headed mountain,
    The rivers running by,
The sunset and the morning,
    That brightens up the sky;
The cold wind in the winter,
    The pleasant summer sun,
The ripe fruits in the garden,
    He made them every one.

"The tall trees in the greenwood,
    The meadows where we play,
The rushes by the water,
    We gather every day.
He gave us eyes to see them,
    And lips that we might tell,
How great is God Almighty,
    Who has made all things well."

The Bible as our Helper,
    And Jesus as our friend,
To die on dark Golgotha
    To make us good again.
God gave us hearts to love Him,
    And tongues His praise to tell—
How *good* is God Almighty,
    Who maketh all things well!

V

THE JUDGES' REPORT

Presiding Officer, Judge William Harman Black of the New York Supreme Court, introduced Judge Almet F. Jenks who, on behalf of the judges, announced that they had decided unanimously in favor of Dr. Straton, and the negative.

The judges were Judge Almet F. Jenks, of the New York Supreme Court, Judge Phillip J. McCook, of the New York Supreme Court, and Hon. Frank P. Walsh, former Chairman of the War Industries Board.

THE VIRGIN BIRTH— FACT OR FICTION?

Third in the Series of
Fundamentalist-Modernist Debates

between

Rev. JOHN ROACH STRATON, D.D.
PASTOR, CALVARY BAPTIST CHURCH
NEW YORK

and

Rev. CHARLES FRANCIS POTTER, M.A., S.T.M.
MINISTER, WEST SIDE UNITARIAN CHURCH
NEW YORK

NEW YORK
GEORGE H. DORAN COMPANY

THE VIRGIN BIRTH—FACT OR FICTION?
—○—
PRINTED IN THE UNITED STATES OF AMERICA

INTRODUCTION

By Rev. John Roach Straton, D.D.

I regret the necessity, in preparing an introduction for this debate on the Virgin Birth, of having to say a word of explanation about the decision of the judges.

On account of the fact that two of the regularly appointed judges for the Virgin Birth debate were called out of the city the day before the debate, and because the third judge was sick in bed, it was necessary to secure substitute judges at the last minute. Through a series of unfortunate mistakes, two of these substitute judges were not selected in accordance with the original agreement governing the debates. Because of this fact, and some other seeming irregularities, our side has requested that the Virgin Birth issue be redebated.

With these statements before him, each reader now can decide for himself as to the merits of the decision on the Virgin Birth.

While I do not attach undue importance to the decisions in these debates, as the decisions really do not settle the questions at issue, still I hope that the question can be resubmitted for final decision, in some way that will remove all grounds of complaint in connection with the series of debates on these vital questions.

In the meantime, the debate on the Deity of Christ, which I won by unanimous vote of the judges, is also now in print, and I sincerely hope that every reader of this booklet will get that also, that both of these great fundamental questions may be viewed side by side.

By agreement with my opponent, in this case, as in the case of the other debates, I have included in this printed form of the discussion some quotations, and other illustrative matter, which I did not have time to give in the oral debate. It is felt that this additional matter gives greater permanent value to the discussions.

The further fact that I speak far more rapidly than does my opponent accounts in part for the difference in the length between the two discussions.

JOHN ROACH STRATON.

Study of Calvary, Baptist Church,
  New York City.

INTRODUCTION

By Rev. CHARLES FRANCIS POTTER, M.A., S.T.M.

My opponent has with my consent added to his oral
debate considerable related matter.   Mine appears as given
in Carnegie Hall.

CHARLES FRANCIS POTTER.

CONTENTS

I

FOR THE AFFIRMATIVE[1]

QUESTION:

RESOLVED, THAT THE MIRACULOUS VIRGIN BIRTH OF JESUS CHRIST IS A FACT AND THAT IT IS AN ESSENTIAL CHRISTIAN DOCTRINE.

The heart of our nation has been recently touched by the death of two Presidents of the Republic. It is very significant, as I shall show a little later, that both Warren G. Harding and Woodrow Wilson before they died declared themselves as being in sympathy with the Fundamentalists and as opposed to the Modernists in the present religious situation. This proves not only that the old-fashioned views of religion appeal to both the scholarly and the practical mind, but also that the religious issues of today are being recognized more and more as of vital importance.

I wish to present my side of the debate tonight under three very simple but, I trust, comprehensive heads. I ask you to consider first—the possibility of the virgin birth; secondly, the probability of it; and thirdly the positive proof of it. This will naturally lead us then to a brief consideration of its essential character.

I. THE POSSIBILITY OF THE VIRGIN BIRTH

In asking you to consider the possibility of such an event as the virgin birth of Christ, I shall try to show that it was possible, first in the light of science, and secondly, in the light of faith.

[1] First speech for the affirmative by Rev. John Roach Straton, D.D., Pastor of Calvary Baptist Church.

11

1. To begin with, then, notice that there is no known natural law and no real fact of science, that would make such an event impossible. The author of a recent little book on "Science An Aid to Faith" concludes a scholarly and scientific discussion by saying:

"Modern science affirms nothing that discredits the doctrine of the Virgin Birth. To assert that there is anything in biology or in any other modern science that discredits the Virgin birth, considered as a physiological event, is to display lack of knowledge of the latest advances of science."

One of our New York radical preachers said in a sermon sometime since that "The virgin birth is not to be accepted as an historic fact," because it involves "a biological miracle that our modern minds cannot use." But, we may ask, "Whose modern minds?" This statement is merely an illustration of the colossal vanity and self-esteem of the religious radicals. The wise men of old are not the only wise men who have come to bow before Him who was born of a Virgin and who was first laid in a manger. Such men as Orr, Dorner, Mortensen, Osterzee, Godet, Bishop Lightfoot, Bishop Westcott, Tholuck, Lange, Luthardt, Delitzsch, Rothe, Dr. Sanday, of Oxford, Dr. Sweet, of Cambridge, Principal Fairbairn, of Warfield, Sir William Ramsey, of Aberdeen; Bishop Gore, Canon Ottley, Dr. Robert Dick Wilson, of Princeton University; Dr. E. Y. Mullins, President of the Southern Baptist Theological Seminary and also President of the Baptist World Alliance, and many others, have believed and taught the virgin birth. Are not these minds "modern?" Indeed, the whole great body of the Christian Church from the beginning, including multitudes of clear thinkers, distinguished scholars and great scientists have had room for this faith in their minds.

In addition to such writers, the famous scientist Romanes declared, even while he was an agnostic and before he came back to the Christian faith, that there was no known physiological law which would prevent belief in the virgin birth.

On the other hand, there are some known facts of nature that shed some light on the possibility of such an event. For one thing, parthenogenesis, that is generation by a virgin, is a well known fact occurring occasionally among bees and other such creatures.

Viewed scientifically, there are two sides to the conception of new life: one is the psychological, or thought side, and the other is the biological or material side. As to the psychological side, it is well known that thought profoundly affects the conception and development of new life. The records of prenatal influences, such as fright, joy, etc., and the reaction of dreams on sex functions, have long since proved this. Boris Sidis of Harvard, and other investigators, have proved not only that thought may be registered electrically, but that thought even causes chemical changes in a body. Intangible though thought is, it is now a well known fact that anger turns loose certain poisons in the human system. Fright has been known to produce such radical chemical changes that death followed, and joyful thoughts also profoundly affect the body.

Then, as to the physiological or biological side, it has been demonstrated scientifically in recent times that generation of new life among certain creatures can be brought about without the usual sexual union. Scientists have demonstrated by their experiments that the eggs of sea urchins, star fish, and other such living things, can be and have been fertilized and made to reproduce their kind without the operation of sex forces. Dr. Jacques Loeb, of the Rockefeller Institute for Medical Research, one of the foremost authorities in the field of biology, in his book on "The Dynamics of Living Matter" (page 165), says: "Eggs which naturally develop only when a spermatozoid enters, can be caused to develop artifically by certain physical and chemical means." The scientists have demonstrated that certain forms of electrical energy or light rays are capable of thus stimulating eggs into activity and development, and that these light rays can penetrate living matter and may be definitely directed to produce specific effects in a living body, as, for example, the treatment of cancer by radium or the fertilization of an egg within the body. Further, the amazing announcement was made by Dr. Charles Russ of England a little while ago that, as demonstrated by experiments, the human eye in vision emits a ray that, varying in strength according to health, etc., can actually move ponderable matter.

Because, then, of these scientific truths about the power of thought and the power of light, we may draw a parallel that may help our thinking in connection with the Virgin Birth of Christ.

It is this: Since man's limited understanding and finite power can send rays of light through matter which will fertilize eggs, and since thought has tangible transforming effects upon matter, which bring about actual electrical and chemical changes, and are particularly influential in conception, then what shall we say of the effects of God's light and the application of God's infinite and unlimited power of thought? When we are taught that the Power of Almighty God moved upon a virgin's thought and overshadowed her, that the radiant light of Heaven shone upon her, and that her submissive mind was centered in obedient willingness upon this blessed enterprise of bringing forth a Savior for mankind, even our limited minds can catch some faint glimpse of the way, both psychologically and physiologically, by which God may have brought about the divine conception and virgin birth of Christ.

Dr. Howard A. Kelly, of Baltimore, one of the most

famous physicians and surgeons in the world and a professor in the Johns Hopkins University, in expressing his full acceptance of the virgin birth of Christ, says:

"The Virgin Birth upsets, as the coming of God to live on this earth ought to upset, all our preconceived notions. In this age of discovery it is folly to cry 'impossible,' because the thing proclaimed is new and outside of our own limited experiences. Only a few years ago radium was declared 'utterly impossible' by distinguished scientists, and yet the explanation—that the phenomena of radium are due to the breaking up and setting loose of enormous forces locked up in the 'indivisible' atoms ('those foundation stones of the universe, unbroken and unworn,' of Clerk Maxwell in 1875) —is now universally accepted, and 'the indivisible atom' is not only divided, but found to be made up of many component parts."

Another one of the most famous biologists in America tells us, through the well known publicist of Milwaukee, Mr. L. C. Morehouse, that from the scientific and historical standpoint the virgin birth is easily believable. He says emphatically:

"To the biologist, the method of reproduction known as parthenogenesis is a perfectly familiar one and he finds no difficulty in virgin birth as such. That parthenogenesis in the case of a human being would be unique, and that consequently the birth of Jesus Christ from a virgin mother is unique, I am ready to grant; but then, Jesus Himself was unique, and I am inclined to argue that a unique phenomenon requires a correspondingly unique producing cause. As a scientist I may go farther and say that if the Virgin Birth had never been mentioned in the Gospels I should be compelled to assume it as the only reasonable explanation of what is affirmed and accepted regarding the character of Jesus. But when I find the fact of the Virgin Birth actually recorded by two biographers, one a business man and the other a competent physician who had taken pains to inform himself accurately concerning every detail from the very first; when I find the mind of the church accepting the record at a very early date and affirming it as her continuous belief and as the only reasonable explanation of the fact of the incarnation of the Son of God in the person of Jesus of

Nazareth—then I am compelled to adopt, on historical grounds, the position which I had already reached on scientific grounds."

THE LIGHT OF FAITH

But these considerations have to do only with method, and I do not seek to avoid the fact of miracle in the virgin birth. There is a deeper and more satisfying view of this matter than any naturalistic explanation, interesting though these scientific side lights are. In connection with the virgin birth, the angel declared that "Nothing shall be impossible with God," and it was God's love, backed by His miracle-working power, that gave a Saviour to mankind.

I will just say, specifically and emphatically, therefore, that I believe the virgin birth of our Lord was a miracle and should be accepted as such. There are not only good grounds for believing that miracles are possible, but that in an infinite universe, ruled by a Living God, they are necessary and inevitable. Indeed, every birth is a miracle, in that it is a mystery entirely beyond our human knowledge or understanding.

HARDING AND WILSON FUNDAMENTALISTS

As I remarked in the beginning, it is significant that both Warren G. Harding and Woodrow Wilson expressed themselves as believing with the Fundamentalists and as opposed to the Modernists in the present Theological turmoil which is rending the religious world asunder. Some months before he was taken sick, President Harding openly declared that he was with the Fundamentalists in their defence of the old faith. And Mr. Axson, the brother-in-law of Woodrow Wilson, gave in the New York Times of February 7th, the day after Ex-President Wilson died, a touching and most intimate character sketch, in which he referred to the Fundamentalist-Modernist discussion. He tells us that he asked Woodrow Wilson first what he thought would have been the attitude of his preacher father on these issues, and Wilson, he said, replied with emphasis, that his father, if alive, would have been a Fundamentalist. Then Mr. Wilson added, for himself, that his father would have been opposed to the Modernists, even as he was, because, as he, Woodrow Wilson, put it, *"they are seeking to take all of the mystery element out of religion."*

This remark showed Woodrow Wilson's profound insight into the real religious problems of today. We cannot reduce the world to a narrow system of bald rationalism. To do so, would really destroy all of the poetry and vision, the romance and religion of life. We cannot measure an infinite universe with the yard stick of our finite minds. Eternity cannot be comprehended by time. Shakespeare was right when he said, "There are more things in Heaven and earth than are dreamed of in our philosophy."

Modern life is not being broadened and truly "liberalized" but rather, it is being unspeakably narrowed by the rationalism and scepticism of the times.

The noble scientist Pasteur, on the occasion of his reception at the French Academy, said: "He who only possesses clear ideas is assuredly a fool." Pasteur well knew that if he had had from the beginning only clear ideas to lead him, he would never have been able to make the great discoveries in science which have crowned his name with glory. He well knew that he was led on and on by intuitive belief that the things after which he was striving were real, and thus he won by faith. We cannot rule out the mystery element. Life and the world are too filled with miracles for us so to do.

MIRACLES ENTIRELY RATIONAL

Now my contention is that the virgin birth was both a fact and a miracle. That is to say, it was a miraculous fact.

But what do I mean by that? Well I do not mean that
it was a violation of any natural law. No law of nature
can be violated. God is a God of Law, and the laws of
nature are His laws. It is inconceivable that God would
violate his own laws. A miracle, therefore, from God's
side, is not a violation of any natural law, but merely
something that God does, according to higher laws, that
are known to Him though unknown to men; laws that
are entirely beyond our present comprehension.

Matthew Arnold said (Preface of "Lit and Dogma"):
"I do not believe in the virgin birth of Christ because it
involves a miracle, *and miracles do not happen!*"

We wonder how Mr. Arnold knew that! His dogmatic
assertion reminds one of the African Chief who, it is
said, had a missionary put to death because the missionary
told him that at certain seasons of the year, in his country,
people walked across the rivers. Living in tropical Africa
and knowing, therefore, nothing about such a thing as
ice, the chief thought that the missionary's statement was
such a monstrous lie that he ought to be put to death
for it!

We cannot safely argue from our own ignorance and
our own limitations. If, a generation ago, before the
X-ray and wireless were discovered, I had asserted that
I could see through opaque substances and send my voice
for thousands of miles through space without a wire, I
would have been regarded as a madman and classified as
indeed a blatant "sensationalist." And yet these miracles
of yesterday are the commonplaces of today.

LOOKING THROUGH ONE'S OWN BODY

A little while ago I looked through my own body and
saw my own heart beating. My family physician sent
me down to a specialist of this city for an examination.
He told him to "look me over." He not only looked me
over: He looked me *through* also! He stood me up be-

fore an oak board in a dark room turned a peculiar electric
light on me, and looked straight through my body. Instead of taking an "X-ray" photograph, he just looked
inside with the ray. When he had satisfied his own scientific curiosity concerning my "department of the interior,"
the specialist said to me casually, "Doctor, would you like
to see yourself as others see you?" "Well," I replied,
"I don't know about that. They have said some pretty
hard things about me here in New York, and if I really
see myself as others see me, I do not know that I can
stand the shock."

However, he held a mirror up before me, and I looked
through my own body, and saw the beating of my own
heart.

Then I stepped to one side and another victim took my
place. The specialist turned and said to me, "Doctor,
would you like to look into this gentleman, so as to see
this thing without a mirror?" I said, "Yes, I can stand
it, if the gentleman is not bashful about it." Then the
specialist turned the light on, and I saw everything the
man had! I not only saw *his* heart also, contracting and
expanding as it beat, but I even saw the grain in the oak
board behind the man's back!

To say that we will not believe the virgin birth "because
it involves a miracle, and miracles do not happen," is not
only to assert that we know all the laws of nature, but it
is also to assert that we know what an infinite God could,
would or would not do! I hope, for his own credit, that
my honorable opponent will not take such a vain and foolish position as that.

MIRACLES POSSIBLE BECAUSE OF GOD

The whole question of miracles is settled the moment
we admit that in and behind the material universe there
is a living, loving, wise and powerful God. The God

of the deists—an absentee creator who merely started the world going like a vast machine, cannot be conceived of as working a miracle. Nor can the God of Pantheism —a prisoner God locked up in matter—the mere "principle" or "law" of nature, perform a miracle. But the true and living God—a Being both transcendent to nature and immanent in nature would inevitably be a worker of miracles. I do every day things that to my little child are miracles; and so of our Heavenly Father.

While in the South, sometime ago, I heard the story of an argument on religion between a Christian farmer and a sceptical travelling salesman. They were in a country store. The salesman was through with his orders from the merchant, and he entered into the conversation of the group of men gathered around the stove. In the course of his discussion with the Christian farmer, the sceptic got off, as usual, on to the subject of natural law and its invariable operation. The farmer was whittling a white pine stick with his jack knife, and the sceptic challenged him. He said: "Do you mean to assert that if you turn that knife loose it can go in any direction except downward, in obedience to the law of gravitation?"

The farmer thought for a moment and then said, "Yes, I will assert that." Then he turned the knife loose, but as he did so, he gave it a little flip upward with his finger, and the blade stuck in the wooden ceiling over his head. Now what had he done? He had not violated the law of gravitation. If he had done that he would have wrecked the universe! No! he had simply brought into play another law, namely the law of human will in living personality, and that took precedence, in that particular case, over the law of gravity. In other words, the law of muscular action, backed by the will of a living person, was stronger, so far as that knife was concerned, than the downward pull of gravitation.

PERSONALITY SUPERIOR TO NATURAL LAW

An object lesson is sometimes useful. I hold here in my hand a watch. Now the natural law of this watch is for the hands to move around from right to left. When left to itself, the watch always acts invariably in just that way. Any yet, I can press down this little stem and move the hands of the watch from left to right or from right to left, or stop or start them as I wish and will. In other words, I can make the watch do many things, through the intervention of my personality, which it does not and cannot do merely through its own natural laws. And in doing these unusual, or miraculous things, I have not violated the law of the watch, nor have I injured it in any way.

Oh, yes, my friends, there are more things in heaven and earth than are dreamed of in our poor human philosophy! And the final fact in the universe is not dead matter and blind force, but living, loving Personality. Yes, the final fact is God! And he can both will and do according to His own good pleasure!

If, therefore, we believe that Almighty God created the universe as a whole, then we should certainly have no difficulty in believing that He could create also in part. If God made the first man—Adam—without a human mother, then could not the same God bring into being the second Adam—Christ—without a human father? There is no more difficulty in accepting the recorded birth of Jesus Christ without an earthly father, than in accepting the recorded creation of Adam without an earthly mother. To disbelieve in either means, therefore, simply a rejection of the Bible narrative, and a denial of the living God therein revealed, and that only because of subjective doubts and unbelief!

The possibility of such an event as the virgin birth, when rightly seen, both on grounds of faith and reason alike, is very easy of acceptance by any fair and un-prejudiced mind! The trouble today is that many minds are closed by doubt to this and other great spiritual truths. They no longer have clear faith in the living God. Instead of the eternal, "I Am," it is with them, the great, "What Is It?"

The Angel of the Annunciation truly said, "With God nothing shall be impossible." We will remember, there-fore, in all our discussions that behind the virgin birth of our Lord stands a living God, with His wise and loving purpose of human redemption from sin and the dominion of Satan!

II. THE PROBABILITY OF THE VIRGIN BIRTH

In coming, then, to a consideration of the probability of the Virgin birth, we naturally ask, first, was there any need or occasion for such an event, which would lead us to expect it?

I answer directly, yes—the need of humanity for a Savior or Redeemer. Regardless of any one's views about the Garden of Eden story, the fact stares all men in the face that something is radically wrong with the human race. The need for outside help, for a Savior, has been apparent from the very dawn of history. So among all peoples there has been the hope and dream of a Messiah or Redeemer.

Now the revealed religion of Judaism and Christianity have the only consistent, comprehensive and truly his-torical account of the coming of such a Redeemer, or Saviour, and it is in connection with this precise matter that the narrative of the virgin birth occurs.

THE ANCIENT PROPHESIES

The second ground of probability for anticipating a divine, virgin-born Savior is ancient prophesy. It is a most striking and significant fact that the virgin birth was prophesied hundreds of years before it came to pass. Indeed, the very first prophesy recorded in the Bible seems to deal with it. In the midst of the sin-wrecked Eden, God's voice was heard, saying that the "seed" of the woman was to bruise the serpent's head (Genesis 3:-5). God promised a Redeemer and Savior from sin who was to bruise Satan's head, and He said that this Savior was to be the "seed" of the woman. The whole of the Bible is but the picture of the enlargement and promised final fulfillment of this first prophesy.

It is noteworthy that the prophesy states that it was to be the "seed of the Woman." Only by divine inspiration could such a prophesy as that have been recorded. The thought of the pre-eminence of woman was utterly repugnant to the ancient Jewish mind. The Jew greatly emphasized the importance of the male. The ambition of every ancient Israelite was to be the father of a son. They cared but little for girl children, so great was their emphasis upon the place and importance of the male. Whatever Jew wrote Genesis, therefore, unless he had been inspired and directed of God so to write, would never have written that the coming Messiah or Savior was to be the "seed" of the woman. An uninspired Jew would have written that it would be the "seed" of the man who would bruise the serpent's head and redeem the race.

THE NEW SPIRITUAL HEAD

But God knew that the human race needed a new spiritual head to take the place of the carnal Adam. God knew that if men were to be saved, if they were to become righteous and pure, they must have a new spiritual heredity to take the place of the old sinful heredity from Adam. So God planned and prophesied a sinless spiritual Savior, and such a Savior could only come through the holy power of God as His Begetter and Father.

Therefore, Isaiah, in that rapt and marvelous prophesy, which doubtless went beyond his own human understanding at the time it was uttered, and which had a much wider application than the local conditions under King Ahaz as is evidenced by the fact that it is addressed to the entire house of David, said:

"The Lord Himself shall give you a sign; behold, a virgin shall conceive, and bear a son, and shall call his name Immanuel" (Isaiah 7:14).

The prophesy of this son to be born of a virgin, is not confined to the one verse here in the seventh chapter of Isaiah. This prophesy continues over several chapters, and here in the ninth chapter we see that this Virgin-born son was to go, in the meaning and power of his life, far beyond the days of Ahaz. Here the prophet was manifestly moved and inspired by a Divine afflatus, that flashed before his enraptured vision a coming glory, which was to appear long after the day in which he lived. His vision was so real that it was as though it had already come to pass. So he exclaimed, with well-nigh inexpressible joy:

"The people that walked in darkness have seen a great light; they that dwell in the land of the shadow of death, upon them hath the light shined. For unto us a child is born, unto us a son is given: and the government shall be upon his shoulder; and his name shall be called Wonderful, Counsellor, The Mighty God, The Everlasting Father, The Prince of Peace. Of the increase of his government and peace there shall be no end upon the throne of David, and upon His kingdom, to order it, and to establish it with judgment and with justice from henceforth even forever. The zeal of the Lord of Hosts will perform this" (Isaiah 9:2 and 6-7).

Such a wonderful prophesy as this about a being so marvelous, could not possibly have had in view a mere man, born in the ordinary way.

Nor can unbelief dispose of this matter by saying that the Hebrew word translated here "virgin" may mean

something else. Those who try to dispose of the virgin
birth say that the Hebrew word almah means merely a
young woman of marriageable age, not necessarily a
virgin. They argue that another word, bethulah, is used
for a real virgin. It is a remarkable fact, however, that
this word bethulah, which critics claim is used only of a
real virgin, is actually used in Joel 1:8 of a bride weeping
for her husband, while the word almah, which it is
claimed may not mean an actual virgin, is used in this
and six other places (Genesis 24:43; Exodus 2-8; Psalm
68:26; Proverbs 13:19, Song of Solomon 1:3; 6-8) and
never in any other sense than an unmarried maiden.

Luther said:

"If a Jew or Christian can prove to me that in any other
passage of scripture 'almah' means a 'married woman,' I will
give him one hundred florins, although God alone knows
where I may find them."

Dr. Willis Beecher says that there is no trace of the
use of this word to denote any other than a virgin.

The seventy scholars who produced the septuagint version of the Old Testament translated the word almah
into the Greek parthenos which means "virgin" and nothing else.

In addition to these prophesies in Isaiah, there is a
similar prediction in Jeremiah: "The Lord hath created
a new thing in the earth. A woman shall compass a
man."—(Jer. 31:32.) That this passage refers to the
virgin birth is shown by the preceding context which says:
"Turn again, O virgin of Israel, to these thy cities."

REVELATION TO MATTHEW

Now Matthew takes these ancient prophesies and says
that they were fulfilled in the virgin birth of Jesus Christ.
After telling of the birth of Christ, Matthew says:

"Now all this was done that it might be fulfilled which
was spoken of the Lord by the prophet, saying, Behold a

virgin shall be with child, and shall bring forth a son, and they shall call his name Emmanuel, which being interpreted is God with us" (Matthew 1:22–23).

In the light of well known history, it is apparent that this was not written by Matthew because he wanted to fix up something that would fit in with what Isaiah had prophesied. These things were not in the Jewish mind in Matthew's day. The voice of prophesy had been silent in Israel for over four hundred years, and the race had sunk into the spiritual dearth and death of Phariseism. Common sense, therefore, as well as devout scholarship tell us truly that Matthew must have been inspired in order to see that the virgin birth of Christ did fulfill the ancient prophesies, and to record for us the spiritual significance of that event. Every step in the story and every advance in the record are assuredly and manifestly under the guidance of supernatural, spiritual and heavenly powers.

Because, then, of these marvelous prophesies, which were of old time, we are overwhelmed with the probability that the Savior would be born of a virgin.

FAKE FULFILMENTS

There is also another aspect of this part of the question to which I wish to draw attention. It is that the heathen and pagan myths about the alleged cohabitation of "Gods" with earthly women, to produce Kings and heroes, instead of militating against the credibility of the virgin birth of our Lord as alleged by some, really strengthen it, when rightly understood. It is said that the disciples of Jesus were so impressed by the greatness of our Lord that, after He went away from them, they tended to think of Him more and more as divine, until they finally followed the old pagan custom of attributing supernatural origin to one who was very great. So, it is argued, they added the story of the virgin birth of Christ to the gospel narratives.

This is a subtle and treacherous argument, but its sceptical sophistry deceives only the simple minded and the uninformed. When we remember these ancient prophesies that the Savior was to be virgin born, and when we remember that there is also in the world a great spirit of evil—Satan—who ever seeks to defeat God, we would expect that he would endeavor to nullify the value of the virgin birth by caricaturing it. Just such distortions and perversions of truth as are found in those revolting old myths are to be expected. Only a thing of value is counterfeited; and the great adversary of souls, knowing that the Savior would be virgin born, seems to have endeavored to discount the event in advance by putting these absurd and licentious lies into the minds of men, and giving them currency in connection with human vanity, ambition, and lust.

SATAN'S SUBTERFUGES

Such students of comparative religion as Prof. Max Mueller, Johann Warneck, Le Page Renouf, Emmanuel Rouge, Franz Lenormant, and others, have proved that ancient religions were pure in their beginnings, and that among the very ancient Greeks, Egyptians, Indians, Zoroastrians, and Chinese, and even among the Sumerians and Africans there was monotheism and the worship of one supreme spiritual God. Then, these scholars tell us, all these religions degenerated into polytheism, idolatry, etc.

Thus, W. St. Clair Tisdale closes his study of "Christianity and Other Faiths," with this statement:

"It follows that Monotheism historically preceded Polytheism, and that the latter is a corruption of the former. It is impossible to explain the facts away. Taken together they show that, as the Bible asserts, man at the very beginning of history knew the one true God. This implies a Revelation of some sort, and traces of that revelation are still found in many ancient faiths."

The grotesque heathen creation myths, to which my opponent referred in the last debate, and the foolish legends about the flood which other races than the Hebrews have produced, only prove that the early knowledge about the creation, the flood, etc., which was common to all in the beginning through divine Revelation, became polluted and distorted as time passed, by the sinful and degenerate human mind.

Adam and his descendants would know and take over the world, the knowledge that the coming Redeemer was to be virgin born, (Gen. 3:15). That this is exactly what happened is evidenced by the following:

"In the Egyptian mythology, Pthah was represented with a distorted foot, implying lameness, with allusion to the bruised heel of the seed of the woman. The Hindoo mythology represents, by sculptured figures in their old pagodas, Creeshna— an avatar or incarnation of their mediatorial deity, Veeshnu—in one instance *trampling on the crushed head of the serpent,* and in another, the latter entwining the deity in its folds, and *biting his heel.* In the Scandinavian mythology, Thor, the first-born of the Supreme Deity, and holding an intermediate place between God and man, is said to have engaged in a mortal struggle with *a gigantic serpent,* to have bruised his head and finally slain him. And in the classic mythology Hercules appears in conflict with the dragon which assailed the daughters of Atlas after they had plucked the golden apples in the garden of the Hesperides; he wields a formidable club, and his right foot *rests on the head of the writhing monster."* (Com. on Gen.—Jamieson.)

So Satan seems to have taken the great prophesy, that the seed of the woman was to bruise the head of the serpent—which prophesy was well known to the entire race in the beginning, and he perverted and distorted it in the minds of men by spreading among them these coarse, crude myths. He manifestly thus sought to forestall and discount the virgin birth of the world's Savior.

But Satan has bungled and blundered, as he always does, in spreading these absurd and silly old myths, even though some rationalists and modernists, because of their superficial thinking, have been caught by them. They not only tend to prove, as just said, that the devil counterfeited true prophesy, but, as Bishop Gore and others have pointed out, they have another value. Dr. James Orr, recognized by liberals and conservatives alike as one of the greatest scholars of this generation, in his famous book on "The Virgin Birth," well said of these old myths:

"Vile as many of them are, they have a value as showing the natural workings of men's minds—the universality of the instinct which connects superhuman greatness with a divine origin, and may be construed in our favor as leading us to expect that, if there is a real incarnation, it will be accompanied by a miraculous origin" ("The Virgin Birth of Christ," page 166).

These old myths are so completely foreign to the Jewish mind, so utterly lacking in any historical facts as to time, place, persons, etc., in connection with their alleged occurrence, that they could not possibly have influenced the thinking of the disciples about the virgin birth. Indeed, they are so manifestly grotesque and ridiculous as to render it utterly impossible to connect them with holy things. In the case of Buddha, for example, the story is that while his mother (not a virgin, note you) slept, she dreamed that a white, six-tusked elephant entered her side, and then, ten months later, a child was born, who was Buddha! Can any fair and well-balanced mind find even an analogy between such an extravaganza and the delicate, restrained, careful narratives of our Gospels?

So far from its being true that pagan birth myths have any source relation to the Gospel stories, it is abundantly evident that the narratives of the Nativity are Jewish-Christian through and through. Dr. Bacon of Yale, says:

"The basal fact for every student of these chapters of

Matthew and Luke is that they are Hebrew to the core.   This is simply fatal to all comparison with heathen mythology."

Dr. Harnack, while he counts the Virgin Birth legendary, nevertheless knocks its pagan derivation in the head. He says:

"Nothing that is mythological in the sense of Greek and Oriental myth is to be found in these accounts; all here is in the spirit of the Old Testament, and most of it reads like a passage from the historical books of that ancient volume"[2]

Every consideration of the rational mind of man and every longing of his aspiring soul lead us, therefore, to the probability of the manifestation of God in human flesh, and this naturally would come to pass through a real incarnation by the virgin birth.

[2] These vulgar and revolting myths tell how some God, like Zeus, for example, would transform himself into a serpent and thus have improper relations with a maiden or a wife, and thus a super-man or God was conceived. Dr. James Orr, completely exploded the application of these pagan and heathen myths to the virgin birth of our Lord. He answers every one of these far-fetched arguments with overwhelming force.   In speaking of the old Greek and Roman Fables he says:

"It is the fact that not one of these tales has to do with a virgin birth in the sense in which alone we are here concerned *with it*. The Gods of whom these impure scandals are narrated are conceived of as being like in form, parts and passions, to mortal men.   If they beget children, it is after a carnal manner. A God, inflamed by lust—Zeus is a chief sinner—surprises a maiden, and has a child by her, but it is by natural generation. There is nothing here analogous to the virgin birth of the gospels.   The stories themselves are incredibly vile.   The better-minded in Greece and Rome were ashamed of them.   Plato would have them banished from his Republic.   They were, as Tertullian tells us, the subjects of public ridicule.   It is a strange imagination that can suppose that these foul tales could be taken over by the church, and in the short space before the composition of our Gospels, became the inspiration of the beautiful and chaste narratives of Matthew and Luke!" (Pages 168–69).

"A direct borrowing of this idea (that is, the idea of virgin birth for Plato, Alexander and Augustus) from contemporary heathenism is now accordingly largely given up, even by extreme writers like Dr. Cheyne and Gunkel, though its rejection disposes of at least three-fourths of the popular analogies" (Page 171).

III. THE POSITIVE PROOFS OF THE VIRGIN BIRTH

This brings us now to a consideration of the positive
proofs of the virgin birth. Did such an event occur in
history? We have seen the possibility of it, and the probability of it; and I ask you to consider now the positive
proofs of it. For such an event not only ought to have
occurred but actually did occur, and we have ample and
conclusive proof of it.

I recognize of course as we all must recognize, that
there is an element of faith in the acceptance of any fact
of ancient history. We were not present to see for ourselves, in connection with the events of ancient history;
nor are there eyewitnesses of the events now living to
tell us by word of mouth that they were present and can
vouch for them. Indeed, there is more or less discussion
and often sharp differences of opinion over many of the
important facts, not only of ancient history but of more
recent events. There is, for example, quite a heated controversy, which has been started by the doubting spirit of
this age, as to whether William Shakespeare really wrote
the plays that bear his name. Some indeed, have even
questioned whether such a character as Shakespeare ever
lived.

Now, in such cases, we can only weigh the evidence
pro and con, and then accept (largely, note you, on our
own faith in the reliability of the witnesses and the documentary evidence) the fact in which we come to believe.
Yet, I rejoice to be able to say, that the facts proving the
virgin birth are unusually clear, specific and trustworthy.

RELIABLE DOCUMENTS AND WITNESSES

What are the proofs, then? Here they are! First,
historical documents that have come down to us, intact
and reliable, tell us plainly of the virgin birth. There
can be no real controversy over the reliability of these

documents. Whereas we have only a few sources for
many classical writings that have come down to us, we
have the greatest abundance of reliable sources containing the account of the virgin birth. Nestle reminds us, for
instance, that all we possess of Sophocles depends on a
single manuscript of the eighth or ninth century. Ten or
fifteen is thought a large number for others; and few of
these go beyond the tenth century, or are even so old.
In contrast with this, the manuscripts of the Gospels, whole
or parts, are reckoned by scores; if you include cursives,
by hundreds. *The accounts of the virgin birth are in all the
original unmutilated manuscripts of the Bible which we
possess. They are also in all the trustworthy versions of
the Bible;* and the preaching and teaching of the early
church fathers were full of the doctrine of the virgin
birth. There are but two versions in which the accounts
of the virgin birth do not occur. One is known as the
"Gospel of the Ebionites," a version used by a sect in
the early Church which denied the divinity of Christ, and
therefore could not admit that He was born in an unusual
manner. The other is the "Gospel of St. Luke," used
by a man named Marcion, a strange person, who held that
the God of the Old Testament was different from the
God of the New, and who taught that matter was
essentially evil. Therefore, he could not consistently
accept the doctrine of the Incarnation at all.

Dr. C. C. Martindale, in his scholarly treatise on the
Virgin Birth, points out that the Ebionites copy of Matthew began only at chapter three. He then shows how
they arbitrarily cut off the first two chapters because of
their unbelief about the virgin birth. He says:

"But we know this only from Epiphanius; if then we
accept it, we must also accept his statement that they had
struck off Chapters 1 and 2 in the interests of their heresy.
He also says that the Nazarene Ebionites used the full text,
as did the early heretics Cerinthus and Carpocrates. So

there is no extrinsic evidence that Matthew began, originally, with the Mission of John."

The more recently discovered "Sinaitic Version" caused some interest at first because, though it contained the word "virgin," it also seemed to make Joseph the natural father of Jesus. But it was soon seen that it was another Ebionite version, which had been mutilated by unbelievers. And while Moffat uses the word "begat" in his translation of the New Testament, he does it only on the ground that "begat" in Jewish usage was used either for natural or legal descent.

Dr. James Orr, from whom I quoted before, has conclusively established the complete reliability of these Bible documents in his great book on "The Virgin Birth." After surveying the entire field of MSS. and versions, and showing how complete is the evidence that these early chapters of both Matthew and Luke—the chapters that contain the account of the virgin birth—are genuine parts of the Gospel, Dr. Orr. points out how arbitrary, unjustifiable and even at times dishonest are the efforts of critics and sceptics to get rid of the record of the virgin birth. Wellhausen, for example, simply cuts out the first two chapters of Matthew and Luke, in his books on those Gospels, without even attempting any critical justification for such a high handed proceeding![8]

*Dr. Orr says: "I have thus surveyed the field of MSS. and versions, and have sought to show you how absolutely unbroken is the phalanx of evidence that these first chapters of Matthew and Luke are genuine parts of the Gospels in which they are found. Well, but, I have no doubt you are not long ere this asking in surprise: If the facts are thus undeniable, what do the objectors say to them? How are they dealt with? One characteristic example of how they are dealt with may perhaps suffice. Here are two recent publications of the great Old Testament critic Wellhausen.—'The Gospel of Matthew, Translated and Explained,' and 'The Gospel of Luke, Translated and Explained.' I take up his version of the Gospel of Matthew, and what do I find? It begins with Chapter 3:1. What has become of the first two chapters? There is not a word of note or

The critics were not able, therefore, to get rid of the chapters containing the account of the virgin birth, and so they next resorted to the scheme of trying to mutilate these chapters, by dropping from them the words or clauses which specifically state the divine conception and virgin birth of Christ. Prof. Harnack, for example, while having to admit many of the main facts about it, nevertheless tries to get rid of the virgin birth itself, simply by deleting a part of the narrative. Just remove such verses as 34 and 35 in the first chapter of Luke, says Harnack, and the matter is settled! The verse, for instance, which records Mary's question to the angel: "How shall this be, seeing I know not a man?" and the angel's answer: "The Holy Ghost shall come upon thee, and the power of the most High shall overshadow thee," etc. Cut these out, says Harnack, and other sceptics, and the virgin birth is disposed of.

But the answer to this is that there is no ground for cutting these verses out, except the doubts of unbelievers, and their desire to alter even the Bible to make it fit in with their sceptical theories of naturalism, as opposed to super-naturalism, and evolution rather than Revelation. On this matter, old Augustine, in one of his vigorous and

comment to explain. The critic thinks they should not be there, so, MSS. and versions notwithstanding, out they go. It is the same with the Gospel of Luke. I open it as before, and I find it begins with Chapter 3:1. Where have the first two Chapters gone to? Again they are simply dropped out, and again without note or explanation. Here, however, is a third work from the same author— an introduction to the First Three Gospels. Perhaps we shall find what we want there. But no, there is a minute and destructive criticism of the Gospels; much about Q, the alleged common source of Matthew and Luke; but not a word in explanation of why these chapters are dropped from what professes to be—and in the main is— a version of our existing Gospels. It is, no doubt, easy enough to get rid of the evidence for the virgin birth in this way. But is it scientific? Is it right? Would a similar treatment be tolerated of any classical work?" (Pages 47–48).

striking metaphors, describes this plea for deletion as "the last gasp of a heretic in the grip of truth."[4]

These records cannot be gotten rid of by scepticism, infidelity and gross dishonesty. Here they are after all these thousands of years, intact, trustworthy and still powerful in their influences over men.

TRUSTWORTHY WITNESSES

2. Again we have in these reliable records the testimony of trustworthy witnesses concerning these matters, and these witnesses tell of the fact of the virgin birth with circumstantial detail, and a persuasiveness that compels the believing mind and heart to accept it as truth.

[4] Dr. Orr points out that even these deletions of verses if allowed, would not really dispose of the virgin birth, because the entire context, in both Matthew and Luke, would remain, and would be inexplicable without these verses that directly assert the virgin birth. Dr. Orr goes further and says "emphatically" that this cutting out of verses is "on no good textual grounds." Here again the evidence of MSS. and versions is decisive (Page 54, "The Virgin Birth").

These sceptics just arbitrarily and dishonestly try to cut the verses out when they do not fit in with their unbelief and infidelity.

Prof. John McNaugher, of the Pittsburgh Theological Seminary, in his book on "The Virgin Birth," page 13, well says:

> "These verses are retained as indubitably genuine by the most distinguished editors of the Greek New Testament, both in England and Germany. Verse 34 is omitted in one codex of the Latin version, but that arises apparently from a confusion of the text, and anyhow no canon of textual science would warrant the rejection of a passage on such beggarly authority. As for verse 35, not only is there no evidence for its omission but it is one of the earliest supported verses in the New Testament, being quoted by Justin Martyr. It is plain, therefore, that the criticism which adjudges these verses to be interpolated is purely subjective and arbitrary. If passages are to be expunged after that fashion, the method might be followed until little of the Gospel narratives would remain. Were the upholders of orthodox doctrine to indulge in such capricious text emendation, they would be laughed to scorn; and we have an equal right to be contemptuous. There are fixed rules of evidence and established principles of textual criticism, and it is not legitimate to ignore these rules and play fast and loose with these principles, even for the sake of dislodging an article of the Christian creed."

Here is no vague tradition of some human emperor with some gross "God" as father, when it was known to all people who His mother and father really were. Here is no empty myth, passed from mouth to mouth until it found a resting place upon some obscene page of human lust and folly. No. Here is historic detail as to time and name and place. Here is great reserve and delicacy of statement. Here is exquisite beauty of narration, and a nobility of sentiment so sublime that it moves the heart to tears. Here, in a word, is the very glory of heaven, flashed for a moment on the gray gloom of our sin-cursed earth!

THE BEAUTIFUL STORY

Listen again, honorable Judges and friends, to but a part of this sweet and compelling narrative, this old, old story of heavenly goodness and divine grace. Listen, first to the Annunciation to Joseph in Nazareth, as recorded in Matthew 1:18–25:

"Now the birth of Jesus Christ was on this wise: When as his mother Mary was espoused to Joseph, *before they came together,* she was found with child of the Holy Ghost. Then Joseph, her husband, being a just man, and not willing to make her a public example, was minded to put her away privily. But, while he thought on these things, behold, the angel of the Lord appeared unto him in a dream, saying, Joseph, thou son of David, fear not to take unto thee Mary thy wife, for that which is conceived in her is of the Holy Ghost. And she shall bring forth a son, and thou shalt call His name Jesus; for he shall save his people from their sins. Now all this was done, that it might be fulfilled which was spoken of the Lord by the prophet, saying, Behold, a virgin shall be with child, and shall bring forth a son and they shall call his name Emmanuel, which being interpreted is, God with us. Then Joseph being raised from sleep, did as the angel of the Lord had bidden him, and took unto him his wife; and *knew her not till she had brought forth her first born son;* and he called his name Jesus."

Listen next to the Annunciation to the Virgin Mary at Nazareth, as recorded in Luke 1:26–38:

"And in the sixth month the angel Gabriel was sent from God unto a city of Gallilee, named Nazareth, to a virgin espoused to a man whose name was Joseph, of the house of David; and the virgin's name was Mary. And the angel came in unto her and said, Hail, thou that art highly favored, the Lord is with thee; blessed art thou among women. And when she saw him, she was troubled at his saying, and cast in her mind what manner of salutation this should be. And the angel said unto her, Fear not Mary; for thou hast found favor with God. And, behold, thou shalt conceive in thy womb, and bring forth a son, and shall call his name Jesus. He shall be great and shall be called the son of the Highest; and the Lord God shall give unto him the throne of his father David; and he shall reign over the house of Jacob forever; and of His kingdom there shall be no end. Then said Mary unto the angel, *How shall this be, seeing I know not a man?* And the angel answered and said unto her, The Holy Ghost shall come upon thee, and the power of the Highest shall overshadow thee; therefore, also that holy thing which shall be born of thee shall be called the Son of God. And, behold, thy cousin Elizabeth, she hath also conceived a son in her old age; and this is the sixth month with her, who was called barren. For with God nothing shall be impossible. And Mary said, behold the handmaid of the Lord; be it unto me according to thy word; and the angel departed from her."

Listen now to the song of Elisabeth upon Mary's visit to the hill country of Judea, and Mary's reply, called the Magnificat, as recorded in Luke 1:39–56:

"And Mary arose in those days and went into the hill country with haste into a city of Judah; and entered into the house of Zacharias, and saluted Elizabeth. And it came to pass, when Elizabeth heard the salutation of Mary, the babe leaped in her womb; and Elizabeth was filled with the Holy Ghost; and she spoke out with a loud vioce, and said, Blessed art thou among women, and blessed is the fruit of thy womb. And whence is this to me, that the mother of my Lord should come to me? For lo, as soon as the voice of thy salutation sounded in mine ears, the babe leaped in my womb for joy. And blessed is she that believed; for there shall be a performance of these things which were told her from the Lord. And Mary said, my soul doth magnify the Lord, and my spirit hath rejoiced in God my Savior.. For he hath regarded the low estate of his handmaiden; for, behold, from henceforth all generations shall call me blessed. For he that is mighty hath done to me great things, and holy is his name."

Was ever anything, my friends, so consistent and sublime and beautiful as that? Is it not perfectly evident that here we are walking in the realm of reality and not of falsehood and deception? Does not the very manner of the telling prove, to both our minds and hearts, that Joseph related his part of these incidents and told what happened to him, and thus the truth was passed down until Matthew recorded it; and that Mary, with sweet and modest reserve, but with a rapture of heart that burst in places into poetry, told of the marvelous and miraculous experiences through which she passed, and thus her narrative passed on in the inner circle of believers, until Luke, the beloved physician, recorded it in his exquisite Gospel, and thus gave it to bless us and all the after ages?

For myself, I confess to you, that this narrative, with its simple dignity and transparent truthfulness, not only enraptures my heart but delights my mind; and though I have read the critical and sceptical books about it, I feel no hesitation or embarrassment in saying that I accept it, in toto, just as it is written, and believe it with every faculty of my intelligence and every drop of my blood!

WERE THE WITNESSES FOOLS OR LIARS

And I wish to say that if we cannot accept and believe this fact of the virgin birth on the statement of records as reliable as these and on testimony as trustworthy as this, then there is no fact of ancient history that can be believed.

It should be noted that the virgin birth of Christ is not founded on a vague rumor or detached myth without

local connections of persons, time and place. On the other
hand, it is given in connection with other facts that are
admitted to be historical, as, for example, the date of the
birth, the fact that it occurred in the reign of 'Herod,
and that it came in connection with the public census,
etc. So firmly convinced has the entire Christian world
been of these facts, that we date our letters from them.
The "Anno-Domini"—that is the year of His birth—at
the head of our letters is, in itself, a standing proof of
the historical reality of that event.

Furthermore, if words can make anything plain at all,
the facts in this case are made plain by these witnesses.
The first fact is that Joseph was not the father of Jesus.
The record tells us that Joseph, instead of being the
father, was so shocked when he found that Mary, his
lover,—not yet his wife—was with child, that in righteous
indignation and surprise, he was thinking of sending her
away privately to hide her shame, until in a dream the
angel told him the truth about the matter, namely, that
the child was begotten by the Holy Ghost. And the
record further explicitly states, that then Joseph married
Mary, *but did not know her in the relation of husband
and wife until after she had "brought forth her first born
son."*

If, therefore, Jesus had a human father, it was some
unknown man and some one who had not been the husband of Mary. If this is the state of the case, then both
Joseph and Mary were utterly immoral, tricky, deceitful
and sinful.

Such a conclusion, however, is monstrously false, for
the facts are just as plain and simple in the case of Mary
as in the case of Joseph. When the angel first spoke to
Mary and began telling her what was to happen to her,
it is recorded here that she was perplexed and troubled in
her mind. Mary knew that she was a pure woman. She
also knew that to give birth to a child her purity would

have to be violated, if the birth came before her marriage. So, in absolute bewilderment, she told the angel that she was a pure woman, that she had never known a man, and in the light of that fact she asked the angel how the thing he had said to her could possibly come to pass. Then the angel told her that the Holy Ghost would come upon her and give her conception by divine power, and that, therefore, the child born of her virgin womb would be "The Son of God."

Mary was evidently still puzzled and distressed, and it was because the angel saw this perplexity, that he told her God could do things that to human minds seemed impossible; and the angel illustrated this with the statement that Elisabeth, though she was old and barren, had conceived a son in her old age. This son was John the Baptist, the forerunner of Christ, and all the circumstances taken together prove the angel's words that "With God nothing shall be impossible."

Here, then, is the direct testimony and it is recorded for us by unimpeachable witnesses. Who, with a fair and open mind, can read these accounts, noting Joseph's chagrin and sorrow, and observing Mary's doubts and questions, and ponder the plain statements of the angel, that God, who made man and woman, would beget a holy being by His own creative power, and then deny the Virgin Birth? The great legal authority, Greenleaf, author of "The Law of Evidence," one of the leading legal classics of the world, in another remarkable book on "The Testimony of the Evangelists Examined by the Rules of Evidence Administered in Courts of Justice," approves as good witnesses those whose testimony is recorded in the New Testament. He points out that they have all the qualities of good and reliable witnesses, namely, vigorous, understanding minds, good moral character, and no possible motive or reason for telling lies

about these matters, even if they had been disposed so
to do.

I present here these reasonable presuppositions, these
venerable records, and these good people as witnesses;
and if my opponent is to overthrow this age-long and
holy faith of the Christian Church, then I demand that
he come into court with evidence more tangible and facts
more plain than these. It will not suffice for him to present mere doubts or sceptical speculations or guesses of
unbelieving so-called "scholars." I present these objective realities, these venerable records and true witnesses.
What are his records and who are his witnesses?

THE TWO GENEALOGIES

So powerful and overwhelming is this documentary
evidence, that its very difficulties are proofs of the virgin
birth when they are rightly understood. Take, for example, the idea that the virgin birth did not occur because
there are alleged difficulties in connection with the two
genealogies of Jesus, as given by Matthew and Luke.
There is no force to this because, even if there were minor
difficulties in the genealogies, nevertheless, Matthew and
Luke, the ones who give us the genealogies, are also the
very ones who tell us specifically that the virgin birth is a
fact! They are not so absurd as to thus contradict themselves; and minor difficulties about the genealogies could
not invalidate the larger fact of the virgin birth, which is
definitely and specifically stated.

Instead of these difficulties in the genealogies disproving the virgin birth, however, they really constitute in
themselves a proof of that event.

Dr. R. A. Torrey, Dean of the Los Angeles Bible Institute, in his work on "The Difficulties of the Bible," clearly
states the whole case. He says:

"The genealogy given in Matthew is the genealogy of
Joseph, the reputed father of Jesus, his father in the eyes

of the Law.   The genealogy given in Luke is the genealogy
of Mary, the mother of Jesus, and is the human genealogy
of Christ in actual fact.   In Matthew, Jesus appears as
the Messiah.   In Luke He appears as 'the Son of Man,'
our brother and redeemer, who belongs to the whole race
and claims kindred with all kinds and conditions of men."*

*Dr. Torrey says further: "So in Matthew, the genealogy descends
from Abraham to Joseph and Jesus, because all the predictions and
promises touching the Messiah are fulfilled in Him. But in Luke the
genealogy ascends from Jesus to Adam, because the genealogy is
being traced back to the head of the whole race, and shows the
relation of the Second Adam to the first. Joseph's line is the strictly
royal line from David to Joseph. In Luke, though the line of descent
is from David, it is not the royal line. In this Jesus is descended
from David through Nathan, David's son indeed, but not in the
royal line, and the list follows a line quite distinct from the royal
line. The Messiah, according to prediction, was to be the actual
son of David according to the flesh (II Sam. 7:12-19; Ps. 89:3, 4,
34-37; 132:11; Acts 2:30; 13:22, 23; Rom. 1:3; II Tim. 2:8)
These prophecies are fulfilled by Jesus being the son of Mary, who
was a lineal descendant of David, though not in the royal line.
Joseph who was of the royal line, was not his father according to
the flesh, but was his father in the eyes of the law. Mary was a
descendant of David through her father, Heli. It is true that Luke
2:23 says that Joseph was the son of Heli. The simple explanation
of this is that, Mary being a woman, her name according to Jewish
usage could not come into the genealogy, males alone forming the line,
so Joseph's name is introduced in the place of Mary's, he being
Mary's husband, Heli was his father-in-law and so Joseph is called
the son of Heli, and the line *thus completed*. While Joseph was
son-in-law of Heli, according to the flesh he was in actual fact the
son of Jacob (Matt. 1:16). *Two genealogies are absolutely necessary*
to trace the lineage of our Lord and Savior Jesus Christ, the one
the royal and legal, the other the natural and literal, and these two
genealogies we find, the legal and royal in Matthew's Gospel, the
Gospel of law and kingship; the natural and literal in Luke's, the
gospel of humanity. We are told in Jer. 22:30 any descendant of
Jeconiah could not come to the throne of David, and Joseph was of
this line, and while Joseph's genealogy furnishes the royal line for
Jesus, his son before the law, nevertheless, Jesus strictly speaking
was not Joseph's descendant and therefore was *not of the seed of
Jeconiah*. If Jesus had been the son of Joseph in reality, He could
not have come to the throne, but He is Mary's son through Nathan,
and can come to the throne legally by her marrying Joseph and so
clear His way legally to it."

If Jesus had come by ordinary human descent, there would have been no difficulty in making up the genealogies. Matthew, therefore, who gives one of these genealogies, says that the birth of Jesus was "on this wise," which shows that he recognized a difference between the generation of Jesus Christ and all those who had preceded Him. No law of human generation could account for Christ's birth. Therefore, Matthew says it was "on this wise." How could it be otherwise, since "that which is born of the flesh is flesh?" Since Christ is the last Adam, the Lord from heaven, His generation must be from heaven, for otherwise he would be like the first Adam, earthly, sinful, fallen like us all.

Matthew, therefore, writing strictly from the Jewish standpoint, sets forth in his genealogy the fact that through Joseph—the *legal* father of Jesus, though not his father according to the flesh—Jesus is entitled to inherit the throne of David. Matthew, therefore, gives the genealogy of Joseph to show that Jesus, his adopted son, had the legal right of succession.

Luke, on the other hand, gives the natural genealogy of Mary, the mother of Jesus, through Heli, her father, who was also a descendant of David, and thus the claim of Jesus to David's throne is established both naturally and legally. The Bible teaches that this claim will be realized when Christ comes back again.

So it is true that both Matthew and Luke explicitly avoid the statement that Jesus was Joseph's natural son. Matthew changes his regular expression that one "begat" the next, etc., and when he comes to Joseph he does not say, "Jacob begat Joseph and Joseph begat Jesus." No, he says, "Jacob begat Joseph, the husband of Mary, *of whom* was born Jesus, who is called Christ" (Matthew 1:16).

And Luke, also, deliberately avoids the statement that

Jesus was Joseph's natural son.   He says: "But Jesus himself, began to be about thirty years of age, being (as was supposed) the son of Joseph, which was the son of Heli" (Luke 3–23).

Nor is there any weight to the objection that some critics, make to these genealogies, because Matthew says Joseph was the son of Jacob while Luke says that Joseph was the son of Heli.   It is evident, however, that Joseph was the natural son of Jacob and the son-in-law of Heli, the father of Mary.   Dr. Scofield clearly states the matter as follows:

"He could not be by natural generation, the son of both Jacob and Heli.   But in Luke it is not said that Heli begat Joseph, so that the natural explanation is that Joseph was the son-in-law of Heli, who was, like himself, a descendant of David.   That in that case he should be called the son of Heli, would be in accord with Jewish usage" (C. I. Scofield's Reference Bible, footnotes on Luke 3:23).

Dr. Scofield refers here to the custom of the Jews to trace the line of descent through the father who was the legal head of the household, or in some cases through the father-in-law.   This naturally explains the apparent discrepancy in this case.

The fact that Joseph became the legal father of Jesus when he married Mary, also quite naturally accounts for the reference by Mary, and some others who were critics, to Joseph as Jesus' "father."   We speak today in the same way.   A wife, in speaking to an adopted child about her husband, still says "your father, so and so."   I shall deal with this more at length in my rebuttal, if necessary.

Thus, there are no real facts in the genealogies which even reflect on the direct statements of Matthew and Luke that Jesus was born of the virgin and that Joseph was not his father.   On the other hand, the very difficulties rather confirm the virgin birth.

THE ARGUMENT FROM SILENCE

"But," it is said again by doubters, "only two of the Gospels—Matthew and Luke—record the narratives of the virgin birth." Therefore, it is argued, it did not occur, since Mark, John, and Paul, as it is claimed, say nothing about it. I shall show that they all assume the virgin birth in all their writings, and do refer to it, but I merely remark now that even if Mark and John and Paul did not refer to it, directly or indirectly, it would not alter the fact of the virgin birth at all. Argument from silence—ex-silentio cannot be depended on. The thief who claimed he ought to be acquitted because, while only two men saw him steal, he could bring forward a hundred who did not see him steal, was not acquitted but convicted. Two good witnesses are enough, unless there is definite and positive evidence contrary to their testimony.

The argument from the silence of others cannot overthrow the direct testimony of Matthew and Luke. If so, then we would have to give up much more of the Bible than those beautiful pages containing the record of the virgin birth. Only two of the Gospels record the Lord's Prayer. The complete sermon on the Mount is found in only one Gospel. Only one Gospel tells of the visit of the wise men, the Flight Into Egypt, the visit of Christ as a child to the Temple, the stories of the Prodigal Son, the Good Samaritan and other incidents of interest and value.

Indeed, these things are just what we should expect in a book like the New Testament, inspired by one author, namely the Holy Spirit. The Holy Spirit is not guilty of redundancy. In inspiring the Gospels, He led Matthew to tell the story of the virgin birth fully from Joseph's viewpoint, and Luke in "the Woman's Gospel"— fully from Mary's viewpoint, and that was enough.

And these, note you, are the only two Gospels which deal with the childhood of Jesus at all. Instead, therefore, of saying "The story of the virgin birth is found in only two Gospels," it is more truthful and fitting to say, "All the Gospels which deal with the childhood of Jesus tell of the virgin birth."

But it is not true, as asserted by some, that the New Testament has no even indirect reference to the Virgin Birth, outside of Matthew and Luke. The truth is that the virgin birth was known to all and accepted by all. They, therefore, built upon it as a fact in all their teachings, especially the teachings that touched upon the diety of our Lord. It was not necessary then, just as it is not necessary now, for Christian preachers and teachers to be constantly referring to, defending, and expounding a fact of doctrine that was accepted and believed by all. After the adequate statement in detail about the matter by Matthew and Luke, even if it were a fact that other New Testament writers do not refer to the virgin birth, it would be rather an argument for than against it, because it would prove that it was so universally accepted and believed that the Holy Spirit did not deem it necessary to use up additional space in the New Testament referring specifically to it.

But it is not true that there are no references to the virgin birth outside of Matthew and Luke. The New Testament writers, in all their utterances, build upon the fact of the incarnation and the deity of Christ, and therefore, on his virgin birth. This is what we would expect the Holy Spirit to lead them to do about a universally accepted truth, and that is just what we find. If necessary, in my rebuttal, I can point instances illustrating this truth.

THE CHURCH FATHERS

I call attention also to the established fact that the church fathers, immediately after the apostolic age, believed and taught the virgin birth of Christ. It is in the old Roman form of the Apostles Creed. Ignatius, Bishop of Antioch, who is believed to have been a disciple of the Apostles, and who lived from 90 to 150 A. D., in his epistles speaks emphatically of the virgin birth. In his epistle to the Ephesians he writes:

"Hidden from the prince of this world were the Virginity of Mary and her child-bearing, and likewise also the death of our Lord—three mysteries of open proclamation, the which were wrought in the silence of God."

In his epistle to the Symareans, he says:

"I give glory to Jesus Christ, the God who bestowed such wisdom upon you; for I have perceived that you are established in faith immovable firmly persuaded as touching our Lord, that He is truly of the race of David according to the flesh, but son of God by divine will and power, truly born of a virgin and baptized by John—truly nailed up for our sakes in the flesh, under Pontius Pilot and Herod the tetrarch."

Aristides of Athens, in his Apology, written about the year 130, writes:

"The Christians trace their descent from the Lord Jesus Christ; now He is confessed by the Holy Ghost to be the Son of the Most High God, having come down from heaven for the salvation of men, and having been born of a holy Virgin—He took flesh and appeared to men."

Justin Martyr in his first Apology, written between 140 and 150, says:

"We find it foretold in the Books of the Prophets that Jesus our Christ should come born of a virgin—be crucified and should die and rise again, and go up to heaven and should both be and be called the 'Son of God.'"

And so we might quote Irenaeous (190), Tertullian (200), Clement (190), Origen (230).

I have given now, I submit, adequate grounds for accepting first the possibility of the virgin birth and, secondly, its probability. I have given next the simple but overwhelming documentary and personal evidence, proving it as an actual occurrence, and showing that it was believed and proclaimed by the Christians from the very beginning. I claim, therefore, that it is proved to be a fact, as much as any fact of ancient history can be proved.

IV. AN ESSENTIAL DOCTRINE

If, then, the virgin birth of Christ is a fact, it is an essential Christian doctrine, as the affirmative of our debate subject says; for who will dare declare that any established fact of the Christian system of truth is nonessential?

1. The virgin birth is an essential Christian Doctrine, first, because to deny or reject it is to deny the integrity of the Bible and to reject its authority. The facts of Christianity are deposited in the records of Christianity, and those records are in the Bible. To reject one part of the New Testament as untrustworthy, is to invalidate it all. It is self-evident to any logical mind that if some have the right to tear out of the Bible the clear, detailed, and elaborate record of the conception and virgin birth of Christ, then others may claim the right to tear out the record of the crucifixion, the resurrection, or any other part not acceptable to their whimsical taste. Thus, we would soon have no Bible—no fixed spiritual standards, and no reliable guide for our souls.

The Bible cannot be thus torn to pieces, because congruity in the life of Christ demands the virgin birth. The Christian Church believes that Christ was a divine as well as a human being. If this is true, it makes it unscientific to argue that He entered the world by purely human means! A supernatural being requires a supernatural birth. Therefore, it is not surprising that Jesus Christ was born of the Virgin. It would have been far more surprising if he had not been virgin born.

Furthermore, the entrance of Christ into the world must be in keeping with His exit from the world. We cannot take the biography of Jesus piecemeal. We cannot separate the beginning and the ending of His marvelous life. According to the record, He left the world by a resurrection and an ascension into heaven. Logic, and sound science also, therefore, require that He should have entered the world by a descent from Heaven and incarnation through the virgin birth. Consequently, the resurrection and the virgin birth are forever connected. One cannot be destroyed without destroying the other. We cannot reject one part of the miraculous life of Christ without invalidating all the rest. A Divine being requires a divine entrance into the world.

It just evidently comes down to this, that if we will not abide by the record as it is written, and accept the history, and if we demand the right to read into the record any idea that we may individually like, then we really make our own history, and all the recorded history is rendered, therefore, utterly worthless. But some of us—the great overwhelming majority indeed—believe in and are fully satisfied with the record as it is written, and we simply refuse to allow the Modernistic tail to wag the Fundamentalist dog!

UNIVERSALLY ACCEPTED

Secondly, the virgin birth of Christ is an essential Christian doctrine because it has been declared so to be by all the great branches of the Christian Church. Canon Randolph, in his little book, "The Virgin Birth of Our Lord," quotes Professor Zahn of Earlangen as saying:

"This, (the Virgin Birth) has been an element of the Creed as far as we can trace it back; and if Ignatius can be taken as a witness of a Baptismal Creed springing from early Apostolic times, certainly in that Creed the name of the Virgin Mary already had its place. We may further assert that during the first four centuries of the church, no teacher and no religious community which can be considered with any appearance of right as an heir of original Christianity, had any other notion of the beginning of the human life of Jesus of Nazareth. The theory of an original Christianity without the belief in Jesus the Son of God, born of the Virgin Mary, is a fiction."

Not only has the doctrine of the virgin birth been in the Apostles Creed from the very beginning, but it has been reasserted and reaffirmed in all the great creeds, doctrinal statements and confessions of faith in Christendom. It is in the Nicene Creed, the Westminster Confession, the Thirty-nine Articles, the Augsburg Confession, the Heidleberg Catechism, the Formula Romana, the Formula Graeca et Russica, and the Confessions of faith of the Methodists, the Presbyterians, the Baptists and other great communions.

In preparation for this debate I sent letters of inquiry to the heads or accredited representatives of the Roman Catholic Church, the Greek Orthodox Church, and the outstanding Protestant communions. The replies are emphatic in their assertions that all of those great groups of Christians accept the virgin birth as a fact, and regard it as an essential Christian doctrine.

Here is a personal letter, for example, from Cardinal Hayes, of the Roman Catholic Church, in which he says most emphatically that his great world-wide church accepts "absolutely" as fact the virgin birth, and regards it as an essential Christian Doctrine. He then takes the trouble to point out to me the historic creeds and utterances of their councils from the beginning which have set forth this doctrine of the virgin birth.

The great creeds and confessions of faith of Protestantism, as before stated, have likewise set forth this doctrine, and affirmed and reaffirmed its essential nature.

Bishop W. T. Manning has given me for his church a clear and decisive statement, which may be accepted as typical of all others. He says:

"We are told today that belief in the virgin birth is unimportant. But the church in whose name we speak does not so teach. Brief as the summary of her essential faith is, the Church has included in it the affirmation 'born of the Virgin Mary.' The importance of this article of the creed is indicated by the fact that wherever the belief in the Virgin Birth becomes weak, belief seems also to become weak in the Resurrection and Ascension of our Lord. This present movement does not mean only rejection of the Virgin birth, of this or that miracle of the Gospel. As Bishop Gore has so ably shown, it has its roots in a determined presupposition against the possibility of miracle, against the supernatural as such, and so against the very message of the Gospel as declared in the New Testament. A Christ who was not born of the Virgin, who did not rise in the body on the third day, and who did not ascend into heaven is not the Christ in whom this Church believes and has always believed."

These things simply mean that practically the whole Christian Church from the beginning has declared itself as believing, not only in the fact, but also in the essential doctrinal value of the virgin birth.

There is an old maxim of both law and theology which teaches that that which is of universal acceptation,—believed semper, ubique, et ab omnibus—always, everywhere, and by all—carries prima facie proof of its truth. As completely as any other doctrine, the doctrine of the virgin birth of our Lord meets the conditions of this maxim. *Here is one doctrine upon which Protestants, Roman Catholics, and Greek Catholics all stand together.* Only a few dissenters, like the ancient sceptical Gnostics and Ebionites—and some small denominations of today, and a handful of individual doubters in each age, like Marcion, Celcus, Voltaire, Schrempf, and Thomas Paine, have set themselves against it.

I wish, therefore, to ask my honorable opponent two simple but very practical questions: First, if the church has not the right to say what is her true and essential Christian doctrine, then pray who has such a right? And, second, if all the great branches of the Church universal have declared the virgin birth as true, and as an essential doctrine, then *what authority* is there in the hands of a small minority to nullify and overthrow her faith and practice?

Thirdly: The virgin birth is an essential Christian Doctrine because upon it depends in part the reliability and efficiency of the Christian atonement. Only a God-man could mediate salvation between God and man. A universal Savior must have been capable of an infinite suffering to cover the infinite sins of all men from the beginning of time to the coming Judgment day. Now an infinite being must be a Divine Being; that is to say, God only must have been His Father, and, to provide His human side, the virgin Mary must have been his mother.

Fourthly: The virgin birth is an essential Christian doctrine because it alone gives us an adequate object of worship. Some say that the Deity of Christ is not dependent on the virgin birth. Well, God might have given His Divine Son to the world by some other miracle than the virgin birth, but the Bible,—the record book—says that He did give His Son by the virgin birth, and in Him we find a fit subject for our devotion.

What we want and what we need is not a mere model or example, but an object of worship; One *to whom we can look up;* One whom we can adore in wonder, and to whom we can bring the utmost gratitude of our hearts for His saving grace and power! Such a One we find in the virgin-born, Christ,—a Being both human and divine—over whom the hearts of holy prophets burned with divine fervor; about whom angelic visitors sang their songs of peace and good will; to whose manger-

throne, the wise and the good came from far countries
to bring their gifts of gold and frank incense and myrrh;
One for whom the very heavens opened and the voice of
the Father was heard saying: "This is my beloved Son";
One whose body was touched by transfiguration glory
until "His face did shine as the sun and His garments
became white as the light"; One who could not only call
back the lifeless tenant of Lazarus tomb, but who, Himself, after a brief repose in the cold embrace of death,
smashed to pieces its iron bars, broke its bands asunder,
and stepped forth as *Victor over the grave.* Yes, One who
then ascended to the right hand of the Divine Majesty,
and who is coming again to defeat the Devil, end the sorrows of earth, and establish the reign of unending peace
and eternal love in "a new Heavens and a new Earth,
wherein dwelleth righteousness!"

This is the Being before whom the sinful and weary
children of men may well come for worship; and such a
being demands the acknowledgment of entrance into this
world, not through the channels of sinful conception but
by way of the altar of a virgin's womb and through the
power of the Most High God!

II

FOR THE NEGATIVE[1]

RESOLVED: That the miraculous virgin birth of Jesus
Christ is a fact and an essential Christian doctrine.

Jesus Christ is the most inspiring character that the
world has ever known. Although he was brought up in
an obscure carpenter's home nineteen centuries ago, and
never traveled a hundred miles away from it; although
he never wrote a book, nor led an army, nor championed
a reform of social wrong, nor did any of the things
by which men usually attain greatness and influence, he
is nevertheless by common consent recognized as the
greatest being who ever walked this planet. Men of all
sorts have rejoiced to be numbered among his followers
and have proudly met death rather than renounce their
allegiance to him.

Ever since he first appeared men have wondered as
to the *reason why* he seemed to be greater than other men.
As the years and centuries have passed and the influence of
his dynamic personality has seemed to increase in force
rather than to lessen, the question is asked with more and
more insistence by thoughtful men.

From the early days there have been different opinions
as to the source of Jesus's greatness, and there is great
difference of opinion today. On one point, however,
most Christians agree, namely, that *Jesus was what he
was because the spirit of God was in him.* Even my
worthy opponent and I would agree upon that point, I

[1] First speech for the negative by Rev. Charles Francis Potter,
Minister, West Side Unitarian Church, New York.

think. Now I am content to let the matter rest right
there, but my opponent wants to go further. He insists
that the spirit of God entered Jesus in a particular way,
in a most unusual way, in fact, in a miraculous way. He
insists, moreover, that belief in this miracle is an essential
Christian doctrine; that is, that unless you believe in it
you are not a Christian!

Get that point very firmly and clearly in your mind.
It doesn't matter to my opponent whether or not you and
I agree with him that Jesus was what he was because the
spirit of God was in him; it doesn't matter whether or
not we follow Jesus' teachings to the very best of our
ability and try to live a Christian life; it doesn't even
save us to believe in the deity of Jesus;—unless we agree
with my opponent as to the particular *way* in which Jesus
became divine then we are heretics and cannot be Christians, because we will have rejected what he calls an
essential Christian doctrine.

Consequently my worthy opponent has undertaken the
Herculean task of proving, in the first place, that the
miraculous virgin birth of Jesus Christ is a fact and in the
second place, that it is an essential Christian doctrine.
I certainly admire his courage in defending his creed,
but if he succeeds in proving either of these contentions,
I shall be tempted to believe that miracles are possible
today.

IS THE VIRGIN BIRTH A FACT?

For, look you, what he must do to prove the first part
of the resolution, namely, that the virgin birth is a fact.
It is not enough to prove that such an extraordinary occurrence is possible scientifically: he must demonstrate that
it actually occurred historically.

Let us take the scientific possibility of the virgin birth
first. I shall not attempt to prove that it is impossible.
I do not have to do that, fortunately, for the true scientist

is very careful about declaring anything impossible. It
will be sufficient to show how very rarely, if ever, virgin
births of humans occur. The extreme scarcity of virgin
births lays a very great burden of improbability on the
argument which would try to prove the actual historical
occurrence of one.

Now the scientific name for virgin birth is parthenogenesis, from "parthenos," virgin, and "genesis," birth,
and cases of parthenogenesis are recorded by scientists
among the lower forms of life. That is far from proving
the possibility of virgin birth among human beings, however. The fact that a female codfish has been known to
lay eight million eggs (according to the Encyclopedia
Brittanica) does not prove the possibility of a human
mother having eight million children.

The chance of a human being being produced by a
virgin is very very remote. The normal method of reproduction in humans is by a male parent and a female
parent. The separate new individual begins to develop
when a cell from the one joins a cell from the other.
Parthenogenesis would be the development of an unfer-
tilized egg-cell. The best known instance of parthenogenesis is the case of the common Aphis, or plant louse.
It has been known also to occur among mites, beetles,
bark-lice, caddis-flies, silk-worms, saw-flies, currant-
worms, and certain maggots.

It is never known to have occurred among the higher
animals or men. There is no parthenogenesis in mam-
malia. For that statement I refer you to almost any
biologist in the world. I will quote you the highest
scientific authority I know, the man who was chosen to
write the article on parthenogenesis in the Encyclopedia
of Religion and Ethics, Dr. J. Arthur Thomson, Regius
Professor of Natural History in the University of Aberdeen, who says (vol. 9, p. 651): "As yet, no instance of
either artificial or natural parthenogenesis has been ob-

served in the animal kingdom above the level of amphibians."

Now that does not mean that virgin birth among human beings is impossible, but it does mean that it is very improbable and it makes a truth-seeker rather suspicious of any alleged virgin birth. The evidence must be very convincing indeed to make us believe that any child was ever born of one parent alone.

What is the evidence that is offered to us? Remember now that the question before us is not one of possibility, it is a question of fact: not whether God could have caused a virgin, unknown of man, to bring forth a child, but whether he actually did so.

WHAT DOES THE NEW TESTAMENT SAY?

Let us examine the evidence. The New Testament includes it all. Let us take it chronologically, in order to begin with the evidence nearest the event in question. Our points would be just as true if we took it in any other order, but since this is a question of historic fact, it is better to take the books in historic order, and that order is generally agreed upon by scholars, conservative and liberal alike to have been as follows,—

The earliest part of the New Testament is Paul's letters, written between 52 and 67 A.D. Then come in order, Mark (67), I Peter (67), Revelation (68, at the earliest), Hebrews (68), Matthew (69), Luke (71), Acts (75), Jude and II Peter (between 75 and 90, at the earliest), John and I, II, and III John (between 90 and 100 A. D.). The date of James is unknown.

What does Paul have to say about the Virgin Birth? He must mention it a great deal for it would work in well with his line of argument. But what do we find? Absolutely no mention of the Virgin Birth at all in all the 13 letters ascribed to Paul, and Paul was the greatest missionary preacher of the early Christian church. Not only do we find no affirmation of the virgin birth, but we find the direct opposite stated. In Romans 1:3, Paul says that Jesus was "made of the seed of David according to the flesh." Now it was Joseph, not Mary, who was of the seed of David. Mary was of the house of Levi, for she was the kinswoman of Elizabeth, who was of the house of Levi. In II Timothy 2:8 Paul repeats that Jesus was "of the seed of David, according to my gospel." In Galatians 4:4 Paul says "God sent forth His Son, made of a *woman,* made under the law, to redeem them that were under the law." That is the same idea which he uses in Romans 8:3 where he says God sent His own Son "in the likeness of sinful flesh." Now anyone who believed that the Holy Spirit was the father of Jesus would not write in that fashion. Paul believed that Jesus was really human and based his whole plan of salvation on that fact. If he believed that Jesus was born of a virgin by the Holy Spirit, he could not write, "made of a woman, made under the law."

The earliest gospel is Mark's, which begins very significantly as follows:

"The beginning of the Gospel of Jesus Christ," and goes on to tell of his baptism by John. Absolutely no mention of the virgin birth at all, throughout the entire gospel of Mark, regarded by scholars as the oldest account of the life of Jesus, and the most trustworthy. And remember that it was written over thirty years after Jesus' death.

The next books in order, I Peter, Revelation, and Hebrews say nothing of the virgin birth whatsoever. On the contrary Hebrews says, Chapter 4, verse 15, that Jesus was "in all points tempted like as we are, yet without sin." Also in Hebrews 2:17, "Wherefore it behooved Him (Jesus) in all things to be made like unto His brethren," and as Professor Frederick Palmer of Harvard says in a book just printed on "The Virgin Birth," page 14:

"If a special nature, conveyed through a special method of generation, rendered him immune to temptation, then every suffering human being might exclaim. 'No comfort nor uplift for me can come from him.—His goodness was conveyed to him from without, but mine is not so conveyed to me.' The doctrine of the Virgin Birth does thus in fact reduce Jesus to the status of an Arabian genie or a Greek demi-god, a being whom we can contemplate with wonder but with whom we can have no essential connection."

We come next to Matthew and there we have one verse, chapter 1, verse 18, which states the virgin birth. It is the only verse which states it in Matthew, and I might as well say here that this is the one verse in the whole Bible which states it directly and clearly. Other verses in Matthew and Luke refer to it by prediction but this is the only verse which states the virgin birth as an historical fact. The verse reads:

"Now the birth of Jesus Christ was on this wise: When his mother Mary had been betrothed to Joseph, before they came together she was found with child by the Holy Spirit."

Upon this verse, and in spite of numerous verses which state the contrary, the whole doctrine of the virgin birth is based.

The singular thing is that in this same chapter it is stated that Jesus was the son of Joseph. The chapter opens, you will remember, with the verse,

"The book of the generation of Jesus Christ, the son of David, the son of Abraham," and goes on to state the genealogy of Jesus, from Abraham, through Isaac and Jacob, to David, down to Josiah, down to Eleazar.
"And Eleazar begat Matthan; and Matthan begat Jacob; and Jacob begat Joseph the husband of Mary, of whom was born Jesus, who is called Christ."

Now since it is stated in the first verse that Jesus was the son of David, that is, his descendant, it is very plain that he must have been the son of Joseph, otherwise there is no sense to the genealogy at all. One of the oldest manuscripts, the Sinai-Syriac, supported by four Latin and two Greek manuscripts, gives this verse as follows:

"Joseph, to whom was betrothed Mary the virgin, begat Jesus, who is called the Christ," and the whole first part of the chapter in the regular text has no meaning unless we understand Joseph to have been the real father of Jesus.

I submit then that the only verse stating the virgin birth cannot be submitted as testimony because in the same chapter the fact is distinctly denied. We find Matthew a flatly contradictory witness and we must rule out his testimony, for no court of law would accept a witness who contradicts himself on the crucial point of the whole case.

But let us go further. In Matthew 13:55 the neighbors of Jesus say, "Is not this the carpenter's son?" and Jesus does not contradict them, practically admitting their charge, when he says:

"A prophet is not without honor, save in his own country, and in his own house."

Luke comes next chronologically, and Luke 4:22 repeats this last incident, phrasing the question, "Is not this Joseph's son?" and again Jesus does not deny his parenthood. Why should he? He never once in all his quoted utterances suggests anything but that Joseph is his earthly father and God his heavenly father.

Luke in his first chapter has something to say about the virgin birth, but he does not say that it actually occurred. He says that the angel Gabriel told Mary that it would occur. Not once does Luke say plainly and directly that Jesus was born of the Virgin Mary by the Holy Spirit of God without a human father. Remember that we are debating on the *fact* of the virgin birth, and are summoning the witnesses, and I ask any lawyer in the audience how much value he would place on Luke's story that an angel told Mary that it would occur, especially when Luke's gospel was written at the very earliest seventy years after the birth of Jesus?

Let us be generous to the other side, however, and say that perhaps Luke intended his readers to think that the virgin birth was a fact, even if he doesn't say so outright. Then why does he flatly deny it in the third chapter with another of those dangerous genealogies? He goes Matthew one better and traces Jesus' genealogy way back to Adam and God, and he traces the line, not through Mary but through *Joseph*, just as Matthew did. That is, in one place Luke tries to prove that Jesus is the son of God by intimating that God, through the Holy Spirit, caused Mary to conceive without having had an earthly husband. Then only two chapters later he tries to prove that Jesus is the son of God by tracing his birth-line through *Joseph* back to Adam, "who was the son of God." Here again is very contradictory evidence and the witness is a very poor one to prove a miracle by, to say the least.

Read the rest of Luke after the first chapter and there is no mention of the virgin birth. You would think it had never been mentioned. Why, in the second chapter, verse 33, after old Simeon had made a little prophecy about the child Jesus, we read that his *father* and mother (note that it doesn't say Joseph and his mother), marveled at the things which were spoken of him. Why should they marvel if the angel had told them more wonderful things only a little while before?

And in the same second chapter, note that Mary was astonished again at his teaching in the temple at the age of twelve, and that she said, "*Thy father* and I have sought thee sorrowing." If the Holy Spirit was his father, wasn't this blasphemy against the Holy Spirit?

And in the third chapter, verse 22, we read that when

Jesus was baptized, "the Holy Spirit descended in a bodily form, as a dove, upon him, and a voice came out of heaven, 'Thou art my beloved Son; in thee I am well pleased.'" There were two current explanations in the early church, one that divinity entered Jesus when Mary conceived him, and one that it entered him at his baptism. A person could accept either explanation and be an equally good Christian. Neither was an essential Christian doctrine. Personally I prefer another explanation, an evolutionary one, also found in Luke 2:52, "And Jesus increased in wisdom and stature, and in favor with God and man." But I forgot for a moment that it has been proved on this very platform that there is no such thing as evolution.

And as for the remaining books of the New Testament, there is no testimony to the virgin birth in them. That includes the fourth gospel, John. Even Dr. Jefferson of this city, who says he believes the virgin birth, although (evidently) not considering it an essential Christain doctrine, admits the scant evidence for it in the Bible, saying, "The Gospel of John is credited to the most intimate and best-loved disciple, to whom Jesus committed his mother as he hung on the cross. John of all disciples must have known about the virgin birth, but he never mentions it." He might have added that in John 1:45 and 6:42, Jesus is called distinctly the son of Joseph, by Philip and others.

SUMMARY OF NEW TESTAMENT EVIDENCE

To summarize then the evidence for the virgin birth, the New Testament evidence, which is all there is, what have we? There is no evidence in any part of the New Testament save in Matthew and possibly Luke, while there is much against it in many places, including Matthew and Luke. Paul distinctly says that Jesus was "made of the seed of David, made of a woman, made under the law, in the likeness of sinful flesh." Dr. Palmer, previously quoted, says on page 15, after an exhaustive and reverent scholarly examination of all the evidence, that one who holds the view that Joseph was the real father of Jesus "may claim for it more extensive Scriptural authority" than the person who holds to the view that Jesus was miraculously virgin-born.

Any attempt to prove from the New Testament that the virgin birth was a fact has on its side only one document, the first part of the gospel according to Matthew, and really only one verse of that first chapter. Luke has to be ruled out as direct evidence: it can only be considered secondary in the light of its being a prophecy by an angel rather than a direct statement. The sections in Matthew and Luke, where references to the virgin birth occur, have by some of the greatest scholars been considered later additions to the gospel story. Dr. Leighton Parks of St. Bartholomews of this city in his book "What is Modernism?" published this week, says on page 64, "there are many scholars of repute who are convinced that the definite statements that Jesus was born without the agency of a human father—are a later insertion worked into the earlier tradition."

Furthermore, to get at the exact facts before us for evidence, the only document of importance as evidence in the case is an unsigned, contradictory statement, made by one who was not an eyewitness, giving hearsay rumors, and written down over sixty years after the event, not as a record of facts but confessedly as a theological tract to prove that Jesus was the Messiah expected by the Jews. Is that good evidence? Even if you admit Luke as evidence, remember that his book is also unsigned, self-contradictory and that he was not an eyewitness and wrote even later than Matthew.

IS THE VIRGIN BIRTH AN ESSENTIAL CHRISTIAN DOCTRINE?

We come now to the second part of the debate, as to whether or not this doctrine is an essential Christian doctrine.

Immediately the question rises whether any doctrine can be essential to Christianity which is not a fact, and my opponent has certainly not proved it to be a fact. The second part of the resolution of the evening depends upon the first. It is certainly time that mistaken persons stopped making the virgin birth a test of a Christian's faith. No doctrine based on such a flimsy foundation ought to be a test-question for young men entering the Christian ministry. If it is so maintained, there will soon be no Christian ministry, and Christianity will degenerate into a few congregations who do nothing but listen to ministers who do nothing but harangue on ancient theological matters.

EMINENT MODERN CHRISTIANS SAY NO

Not only is the virgin birth not an essential Christian doctrine because it is not based on a historical fact, but its non-essentiality is proved by the fact that many modern Christian theologians, preachers, teachers and laymen do not consider it essential and still retain their membership in churches of practically every Protestant faith.

Here is Bishop Lawrence of Massachusetts, one of the leading Episcopal bishops of this country, a Christian if one ever lived, who says in his book "Fifty Years," page 72,—

"There is no essential connection between belief in the virgin birth and a belief in the incarnation," and stating furthermore that he will not ask candidates in his diocese their position on the historicity of the virgin birth. Certainly he does not consider it essential to Christian faith.

Here is Bishop Gore of the Church of England saying on page 274 of his book "Belief in God" (a book which Bishop Manning commended to his diocese), and referring to the virgin birth,

"Certainly nothing concerning the birth of Christ was part of that assurance on the basis of which faith in Jesus was claimed. I may add that it ought not, to this day, to form part of the basis of the claim."

Further on page 279 Bishop Gore, who has been justly called one of the most scholarly, spiritual and honest-minded prelates of the entire Anglican world, says:

"the question of faith in Jesus must rest still, where it was made to rest from the beginning, on the life, teaching, death and resurrection of Jesus. On these, quite apart from any questions concerning his birth, the faith stood and still could stand."

Canon Storrs, the great English evangelical, in a sermon on the Incarnation delivered in Westminster Abbey recently said that he attached no theological significance to the virgin birth for, "there are today not a few Christians who for one reason or another find themselves unable to accept this article of the creed, and yet are absolutely conviced that Jesus is the Son of God in the sense in which the creeds asserts."

I am sure that Dr. Henry Sloan Coffin would not refuse membership in his church (Presbyterian) to one who believed in Jesus but who doubted whether or not the virgin birth was an essential doctrine. Certainly his book on "Some Christian Convictions" leads one to suppose that. Nor would Dr. Parks of St. Bartholomews, nor Dr. L. Mason Clark of Brooklyn, nor Dr. Woelfkin of Park Avenue Baptist.

In the Encyclopedia of Religion and Ethics, the article in volume 12, page 625, written by Dr. J. A. MacCulloch, whose whole article is in favor of the virgin birth, nevertheless admits that "it is not to be denied that belief in the divinity of Christ, in the Incarnation, is possible without a belief in the virgin birth."

And our great American authority, the revised New International Encyclopedia, has in volume 23, page 177, a very direct statement at the end of the article on the virgin birth, saying:

"Many Protestant churches have ceased to maintain that belief in the virgin birth is essential to Christian faith."

Will my opponent dare to say that the entire Unitarian denomination, which includes Charles W. Eliot and William Howard Taft and which has twenty-two names in the Hall of Fame out of the sixty-five there, and the Universalist denomination and the liberal Quakers, both containing some of the best people alive today, will he dare to say that these are not Christians? Yet if he maintains that the virgin birth is an *essential* Christian doctrine, he must say so. Jesus said, "By their fruits ye shall know them?" and modernists respectfully submit that those who try to follow Jesus, to catch his wonderful spirit of service, to live lives of spiritual consecration to God and humanity, these are really Christians. And there is an increasing number of such souls who cannot honestly believe that the miraculous virgin birth is either a fact or an essential Christian doctrine.

IT HAS ALWAYS BEEN IN DISPUTE

Not only are there many modern Christians who do not consider the Virgin Birth an essential doctrine, but there have always been those who have doubted its importance. The question has always been disputed in the Christian Church. Even in the Roman Catholic Church there has been considerable difficulty over the doctrine. Its theologians recognized that to eliminate the human father was to close only one door to original sin, so about the middle of the last century one of the popes announced the opinion of the church that Mary herself was conceived by her mother without sin. I honor the Roman Catholics for having taken this stand, for it is a more consistent position than the Protestant one, which is only a half way measure.

As I have said, the matter of the Virgin Birth has always created a great deal of discussion in Christianity. My opponent was misinformed when he stated that it was in all the great creeds. The Athanasian creed, the longest and most carefully detailed of the ecumenical creeds of Christendom, did not contain it, nor did the earliest form of the Nicene creed have it.

It is when we get back to the origins of Christianity that we find the relative unimportance of the Virgin Birth indicated by its absence from the theology of the founders of Christianity. The argument from silence may sometimes have its defects, but certainly in the second half of this debate, when the question before us is as to whether or not the Virgin Birth doctrine is *essential* to Christianity, the negative has almost overwhelming proof from the fact that Paul, Peter, Mark and John did not consider it important enough in their theology to mention it. Certainly these four men were Christians if ever there were Christians. The earliest Christians did not consider the Virgin Birth essential. Paul was the greatest missionary Christianity has ever had. Peter, Mark and John were in close touch with Jesus. If they did not consider it important enought to mention it, certainly it cannot be held an essential Christian doctrine.

It would seem natural for a person who was looking to find out whether or not any doctrine was essential in Christianity, if that person should turn to Jesus' teaching itself. Search as you will in the recorded sayings of Jesus, you will find the Virgin Birth never mentioned. When they came to him and asked him the source of his power, then was the time for him to point to his miraculous virgin birth, as the Fundamentalists do. Yet the records say that he pointed rather to the good works which he was doing, healing the sick and helping poor people. Are modern Christians wrong when they follow Jesus in finding the evidence for his own divinity in his life of useful service to his fellow men? I ask again the question, can any doctrine be essential to Christianity which is never mentioned in Jesus' own teachings?

THE VIRGIN BIRTH STORY IS AN INSULT TO THE MARRIAGE RELATIONSHIP

When in the course of my ministry I unite a blushing bridegroom to a clear-eyed, calm and steady bride, I use a ceremony which begins just as my worthy opponent's marriage ceremony begins, with the words, "Marriage is an institution ordained of God." Are we telling a lie when we say this? If marriage is an institution ordained of God, if from the very beginning God intended man and woman for each other and instituted marriage as a "sacred union of hearts," can it be that when an exceptionally good man was to have been born, it was "essential" to select some other method for his birth? To say so is to imply that marriage is not an "institution ordained of God."

I maintain that there is nothing higher or holier than the love of a pure man for a pure woman, and the fact that from that love another individual comes into the world. For better babies to be born, what we need is more love in the heart, rather than some unnatural, abnormal method of birth.

THE VIRGIN BIRTH IS MATERIALISTIC

Another strong criticism of the Virgin Birth doctrine, which proves that it is contrary to the spirit of Christionity, is the fact that this doctrine is essentially materialistic, and anything materialistic is not only not essential to Christianity, but distinctly contrary to its spirit.

The materialism of the Virgin Birth doctrine is revealed by the fact that it places the emphasis upon a method of physical conception rather than upon the spirit of Jesus. This is quite in line with all the other Fundamentalist doctrines: The resurrection of the body of Jesus, for instance, and his bodily return upon the clouds of Heaven. I would say openly that Fundamentalism is a materialistic heresy which is trying to creep into spiritual Christianity.

Jesus' character, devotion and spirituality do not depend upon the method of his birth. It is rather in the sublimity of his life that we are to find the explanation of his power. An ignorant age may have attributed his greatness to a peculiar and miraculous form of birth, but, more and more, thoughtful Christians are inclined to find in his character itself the explanation of his worth. Indeed, if we had never known anything about Jesus' birth; if we began where Mark, the earliest Gospel begins, we would still hold Jesus as our divine leader.

Wherefore, Honorable Judges, and ladies and gentlemen, I submit that my worthy opponent has not at all proved his case. The Virgin Birth of Jesus is neither a fact, nor is it an essential Christian doctrine. It is not a fact because there is more evidence in the New Testament against the Virgin Birth than there is for it. It is not an essential Christian doctrine because the growing sentiment of modern Christianity is against it, because it has always been a matter of dispute within the Christian Church, because it is not found in all the creeds, and because the founders of Christianity, Paul, Peter, Mark and John, and especially Jesus himself, knew nothing about it. It is not an essential Christian doctrine because it is a slur on the marriage relationship, which was ordained of God, and because it is too materialistic to be in harmony with the spiritual character of Jesus and of Christianity.

III

REBUTTAL FOR THE AFFIRMATIVE[1]

In the beginning, I wish to point out that my opponent has misstated the ground of my contention that the Virgin Birth is an essential Christian doctrine. He has sought to make it appear that I am arguing that no man can be a Christian who does not believe in the Virgin Birth. I argued no such thing. The question for debate is: "Resolved that the Miraculous Virgin Birth of Jesus Christ is a Fact, *and that it is an Essential Christian Doctrine."* *An* "essential Christian Doctrine" not the *only* essential Christian doctrine. There are varieties of view on all of the Christian doctrines. And I have not and do not argue that the Virgin Birth is an essential Christian doctrine, in the sense that unless one believes it absolutely he cannot be a Christian. It is an essential to the full rounded system of Christian doctrine, and that is all that I or any other Christian teacher, with whom I am familiar would hold about it. I must express my surprise, therefore, that my opponent seemingly seeks to twist what I said upon this point. He has not shown wherein the Virgin Birth is non-essential, and I have shown that it is certainly essential in some ways.

Secondly, there is no disagreement between us as to the scientific possibility of the Virgin Birth. As Mr. Potter admits that parthenogenesis is a fact among some forms of animal life, I pass that by without comment.

NOT JUST IN ONE VERSE

Again, my opponent argued that the Virgin Birth can be dismissed because, as he alleges, it is really taught in

[1] By Rev. John Roach Straton, D.D.

only one verse of the New Testament. This is not true. As I showed in my opening speech, the doctrine runs like a golden thread through the entire Scripture. It starts with that remarkable prophecy in Genesis that "the seed of the woman"—not the seed of the man—would "bruise the serpent's head." It goes on through the prophesies of Isaiah that the Savior would be Virgin born (and the word in Isaiah means Virgin, regardless of what my opponent may try to say to the contrary), until the teaching culminates in the full and elaborate statements of Matthew and Luke.

As to the point my opponent tried to make about the order in which the books of the New Testament were written, what has that to do with the question? The teaching is in the books, specifically, regardless of the precise order in which they were written; and even if we grant that Mark wrote the earliest Gospel and that the epistles of Paul were also early, it would only mean that the Holy Spirit led those Gospel writers to emphasize the thing that was most prominently up at the time when they wrote and spoke. The urgent testimony in the day of Paul and the earliest Gospel writers was the testimony concerning the resurrection, the atonement, etc. If it is true that Mark and Paul were the earliest writers, then it becomes clear that the Holy Spirit emphasizes the thing that was then most urgent. So Mark's Gospel did not deal specifically with the childhood of Jesus at all, but started with His baptism and public ministry. The full detailed statement concerning the miraculous Virgin Birth of Christ would thus logically have come along later, when Matthew and Luke were inspired to write their narratives.

I deny emphatically, however, that the teaching of the Virgin Birth depends upon only one verse. Both of these long detailed narratives in Matthew and Luke deal specifically with that event, and all of the circumstances as to

time, place and persons in the narratives simply head
up, as in any other narrative, in the final statement of
the fact itself.   As Dr. Orr pointed out, these narratives
of Matthew and Luke would really be meaningless and
absurd, if the critics had succeeded in deleting the verses
which specifically state the Virgin Birth, because all the
other incidents would be entirely uncalled for, without
that central event around which they cluster.   As, for
example, the statement that Joseph did not know Mary
as his wife until after she had brought forth her first born
son, namely, Jesus.   One might as well say that the
baptism of Jesus in the River Jordan by John the Baptist
is not a fact, because the direct statement of the event
itself is given only in one verse.   But everything that
leads up to that statement is really a part of it, as, for
example, that He came from Galilee down to the Jordan,
and that He came for the express purpose of being baptized, and that John the Baptist expressed His feeling of
unworthiness to baptize the Son of God, etc., etc.

MISQUOTING MARK

I wish to say, again, however, and most emphatically,
that I do not admit that Mark and John and Paul did
not know of the Virgin Birth and did not teach it.   All
that these men knew and taught is not given in the New
Testament, but there are touches of this doctrine in
what is given.

My opponent, for example, quoted a part of the first
sentence from Mark's Gospel, but I wish to ask pointedly
why he did not quote it all.   He said that Mark's Gospel
starts with the statement: "The beginning of the Gospel
of Jesus Christ."   But that is not all of that first sentence of Mark's.   Here is the complete sentence: "The
beginning of the Gospel of Jesus Christ, *the Son of God.*"
Why did not my opponent put in that phrase, "The Son
of God"?   That plainly proves that Mark knew who

Jesus was, and that He was not the son of Joseph but the Son of God. And why did not my opponent quote that other verse in the first chapter of Mark's Gospel where it is asserted, in connection with the baptism of Jesus: "There came a voice from heaven saying, *thou art my beloved Son in whom I am well pleased*" (Mark 1:11)? And why did not my opponent give all three of the first verses of Mark's Gospel? Here they are:

"The beginning of the Gospel of Jesus Christ, the Son of God; as it is written in the prophets, Behold, I send my messenger before thy face, which shall prepare thy way before thee. The voice of one crying in the wilderness, Prepare ye the way of the Lord, make his paths straight" (Mark 1:1-3).

In every line of this, there is not only the plain implication of the miraculous conception and birth of Jesus, as the prophets had foretold, and as Mark evidently believed, but there is the direct adoption by Mark of the divine name for Jesus—"*Lord.*"

JOHN'S TESTIMONY

And so, also, of John's testimony. Listen, please, to the first sentence in John's Gospel:

"In the beginning was the word [the Logos, the Divine Voice, the Christ] and the word was with God, and the word was God. All things were made by Him; and without Him was not anything made that was made. In Him was life; and the life was the light of men, And the word was made flesh, and dwelt among us (and we beheld His glory, the glory as of the only begotten of the Father) full of grace and truth" (John 1:3-4-14).

Who dares say that John did not know anything about the Virgin Birth and that he made no reference to it, when here he says that the "Word was made flesh"—not conceived in human desire, but "*made* flesh"—by the power of God, and, therefore, that the Christ was the "only *begotten* of the Father"? That means just what

it says,—that God begat Jesus. If that is not a statement
of the miraculous conception, carrying with it, of necessity, the Virgin Birth of Christ, then what is it?

Further Mary, the mother of Jesus, made her home
with John after the crucifixion. Now it is well known
that John's Gospel is the latest of the Gospels. If, therefore, Matthew's Gospel and Luke's Gospel did not tell
the truth about the virgin birth, John would have known
the truth from Mary, and he would have corrected such
a wrong statement when he wrote his Gospel.[2]

PAUL'S "SILENCE"

The same thing may be said in regard to the argument
that Paul did not know anything about the virgin birth,
because he is alleged to have remained silent on the subject when he wrote his epistles. But Paul's great purpose
in writing his epistles was to emphasize, to make clear
and to defend other great facts of the Gospel message.
Like John, Paul knew that the virgin birth would be
adequately set forth, and that all the followers of Christ
in that day knew about it. Once more, the fact that Paul
does not use the actual term "virgin birth," is an argument
for the truth of it rather than against it, because it proves

[2] Well does Dr. Orr say concerning this matter: "John, had un-
questionably the Gospels of Matthew and Luke in his hands; he
wrote, as we shall see, at a time when the Virgin Birth was already
a general article of belief in the Church; it is generally understood
that one part of his design, at least, was to supplement the other
Gospels with material from his own recollections. What, then, is
John's relation to the narrative of the birth of Christ in these earlier
Gospels? He knew them. Does he repudiate them? Or contradict
them? Or correct them? If he does not—and who will be bold
enough to affirm that he does?—what remains but to believe that he
accepted and endorsed them? Remember that Mary had been placed
under John's guardianship by Jesus Himself, and probably lived in
his house until she died. Remember also that these stories, if not
true, could only be interpreted in a way which implied a slur on
Mary's good name. Is it conceivable that, if he knew them to be
false, the Evangelist would have met them with no word of in-
dignant denial?" ("The Virgin Birth of Christ, Page 109).

that the doctrine was so well known and so universally accepted that it needed neither elaboration nor defense.

Paul does not refer specifically to the miracles of our Lord, and to many significant events in His life.   But we could not argue from this that he did not believe in the miracles, or that he had no knowledge of the events to which he does not refer.   The truth is, that, as with John, the Holy Spirit inspired Paul to specialize on the great truths of the atonement, the resurrection and the return of Christ, as these were liable to misunderstanding and abuse.   But also, as with John, everything that Paul wrote or spoke was founded on the truth of the deity and the virgin birth of Christ.   I fully anticipated my opponent's argument that Paul knew nothing about the Virgin birth because he says that Jesus "was of the Seed of David according to the flesh."

I showed that Jesus *was* of the seed of David, according to the flesh, *through Mary his mother,* who was a descendant of David through Heli her father, Nathan, etc.

Instead of Paul's stating the opposite of the Virgin Birth, as my opponent asserted, his references to Jesus' coming into the world are manifestly founded on the fact of the Virgin Birth.   Hear him in Colossians speaking of Christ as the "first born of every creature,"— thus giving Him preeminence over all, because He was the only one *born* directly by the Father's power.   Hear this passage as a whole:

"Who is the image of the invisible God, the first born of every creature; for by Him were all things created, that are in heaven and that are in earth, visible and invisible, whether they be thrones, or dominions, or principalities, or powers; all things were created by Him, and for Him; and He is before all things, and in Him all things consist," or hold together (Col. 1:15-17).

Think of the absurdity of Paul speaking in such terms as those of any person who he thought had been conceived and born in the usual human way.

Other utterances of Paul, beyond any question, assume the fact of the virgin birth.   Hear him as he speaks in Romans:

"For what the law could not do, in that it was weak through the flesh, God sending His own son [not having a man conceive a son] in the likeness of sinful flesh, and for sin, condemned sin in the flesh." (Roman 8:3.)

Hear him again:

"But when the fullness of the time was come, God sent forth His Son, *made of a woman* [not born of natural human conception, but "made of a woman"], made under the law, to redeem them that were under the law that we might receive the adoption of sons."   (Gal. 4:4–5.)

Hear him again as he says:

"Let this mind be in you, which was also in Christ Jesus; Who being in the form of God, thought it not robbery to be equal with God: But made himseldf of no reputation, and took upon him the form of a servant, and was *made in the likeness of men:* [again "made" not conceived] And being found in fashion as a man, he humbled himself, and became obedient unto death, even the death of the cross. Wherefore, God also hath highly exalted him, and given him a name which is above every name.   That at the name of Jesus every knee should bow, of things in heaven, and things in earth, and things under the earth, And that every tongue should confess that Jesus Christ is Lord, to the glory of God the Father." (Phil. 2:5–11.)

Who can stand in the presence of such majestic words as these from Paul and say that he did not know that Jesus Christ was absolutely unique in His birth and in every other way?

Luke was the bosom friend and traveling companion of Paul, in fact, his biographer. The idea, therefore, that Luke did not tell Paul the truth which he fully knew about the virgin birth, and that the truth is not behind these great statements of Paul, is absurd on the face of it. Paul did know and preached the virgin birth. And the deity of our Lord which went with it, was the foundation beneath his very greatest utterances. It was altogether natural that references to the virgin birth in the preaching and teaching of the early church—especially while Mary was still alive—should be reserved and not bold and open. We would expect just such forms of expression about it as we find in these words of Mark and John and Paul.

Dr. Nolan Rice Best, Editor of "The Continent," well says upon this point:

"The reticence of the evangelists from speculations concerning the virgin birth seems to be but part of a characteristic reticence throughout the early church about the fact of it. While Mary lived at least, the Christians appear to have felt the mystery of her marvellous Child too intimate and sacred a matter to be bruited abroad to the world; it was a sacred knowledge esoteric to the church,—an incident of such delicacy that they would talk of it freely only where they were assured that they would be heard with reverence. Their historians wrote down the true relation of the matter when they undertook to tell of the birth of their Lord; fidelity to truth demanded that, and at any rate these works were expected to be read chiefly among the faithful." ("Beyond the Natural Order," page 122.)

My opponent's appeal, therefore, to the "argument from silence" breaks down. I repeat, however, what I said in my opening speech, that even if John and Mark and Paul had not known in the earlier days of their ministry, the facts about the Virgin Birth, and had not referred to it, it would not change the force of the direct and specific testimony of Matthew and Luke. Two good witnesses, whose testimony stands unimpeached, is enough in any court of law or at the bar of reason anywhere.

THE LATEST VOICE

Nor can my opponent's references to this book by Dr. Leighton Parks break the force of the facts about the Virgin Birth. It happens that I also received a copy of Dr. Parks' book, and I have it here with me. It is just fresh from the press, and it came to my desk only today. It may be regarded, therefore, as the very last word on the question of the Virgin Birth. Though liberal in his views, Dr. Parks' makes an effort to be fair, both to the Fundamentalists and Modernists. He deals with such matters as the argument of the Modernists that the first two chapters both of Matthew and Luke were added to those Gospels at a late date, but he has to admit that this, and all other hypotheses which have been urged for the overthrow of the Virgin Birth, are utterly unproved. He has to admit this even though he is avowedly sympathetic with the Modernistic viewpoints.

Dr. Parks has to admit, for example, that the text of Von Soden, which Dr. Moffatt uses as the basis of his translation of Matthew 1:16, is contested by scholars. Then Dr. Parks says (page 60): "The question has, of course, not been settled." He has to say, further, in discussing the thought that additions had been made to the Gospels or changes in them, by later editors: "There are many difficulties which such a hypothesis must meet. The language is in accordance with the rest of the books, and the suggestion that they are inserted as late as the second century seems an arbitrary assertion" (page 64).

Dr. Parks then, of course, gives the modernistic arguments about the matter, but the point I wish to make is that he has to admit that the critical and sceptical contentions over the Virgin Birth are not proved—or, as he puts it, "settled,"—and that some of their main arguments seem "arbitrary assertions."

Allow me to quote it just the way he puts it. He says:

"What, then, are the conclusions which scholars have reached in regard to the first Gospel? To speak frankly, they have not yet reached definite conclusions" (p. 66). And in speaking again of the effort to mutilate Matthew and Luke by dropping the verses that directly teach the Virgin Birth, Dr. Parks asks "But what right has any man to mutilate the text?" And then he answer his own question by saying: "None at all." And Dr. Parks then admits that it is not true that there is no Scriptural evidence which give grounds for the belief that the doctrine of the Virgin Birth expresses a historical fact. While, therefore, Dr. Parks leans to the modernists, he has nevertheless, to admit that the critical contentions against the Virgin Birth are unproved.

This, then, is the very latest voice on the subject, and I merely add it to the statements of Dr. Orr, and the exposures already given of the arbitrary and unjustifiable methods of such critics as Wellhausen Harnack, etc. These things, I submit, are adequate to dispose of all the critical contentions which my opponent has tried to bring in.

UNJUSTIFIABLE PROCEDURE

It is a revolutionary and unjustifiable procedure to try to deny such a fact as the Virgin Birth by merely endeavoring to reject in whole or to mutilate in part the records which give the account of that event.

Supposing a lawyer should come into court and declare that he no longer individually accepted a certain cardinal principle of the common law, as recorded say, in Blackstone; and that he also refused to abide by the record made in a famous case, which had become an established precedent for all like cases. Supposing he should take that position in trying to win his case, which involved the precise principle and the well established precedent which he was rejecting? Does anyone doubt that court and jury alike would declare against him without a moment's delay? My honorable opponent and the mod-

ernists in general are precisely in that position, in their
efforts to reject one after the other the great facts and
doctrines of the Christian religion.

For any one who has honest difficulties with the miracles
of the Bible there should be charity and patience. Such
an one merits faithful effort on the part of believers to
persuade him of the fundamental fact that the universe
is primarily not a mere material machine but a spiritual
order and, therefore, that miracles are inevitable. But
there is a type of mind that does not believe because it will
not believe. It is predisposed to unbelief, and seeks rather
confirmation of its own doubts than revelation of the
truth. One who demands more proof than naturally
belongs to any matter at issue arouses the suspicion that
he is really seeking to evade belief rather than to attain
it. And surely the proof for the Virgin Birth is clear
and abundant enough for all who will accept it.

Just see what unbelief in the Virgin Birth leads to. If
we reject this record, then we practically assert, that all
of these witnesses are liars. Joseph, who is described
here as "a just man," who alone could have told about
his dream, and the other matters connected with his side
of the incident, who knew that he was not the father of
the unborn child, and who changed his merciful plan to
put Mary away privily, after the angel revealed to him
that God was the father, and who declared that he did
not know Mary in the relationship of husband and wife
until after the birth of Jesus; Mary who alone could
have told of the marvelous experiences through which
she passed, and who declared specifically to the angel that
she was a pure woman—that she had never "known a
man";—Matthew, an experienced business man, who in
the light of the facts presented to him said, "Now the
birth of Jesus was on this wise"; Luke, who has been
commended for his accuracy by Sir William Ramsay,
and other modern scholars, Luke, who was a scientist and

physician, and a historian so careful and exact that he introduces his gospel by saying: "Forasmuch as many have taken in hand to set forth in order a declaration of those things which are most surely believed among us, even as they delivered them unto us, which from the beginning were eyewitnesses, and ministers, of the word. It seemed good to me also, having had *perfect understanding* of all things *from the very first,* to write unto thee in order, most excellent Theophilus, that thou mightest know the *certainty of those things;* wherein thou hast been instructed" (Luke 1:1–4); Elizabeth, who tells us that she was so strangely moved by these miraculous events that she called Mary "the mother of my Lord"; the prophet Simeon, having a reputation, according to the narrative, as a "just and devout man," to whom it was revealed that he should see the Messiah, and, who when he saw the infant Jesus in the temple, recognized Him as the Heaven-sent Messiah, took him up in his arms, blessed God, and said:

"Lord, now lettest thou thy servant depart in peace, according to thy word. For mine eyes have seen thy salvation, which thou hast prepared before the face of all people; a light to light the Gentiles, and the glory of thy people Israel" (Luke 2:29–32).

The aged prophetess Anna, famous for her piety, fastings and prayers, who gave thanks unto God when she saw the infant Jesus and who spake of Him "all them that looked for redemption;" the Angel Gabriel, who said to the Virgin: "The Holy Ghost shall come upon thee, and the power of the Highest shall overshadow thee, and that holy thing which shall be born of thee shall be called the Son of God;"—all of these are either self-deluded, crack-brained fanatics, or else deliberate falsifiers, unless the virgin birth is a true fact, as recorded.

It is not true, as my opponent said, that Luke's narrative concerning the Virgin Birth has nothing stronger than the angel's *prophesy* that Mary the Virgin would conceive and bring forth the Son of God by the Holy Spirit. On the other hand, Luke records Mary's specific statement that the thing which the angel had told her would come to pass *had actually come to pass in her.* Mary said to Elizabeth:

"My soul doth magnify the Lord and my spirit hath rejoiced in God my Savior, for *He hath regarded the low estate of His handmaiden.* For Behold! All generations shall call me blessed. For *He that is mighty hath done to me great things and holy is His name.*" (Luke 1:46–49).

Here is a direct statement that God had actually performed that which the angel had prophesied. The twisting of this matter by my opponent is a capital illustration of how modernists strain and tug to wrest even Holy Scripture, in their effort to make good on their own subjective scepticisms and naturalistic theories. The Modernists even endeavor to make the Bible itself say just the exact opposite of what it is trying to say to us. The glorious truth of the Virgin Birth has suffered more than almost any other Bible doctrine by these unfair methods, and it is because of the fact that the attack here is merely the beginning of a wider attack on Bible doctrines in general. Just as Bishop Manning said in his letter, from which I quoted, the attack is not merely on the Virgin birth, but it is on all miracles—in fact on the supernatural in any form.

NO SELF-CONTRADICTIONS

My opponent's statements that Luke and Matthew contradict themselves in connection with the generalogies, and therefore are not good witnesses, are also wholly without warrant. The facts are, as I set forth in my first speech, that Matthew gave the *legal* genealogy of Jesus through Joseph, his legal father, and Luke the natural genealogy through his Mother, by Heli, her father, etc.

It is simply absurd to argue that a careful business man like Matthew, and a trained scientist and scrupulously exact historian like Luke would contradict themselves within three chapters of their own works. There is no contradiction, and they are both thoroughly competent witnesses. But even if there were difficulties in the genealogies, these difficulties on minor questions cannot possibly nullify the direct and explicit statements of both these authors that the Virgin Birth was a fact.

WHY THE BIBLE REFERS TO JESUS AS "JOSEPH'S SON."

Nor can my opponent's references to the few places where the Bible refers to Jesus as "Joseph's son" break the force of all this. I really anticipated this point in my first speech, and covered it in brief, but I will now cover it more fully in closing. It is perfectly evident that these references to Jesus as "Joseph's son" were founded upon the fact that Jesus was the *legal* or adopted son of Joseph, and that adequately accounts for them all. Take the case of the question in Matthew 13:55: "Is not this the carpenter's son?" This question was asked by the unbelieving Jews of Nazareth. The community of unbelievers there, of course, would not know the inside facts about Jesus' miraculous birth. It was natural for them, therefore, to ask the question in just that way. Where this expression was used by Philip it was used *when he first met Jesus* and, therefore, probably before he had learned all of the inside facts as to Jesus's miraculous origin. Philip said: "We have found him, of whom Moses in the law, and the prophets did write, Jesus of Nazareth, the son of Joseph" (John 1:45). But at worst this could mean nothing more than in the other cases,—a recognition that Joseph was the legal father of Jesus. As to the question in John 6:42 where it is written: "Is not this Jesus, the son of Joseph, whose father and mother we know?" These words were spoken also by critical, faultfinding Jews who were not disciples,

and they are given in the Bible only as a quotation from
such people.

In the case where Mary herself, when she found Jesus
in the Temple, after he had been lost, said to Him—
"Behold thy father and I have sought thee sorrowing,"
it is evident that there was no other form in which she
could put the statement, since Jesus was Joseph's adopted
son. But that Mary had given to Jesus some information about the miraculous and marvelous manner of His
birth is indicated in Jesus's reply to her statement that
she and His "father" had sought Him sorrowing. It is
written here: "He said unto them, how is it that ye
sought me; wist ye not that I must be about *my* Father's
business." Did not Jesus quite delicately here remind
His mother that He knew that His real father was the
heavenly Father? Must he not have put the emphasis on
the word "my"—"*my* father"? That there was some
such deeper meaning in this conversation, is indicated
further by the statement which Luke makes that while
Jesus went back with his parents to Nazareth and was
subject unto them, nevertheless, "His mother kept all
these sayings in her heart" (Luke 2:48-51). In fact,
that Mary all the way saw something of the deeper meaning of the miraculous manner of Jesus' birth is indicated
by this and other such expressions, as, for example, when
she said to those at the wedding feast in Cana of Galilee,
before Jesus performed his miracle of turning the water
into wine: "Whatsoever he saith unto you, do it." (John
2:5).

And that Jesus also understood His unusual earthly
origin is proved by such expressions from Him as "I
am from above" (John 8:23); and "I know whence I
came" (John 8:14); and "the Father that sent me" (John
8:16); and again where Jesus said emphatically to His
foes: "If God were your Father, ye would love me: for
I proceeded forth and came from God; neither came I of

myself (that would be by natural means), but he sent me" (John 8:42).

The argument, therefore, that the explicit teachings of the Bible that Jesus was virgin born and that He was not Joseph's natural son should be rejected because of these references to Him as "Joseph's son"—are simply not tenable. Such references were precisely what we have today under similar circumstances. I once had a family in my church in which there was an adopted son. I did not know until I had been pastor of the church for four years, and had been often in that home, that the boy was really an adopted son. He referred to his foster father as "father," and the father always referred to him as his "son." These references, therefore, to Jesus as "Joseph's son" are perfectly plain, and they are simply overwhelmed by the disclosure of the unquestionable facts in the other parts of the records, where it is plainly taught that He was not the natural son of Joseph but that He came by miraculous conception and Virgin Birth.

SUMMARY·

It all comes down, at last, then, to this: We have here this unbroken, historic record, namely, the Bible; and we have also the testimony of these good men and women concerning the virgin birth and the events that cluster around it. Now on what grounds are we asked to reject these records and to declare the testimony of these witnesses false? On no ground whatever that I have ever been able to find, or that my opponent has given here, except just plain scepticism, stubborn doubts, and a lot of pedantic jargon spun from the nebulous intangibility of subjective ideas, rather than the solid substance of objective reality and historic fact!

On one side, as Dr. Orr, Dr. MacNaugher, and a host of other scholars have proved, are all of the unmutilated manuscripts and all the trustworthy versions containing these accounts of the virgin birth. And on the other side, only two or three documents of doubtful standing, about which the sceptical scholars themselves do not agree, and which were evidently mutilated by doubters. The virgin birth of Jesus is a question of historic fact. The fact is asserted and testified to by witnesses. These assertions and the record of his testimony are in the Bible. To disprove the fact and win this debate it was necessary for my opponent to show that the Bible record of the virgin birth is unbelievable and that the witnesses that testify concerning it are untrustworthy. Now I submit that he simply has not done this. He has made a brilliant effort, and has done just as well as any doubter can do, but the facts are simply against him. Mere minor difficulties over this secondary matter or the other, such as occur in connection with any event of ancient history, cannot break the force of the main facts—

Therefore, I ask a decision for the affirmative.

NO REFLECTION UPON MARY OR MARRIAGE

I wish to say, in closing, that there is no ground for my opponent's contention that the Virgin Birth of Christ is any reflection upon the sanctity of marriage or any "insult," as he expressed it, to that holy estate. Jesus was absolutely unique, and it was necessary that, as the sinless Savior of the world, He should be miraculously conceived and born of the virgin. So far from it being true that there is any reflection upon marriage in the Virgin Birth of our Lord, it is rather true that the respect and veneration which the world has given to Mary, the virgin mother of our Lord, has been one of the greatest bulwarks of the sanctity of the marriage vow and one of the finest influences for increasing humanity's respect for womanhood and motherhood.

I close, therefore, with a further word of defence of the virgin Mary. To deny these Bible records and to assert that Jesus was not virgin born, is really to cast reproach upon Mary's good name. The angel Gabriel said that Jesus was "the Son of God." If now He was the Son of God, then He was God's Son and not Joseph's son. Joseph made it perfectly plain that he was not the father of Jesus, and if Joseph was not the father of Jesus, then, unless Gabriel's statement is true, He was the Son of some unknown man and was born out of wedlock. Therefore, He was a bastard, and Mary His Mother was both a liar and an impure woman.

Such a conclusion is revolting, horrible, and utterly unreasonable, in the light both of the Bible record and the after influence of Jesus of Nazareth and Mary His mother.

Rather than cast such a reproach upon her, therefore, we should stand by the Bible's declaration that all the after ages should "call her blessed." Because she was so highly honored of God: because the very angels of paradise spoke to her face to face; because she was the connecting link between earth and heaven; because her pure body was the channel through which the Son of God came to save the world; because Jesus' first look of awakening consciousness rested upon her beautiful face and His last agonized glance from the cross beheld her; because she was willing to discharge the duties of motherhood; because she did a true woman's work in the world; because her soul walked in fellowship and communion with God; we hold her up as the ideal woman, wife and mother of all the ages. We magnify the Lord with her, we magnify the Lord for her, and with all the generations,—past, present and future,—we "call her blessed!"

IV

REBUTTAL FOR THE NEGATIVE[1]

When the Western Union messenger boy delivered my
copy of Dr. Parks' book, "WHAT IS MODERNISM,"
yesterday, I noticed that according to the slip which I
had to sign, Dr. Straton had already received his copy,
so I was quite aware of the fact that he was familiar with
the book. When Dr. Straton had not arrived tonight at
three minutes to eight I presumed he had read Dr. Parks'
book and had become converted to the Modernist point
of view and that therefore there would be no debate!

In one instance tonight my worthy opponent accused
me of stopping too soon when I was reading a certain
Bible passage. Let me point out to you that he did not
correctly convey Dr. Parks' meaning when he read only
part of what Dr. Parks says on page 64 in this book.
The sentence which follows the last one which my worthy
opponent read reads, "But nevertheless there are many
scholars of repute who are convinced that the definite
statements contained in the first and third gospels—that
Jesus was born without the agency of a human father—
are a later insertion worked into the earlier tradition."
You can easily see why my opponent stopped where he
did. I claim that Dr. Parks' book is a strong argument
on the negative side of the debate.

REBUTTAL OF FIRST SPEECH

Let us take up in order the points made by my opponent in his first speech:

He began by saying that according to the subject to-

[1] By Rev. Charles Francis Potter.

night, the Virgin Birth, we are in the realm of miracle because the phrase "the 'miraculous' Virgin Birth of Jesus Christ" occurs in the wording of the resolution. I challenge that statement immediately. We are not in the realm of miracle; we are in the realm of fact, for the statement of the resolution is "Resolved that the Miraculous Birth of Jesus Christ is a *Fact*." Consequently we must debate on facts and evidence. If we were in the realm of miracle there would be no need of debating at all.

His next point was a statement that our late presidents Harding and Wilson were opposed to Modernism. Even if this statement were true, that is no argument for to-night's debate. And right here let me call the attention of the judges to the fact that at least three-fourths of all the matter introduced by my worthy opponent is utterly irrelevant to the question at issue. He said also that what appears to be a miracle from man's side is not a miracle from God's side, and that therefore we cannot argue from our own ignorance and limitations. Did my worthy opponent forget that that is the only way we can argue? We cannot jump outside our limitations in order to conduct this debate. We must argue from the human side because that is the only side we can see.

My opponent's long dissertation on his X-Ray experience is utterly irrelevant. What argument is it for this debate that he looked through his own body? That proves nothing about the Virgin Birth. He was continually diverting our attention from the issue. For instance, he said "the whole question is, do we believe in a living God?" That is not the question which we are debating tonight. When you ask, do we believe in a living God, you are implying that if we believe in a living God, we think that such a God could have made possible the Virgin Birth, but the debate question is not, *Could* God have done it, but, *did* he do it; not was the Virgin

birth a *possibility*, but was it a *fact*. Simply to say that
with God nothing is impossible, diverts our attention from
the real issue under discussion. There were several
serious gaps in his logic also:

When he said "If God made Adam without a mother,
could he not make Christ without a father?" he neglected
to prove his premise, and I for one am not willing to
grant that God made Adam without a mother.

My opponent's quoting of Old Testament prophecies
was very unfortunate for his side. Genesis 3:15, where
it says that the seed of the woman shall bruise the serpent's head with his heel, can only by a wild flight of the
imagination be taken to have any connection with the
Virgin Birth. Isaiah 7:14, "Behold a Virgin shall be
with child" is not at all helpful for the affirmative tonight. The word translated "virgin" is a Hebrew word
"almah" which means "young marriageable woman." An
"almah" may or may not be a virgin. If the Hebrew
word for virgin had been used it would be "bethulah."
My opponent's reference to Isaiah 9 is not at all convincing. Of this child who is to come the prophecy
which he read says that the government shall be upon
his shoulder, his name shall be called Wonderful, Counsellor, and he shall sit on the throne of David. Not one of
these things was fulfilled in the case of Jesus. The government was never upon his shoulder for he deliberately
refused any connection with politics. He was never called
in New Testament times by the name "Wonderful," or
"Counsellor," nor did he ever sit upon the throne of
David.

My worthy opponent referred to the myths of other
virgin births as being grotesque and ridiculous. I fail
to see the bearing of that upon the argument. Nevertheless, I might say in return that if all the contemporary
stories about the virgin birth of Jesus had been included
in Matthew and Luke, they would now be recognized as

just as ridiculous and grotesque as some of the stories in other mythologies.   In the Apocryphal Gospel according to Mary and in The Protevangelion, books which were once accepted by Christians, but which were left out when the New Testament was finally compiled, you get legends about the birth of Jesus which are quite preposterous.

In his first speech my opponent said that when we come to examine the evidence for the Virgin Birth we should weigh the evidence pro and con, and then accept the story in the light of our own faith.   But faith is a dangerous matter when it comes to a question of fact.   Faith and inclination are very closely associated.   Indeed there are times when I suspect that the small boy was right who said that "faith is believin' what yeh know ain't so."

When my worthy opponent said that the Virgin Birth stories were in all the original unmutilated manuscripts, he may have given you a wrong impression.   Please remember that the oldest of these manuscripts that he refers to is dated 350 A. D.   None of the original manuscripts are in existence.   What we have are only tenth-hand copies.

My opponent says that we must not cut out of the Bible the passages which refer to the Virgin Birth, but in his first speech and in his rebuttal he deliberately refused to recognize the verses to which I called your attention which stated that Joseph was Jesus' father.   We have just as much right to omit the Virgin Birth verses as he has to omit the verses which say that Joseph was his father.

He was treading on dangerous ground too when he said that the date of the birth of Jesus is firmly fixed because our Anno Domini dating is based on the date of his birth.   May I suggest that even in the orthodox churches it is taught that the date of Jesus' birth was B. C. 4, while many scholars place it as B. C. 6.   The

date is not firmly fixed. No one knows exactly when
Jesus was born. The two letters "A. D." by no means
prove the virgin birth.

Do not be deceived either by the false dilemma in which
my opponent tried to place us. He said that if the Holy
Ghost was not Jesus' father, then some other man than
Joseph must have been his father, and that therefore we
make Mary and Joseph cheats and liars. This is not
true. We are not obliged to think that another man was
Jesus' father if we do not believe the legend that the Holy
Ghost was. We can believe that Joseph was his father
and we have more New Testament evidence for it than
for the other view.

My opponent did attempt to explain the several references to Joseph's fatherhood of Jesus by saying that
Joseph was the legal father and Jesus his adopted son.
But that is neither stated nor implied in any part of the
New Testament. When my opponent says that Joseph
was the *legal* father he is interpolating a word. He has
become a higher critic himself. The only place where it
says that Joseph was the *legal* father of Jesus and that
Jesus was Joseph's *adopted* son is in the Gospel According to Straton.

My worthy opponent was so rash as to say in his first
speech that Mark, John and Paul had told of the Virgin
Birth and that he would prove in his rebuttal, if necessary,
that they did. But in his rebuttal he did not give one
instance where Mark, John or Paul stated the fact of the
Virgin Birth. It is impossible to find any place where
they did. I challenge him or any one in the audience to
bring one such verse as evidence, and although I am only
a poor preacher I am willing to give $100 to any one
who will prove that Mark, John or Paul stated the fact
of the Virgin Birth.

In his first speech my opponent attempted to prove the
Virgin Birth was a fact and that therefore it was essen-

tial to Christian doctrine. He did not prove it a fact, but even if he had, that would not have made it essential to Christian doctrine. Foot-washing was a fact in the early church. Jesus, according to the New Testament, practiced it, and there are Christian sects today who practice it, but I do not believe that my worthy opponent would consider foot-washing an essential Christian doctrine.

Furthermore, my opponent made a misstatement when he said that the Virgin Birth is in all the great creeds. Of the three great ecumenical creeds, the Athanasian is the longest and most detailed, and it does not state the Virgin Birth. Neither does the Nicene Creed in its original form. Consequently my opponent was wrong when he said that the Virgin Birth is essential because of its universal acceptation. It has not been accepted "always, everywhere, and by all," as I have sufficiently shown in my main speech.

My opponent put to me a challenging question based upon two premises. He said, "If the church has the right to say what is her true and essential Christian doctrine, and if the church universal has declared the Virgin Birth true and essential, then what authority is there in the hands of an insignificant minority to overthrow her faith and practice?" This is the exact question because I took it down carefully in shorthand. And I answer that question by saying that all progress, both within the church and outside the church, has come at the hands of an intelligent minority. That is the way progress always comes.

REBUTTAL OF THE REBUTTAL

We come now to the rebuttal of Dr. Straton's second speech. My opponent tried to dodge the word "essential" by pointing out that in the phrasing of the debate the word "essential" is preceded by "an," rather than "the," but even with the "an" I am justified in maintaining that if the Virgin Birth is an essential doctrine its omission shuts out from Christianity the one who omits it. If the Virgin Birth is an *essential* Christian doctrine, those who omit it are not Christians.

In my opponent's summary at the end of his rebuttal he made several unsupported statements. In attempting to prove that the Virgin Birth is found all through the Bible he stated that it starts from the beginning of Genesis, but I have shown that the only verse which he mentions has nothing to do with the Virgin Birth whatever. The reference in Isaiah to the "almah" is not germane to the debate, and his statement that we find the Virgin Birth in the entire narrative is only an unsupported assertion.

I fail to see why my opponent brought up the matter of the order in which the books were written, inasmuch as I stated myself that the arguments hold just as well no matter in what order we take the books.

My opponent quoted some phrases of Mark and John and Paul which he says prove the Virgin Birth, but I hope you noticed that not one of the phrases stated that the Virgin Birth was a fact or an essential Christian doctrine. In fact, they do not mention the Virgin Birth. They are only general statements as to Jesus' relation to God, and it is only when they are "interpreted," or misinterpreted, by my worthy opponent that they seem to have any bearing upon the Virgin Birth. Let us take these references in the order in which he stated them:

First, my opponent made a great deal of the fact that Mark's gospel, the first verse, states that Jesus was "the

* Note: According to Webster's Dictionary the word "essential" means.
"That which makes an object what it is."
"Important in the highest degree."
"Indispensably necessary."

son of God." Very well. I do not deny that. But that does not prove the Virgin Birth. He could have been the son of God in some other way. Indeed, in Luke 3:38, it states that Adam was the son of God. Does that prove that Adam was born of a virgin? The beginning of John's gospel states that "the word was made flesh." From that, my opponent, with marvelous lack of logic, deduced that the Virgin Birth is a fact. The verse certainly does not say that Jesus was born of a virgin. When John speaks of Jesus as "the only begotten of the Father," does that prove the Virgin Birth, and when my worthy opponent quotes Paul as saying of Christ "who is the image of the invisible, the first-born of every creature," and that "God sent his own son, who was made in the likeness of man," do any of these verses even suggest, to a logical mind, that Jesus was necessarily born of a virgin?

It was a dangerous thing when my opponent asserted that the Bible is the Blackstone of religion, and that therefore it is proved that Jesus was born of a virgin. I have already shown that there are more verses in the Bible which call Joseph Jesus' father than there are verses which maintain that he was born of a virgin who conceived by the Holy Ghost. If the Bible is the Blackstone of religion, the negative of this debate is therefore proved.

My opponent's closing remarks included the rather rash statement that if the Virgin Birth is not true then all these are liars, namely, Joseph, Mary, Elizabeth, Simeon, Matthew and Luke. But of these six the first four have written no gospel. What comes from them is not direct, but second hand, many times removed.

As for Matthew and Luke I have shown tonight that their testimony is self-contradictory, and therefore cannot be accepted as conclusive evidence.

CONCLUSION

I therefore maintain, Honorable Judges, Ladies and Gentlemen, that both in the first affirmative speech and in the rebuttal, my opponent has not proved that the Virgin Birth is either a fact or an essential Christian doctrine.

V

THE JUDGES' REPORT

Presiding officer Colonel Robert Starr Allyn introduced Mr. Ernest F. Conant of the New York Bar, who, on behalf of the other judges, Mr. H. F. Gunnison, publisher of the Brooklyn Eagle, and Mr. Louis Annin Ames, president of the Sons of the American Revolution, announced that the judges had come to a split decision with the weight of opinion in favor of the negative.

WAS CHRIST BOTH
GOD AND MAN?

Rev. JOHN ROACH STRATON, D.D.
and
Rev. CHARLES FRANCIS POTTER, M.A., S.T.M.

This book contains the only official text of the fourth of a series of five theological debates between Rev. Charles Francis Potter, challenger, and Dr. John Roach Straton, to be published under the following titles:

I: THE BATTLE OVER THE BIBLE
Question: The Bible is the Infallible Word of God

II: EVOLUTION VERSUS CREATION
Question: The Earth and Man Came by Evolution

III: THE VIRGIN BIRTH—FACT OR FICTION?
Question: The Miraculous Virgin Birth of Jesus Christ is a Fact and an Essential Christian Doctrine

IV: WAS CHRIST BOTH GOD AND MAN?
Question: Jesus Christ Was Entirely Man Instead of Incarnate Deity.

V: UTOPIA—BY MAN'S EFFORT OR CHRIST'S RETURN?
Question: Jesus Christ Will Return in Bodily Presence to this Earth and Establish the Reign of Universal Peace and Righteousness.

Dr. Straton takes the affirmative in all but the second and fourth debates. The first debate was held in Calvary Baptist Church, New York, on December 20, 1923, the second in Carnegie Hall, January 28, 1924, and the third and fourth also in Carnegie Hall, on March 22 and April 28, 1924. Copies of each debate will be published separately at 50 cents each and the entire series on completion will be reissued in one volume, cloth at $2.00.

These debates may be obtained from the Religious Literature Departments of the Calvary Baptist Church and the West Side Unitarian Church or at all booksellers.

NEW YORK : GEORGE H. DORAN COMPANY

WAS CHRIST BOTH GOD AND MAN?

Fourth in the Series of
Fundamentalist-Modernist Debates

between

Rev. JOHN ROACH STRATON, D.D.
PASTOR, CALVARY BAPTIST CHURCH
NEW YORK

and

Rev. CHARLES FRANCIS POTTER, M.A., S.T.M.
MINISTER, WEST SIDE UNITARIAN CHURCH
NEW YORK

NEW YORK
GEORGE H. DORAN COMPANY

WAS CHRIST BOTH GOD AND MAN?
—C—
PRINTED IN THE UNITED STATES OF AMERICA

INTRODUCTION

By Rev. John Roach Straton, D.D.

I only wish to say, by way of introduction to my share in this debate on the deity of Jesus Christ, that the hard work which I did in preparation for the debate was a labor of love, and in some faint degree an expression of gratitude to Jesus for lifting me out of my sins and giving me a new heart and putting before me the blessed hope of an eternity of fellowship with Him and my loved ones who have gone before. I was happy, therefore, that the Judges gave me a unanimous decision.

Looking at the series up to date, the interesting fact has been pointed out that the side of old-fashioned religion has won the only two unanimous decisions yet given in the debates. The first unanimous decision was that which I had the honor of winning in the debate on Evolution; and the second was that in this debate on the deity of our Lord. In the case of the other two debates, there was a split verdict.

Hoping that the added illustrations, etc., which I had in my manuscript, but which I did not have time to give in full in the oral debate, may be of value for reference, we have agreed to their use in this printed form of the debate.

As I see it, there can be no question about the value of these discussions to the Lord's cause. While it was painful to hear Mr. Potter's radical views, it needs to be remembered that these views of the Modernists have been paraded now in the New York papers and other papers for a long time. Columns of matter every week are de-

voted to reporting the sermons and addresses of radical
religious leaders, and the opportunity to get the other
side—God's old-fashioned truth—before the people was
a great and valuable opportunity. It is significant that
there have been conversions as the result of the messages
in these debates from time to time, and we know that
God's word will not return unto Him void, even as He
has promised.

A flood of letters and messages has come in from far
and near thanking me for the service rendered and the
hard work done in connection with these debates. The
following extract is typical of expressions that have come
from Christian leaders, not only throughout America, but
from some even across the seas. The famous evangelist
and Bible expositor, from whose letter the following extract is taken, is one of the strongest preachers and one of
the most thorough-going Fundamentalists in the entire
world. In addition to other kind things, he says this
about the debates:

"You did the greatest work of your life in accepting these
debates. It means more for the truth than any other thing
that was ever done in New York. And the influence reaches
far beyond New York. Your address on Evolution is the
greatest thing I ever read on the subject."

If God has used my poor effects, then I rejoice, and
I give Him all the glory.

JOHN ROACH STRATON.

Study of Calvary Baptist Church,
New York City.

INTRODUCTION

By Rev. Charles Francis Potter, M.A., S.T.M.

My worthy opponent has no greater appreciation of
the worth of Jesus of Nazareth than I. He thinks that
Jesus was very God of very God and wished to be so
considered. I find no warrant for acceptance of deity in
the reported words of Jesus and think that could Jesus
return, he would be surprised and pained at the mistaken
ascriptions of deity given to him. The trouble with
those who insist on the deity of Jesus is simply that they
do not rate humanity high enough. Jesus was far greater
than they suspect, but his greatness is an evidence not
of deity but of the great possibilities of spiritually cultivated human nature.

Charles Francis Potter.

Study of West Side Unitarian Church,
New York City.

P. S.—My opponent has with my consent added to
his oral debate considerable related matter. Mine appears
as given in Carnegie Hall.

CONTENTS

I

FOR THE AFFIRMATIVE[1]

RESOLVED: That Jesus Christ was Entirely Man instead of Incarnate Deity.

Mr. Chairman, Honorable Judges, Worthy Opponent, and
    Ladies and Gentlemen of both this visible audience
    and the Greater Invisible Audience:

We are gathered here tonight to consider, pro and con, a most important subject—the Deity of Jesus. Our resolution is—

"RESOLVED: That Jesus Christ was Entirely Man instead of Incarnate Deity."

By the very nature of the theological question my opponent should be taking the affirmative, and I should be upholding the negative. It is, however, my turn to take the affirmative and consequently the question has been phrased in such a way that I may do so. It is understood between my opponent and myself that the issue of this debate is the deity of Jesus Christ. It is admitted by both sides that he was truly man, but my worthy opponent takes the position that he was more than man— that he was also incarnate deity, the God-man. This I deny, and that is the issue of the debate.

DEFINITIONS

In order to avoid any misunderstanding, and in order to profit by the experience of the previous debates, it will be necessary for us to define the words used in this

[1] First speech for the affirmative by Rev. Charles Francis Potter, Minister West Side Unitarian Church.

11

debate.   I shall use the Webster and the Standard Dictionaries.

Both dictionaries agree in defining "deity" as "the Supreme Being: God."   Deity and divinity should be distinguished.   Deity is from *"deus,"* a god; divinity is from *"divus,"* godlike.   Webster defines God as "the eternal and infinite Spirit, the Creator and Sovereign of the universe."

The Standard defines God as "the one Supreme Being, self-existent and eternal; the infinite maker, sustainer, and ruler of the universe."   This dictionary also defines "infinite" as "so great as to be immeasurable and unbounded; limitless; inexhaustible," saying further "Infinite signifies without bounds or limits in any way."

Webster defines "infinite" as "without limit in power, capacity, knowledge or excellence."

Both dictionaries define "incarnate" as "invested with flesh."   It is obvious then that "finite," by its very nature and derivation means the direct opposite of infinite, and nothing can be both finite and infinite at the same time.

My opponent then has the difficult task of proving Jesus to be both God and man, both finite and infinite at the same time.

THE DIVINITY OF HUMANITY

I come here with no idea of tearing down any one's faith.   I come simply to assert my own.   There is a very positive and firm conviction in my heart that Jesus means more to us as man than he could possibly mean as God. It is the divinity of humanity as seen in Jesus and as taught by Jesus, which is my daily inspiration and hope. As Emerson has put it, "One man was true to what is in you and me."

In the sublime figure of Jesus we see the possibilities of human nature.   More than in any other man we recognize in him a development of man Godward. He felt so close to God that he could call him "Father." His consciousness of God was so great that an ignorant age said that he must be God himself, and thereby they removed him from them. He was constantly pointing out that not only was God *his* Father, but that God is *our* Father. His whole teaching emphasizes the fact that the difference between Jesus and us is one of *degree* and not one of kind. He repeatedly asserted the divine possibility in every human soul. Where his contemporaries saw only vileness and corruption, he saw the image of God. It is his sublime faith in men which wrought changes in those with whom he came in contact, and still does.

He dared men to believe in themselves, challenged them to live worthy of their relationship to God, and when they took him at his word, and life opened for them with grand new meanings, they came to him in gratitude. So great was their gratitude that they began considering him more than man. They said a little later, "This one could not have been man. He must have been God come down from the clouds and walking among us."

THE TRAGEDY OF CHRISTIANITY

They deified him and this is the tragedy of Christianity. The deification of Jesus is the very negation of all his teaching. It is the supreme heresy of Christian theology and will so be seen in future ages. There were attempts, even during his life time, to attribute perfection to him, and these attempts he indignantly and sorrowfully repudiated. The saddest verse in the Bible is not "Jesus wept"; it is not the one which tells of the Crucification, nor even the one which depicts the heart-breaking scene in Gethsemane. It is the simple despairing cry, "Why call ye *me* good? There is *none* good but one, that is God" (Mark 10:18). Could God have said that? No. It was the

cry of a very wonderful man who was trying to get
people to realize that they could be human beings and
still be as good as he or better.   And all because of his
very goodness, men have negated his teaching by saying
he was too good to be a man; he must have been God.
Surely it is obvious to thinking men that making him
God takes the very soul out of his message.   Here was no
deity disguised in flesh, no God parading among men,
but a simple, honest, loving man, trying to get men to see
their own infinite possibilities.   "The Kingdom of God
is within you," he cried, "Be ye therefore perfect," he
urged them, "even as your Father in Heaven is perfect."
He was challenging their own latent divinity.

Did you ever seriously consider how really unfair it
would have been for a disguised God to urge men to become perfect?   If he was God he could not sin.   He could
not really be tempted.   If he was God the whole verse is
untrue which says that "he was tempted in all points like
as we are."   It is an utter moral impossibility for a God to
be tempted.   No one can be tempted to do wrong unless
it is possible for him to do wrong.   Therefore, for a
being who could not possibly sin, to urge men to be perfect, would be utterly inconsistent with a loving heart.
If Jesus, our example, was a God come down from
heaven, then he was merely a tantalus.   But if Jesus was
a man who overcame his temptations, who was tempted
and could have fallen but resisted those temptations, and
won through to a sturdy character, then he is forever an
inspiration to the entire human race.   This is the gospel
I preach.   This is the gospel Jesus himself preached.
Men of misunderstanding have attached to the simple
message of Jesus the great body of theology connected
with the doctrine of the deity of Jesus.   No wonder the
world is not yet Christian, when the very message of
Jesus is misunderstood.

DEITY REMOVES JESUS FROM US

The 'deity of Jesus' doctrine removed Jesus so far from men that instead of finding him a helpful inspiration, a leader to bring men to God, he became so far away that the Roman Catholic church very rightly developed the doctrine of the Virgin Mary who was nearer to humanity and did understand humanity. And millions of men have prayed to the Virgin Mary to lead them to Jesus because of the very fact that the deification of Jesus had put him out of their reach. Roman Catholicism is more consistent, and understands human nature better than does orthodox Protestantism. We need some good man or woman to show us how to live, and to point the way to God, some helpful elder brother or sister who has been tempted in all points like as we are.

DEIFICATIONS COMMON THEN

It is not to be wondered at that men deified Jesus in spite of his protests, for deifications were more common in those days than now. In the year 307 B. C. Demetrius and his father, Antigonus, who freed Athens from the tyrant Cassander, were greeted by the thankful Athenians as saviour gods. They even went so far as to say that Demetrius was so good that he must have been born of divine parents, so they attributed divine parentage to him, and called Poseidon, his father, and Aphrodite, his mother. In Syria, Antiochus of the house of Seleucus was called "Theos," the Greek word for God, and his son Antiochus was called Antiochus Epiphane's, or God-manifest. Antiochus Epiphanes lived 175 B. C.

On the famous Rosetta stone 205 B. C. Ptolemy V is called eternal-lived, and the living image of Zeus. At Ephesus, Julius Caesar, 44 B. C., was called God-manifest and the common saviour of human life. Still nearer to the time of Jesus, in the year 11 B. C., the Emperor Augustus was called, Lord, Saviour, Son of God, and "Zeus out of Father Zeus." The day of his birth was called the beginning of good tidings for the world, and the story was current that the Roman Senate had decreed the slaughter of all children born the same year as Augustus. These attributive names of deification in carved inscriptions, were discovered late in the 19th Century by an archaeological expedition at Halicarnassus. It was easy for Jesus' disciples living in the Roman world and influenced by Roman thought-conceptions to attribute deity to Jesus, without realizing the philosophical and theological difficulties they were raising.

HISTORIC PROTESTS AGAINST DEITY IDEA

When you believe in the deity of Jesus you are not believing in the teachings of Jesus himself, but in the doctrine which grew up about him—the explanation given by an ignorant age to account for an unusual man, the same easy thoughtless explanation which has been given for other unusual men, Buddha, for instance. Now, this doctrine of the deity of Jesus caused a great deal of trouble in the early church. Common sense men said then, as they do today, how could Jesus have been God when we know that he was man? Church council after church council was called to solve the difficulty. Long documents were drawn up to explain the inexplainable, so that theology became synonymous with wordy nothings. Even today the common people laugh at theological verbiage.

These councils continued for years, and finally, October 8, 451 A. D., the Council of Chalcedon produced the following remarkable document. It is a statement attempting to reconcile the deity of Jesus with his humanity. I want to read it to you verbatim:

"We, then, following the holy fathers, all with one consent teach men to confess one and the same Son our Lord Jesus Christ: the same perfect in Godhead and also perfect in Manhood; truly God and truly Man; of a reasonable soul and body; consubstantial with the Father according to the Godhead, and consubstantial with us according to the Manhood; in all things like unto us without sin; begotten before all ages of the Father according to the Godhead, and in these latter days for us and our salvation born of the virgin Mary the mother of God according to the Manhood; one and the same Christ, Son, Lord, only begotten, to be acknowledged in two natures, unconfusedly, unchangeably, indivisibly, inseparably, the distinction of natures being by no means taken away by the union, but rather the property of each nature being preserved, and concurring in one person and one hypostasis, not parted or divided into two persons, but one and the same Son and only begotten God, Word, Lord, Jesus Christ, as the prophets, from the beginning have declared concerning him, and the Lord Jesus Christ himself hath taught us, and the Creed of the holy fathers hath delivered to us."

Can you understand that? Does it really explain how Jesus could be both God and man at the same time? It certainly does not. No council and no theologian can ever reconcile those two things.

ABANDONING REASON

If a person accepts the doctrine of the deity of Jesus he must leave his reason behind and accept it as an act of faith. Now, if we abandon reason, where are we? The whole world depends upon reason. Once you abandon it, you find yourself in constant difficulty. Reason has been achieved by the human race at a tremendous cost. Looking back through the long centuries and milleniums of man's evolution we see that reason is the thing which differentiates man from the beasts. If you abandon it, you abandon the legacy of the race. Now, if any one wants to accept the doctrine of the deity of Jesus by faith, or intuition, or any other process, very well and good: I would not for a moment hinder him;

WAS CHRIST BOTH GOD AND MAN?

but this debate is a reasonable discussion, and what we are concerned with tonight is not whether or not a person can accept the deity of Jesus by faith, but whether or not he can reconcile it with his reason. We are debating tonight a matter of fact. The question is not whether we by faith believe in the deity of Jesus—there would be no difficulty about that—you can believe by faith in anything, and the more impossible the thing is, the more some people seem to be ready to believe it. Faith very easily becomes gullibility, and history reports many instances of men who, stirred by emotion, have declared their belief in utter impossibilities. When men declare that their honest reason forbids them to believe that Jesus was both God and man at the same time, that he was both finite and infinite at the same moment, theologians have said, "This is a holy mystery. You must take it on faith." By the same process you can make credulous people who trust you believe almost anything. But our debate is out of that realm. We are debating a straight proposition, and I maintain that human reason cannot accept the statement that Jesus was finite and infinite at the same time. If my opponent steps outside of reason he is begging the question and arguing beside the point. This is a matter for evidence, and I want to point out to you now some of the evidences that Jesus was not God.

A DILEMMA

One passage alone is amply sufficient for our purpose: We read in the 24th chapter of Matthew, and in the 13th chapter of Mark, that one day as Jesus sat on the Mount of Olives his disciples asked him saying, "What shall be the sign of thy coming, and of the end of the world?" Then Jesus told them the signs of his coming, how the Heavens would be shaken and how they should see the son of man coming on the clouds of Heaven with power and great glory. He said that their generation would not pass away until all those things were accomplished, but as to the time, the actual day and hour when this would come to pass, he said as follows (and this saying of his is doubly attested. It occurs in Matthew 24:36 and identically the same in Mark 13:32). The verse reads as follows:

"But of that day and hour knoweth no one, not even the angels in Heaven, neither the Son, but the Father only."

Now here is a plain statement, doubly attested, as I said. Jesus said that he did not know the day or the hour of the coming of the Son of Man. In other words, answering their question, he did not know when the end of the world was coming. Now, he either did know, or he did not know. If he did not know, then he could not have been God, for God knows all things. If he did know, then he was telling an untruth, and therefore he could not have been God. Hence this one verse alone proves my contention.

This verse has always bothered orthodox theologians, for Jesus to admit that there was something which God knew and which he, Jesus, did not know—was to deny his own deity. Consequently, Cyril, an early church Father, said Jesus only pretended not to know. Syrian Ephraim (308 A. D.) said boldly, "Christ, though he knew the moment of his advent, yet that they might not ask him any more about it, said, 'I know it not.'" You see that Cyril and Ephraim defended his deity, even at the cost of his truthfulness. Theodoret, another church Father, answering these two men, said indignantly, "If Jesus knew the day and wishing to conceal it, said he was ignorant, see what blasphemy is the result of this conclusion, the Truth tells a lie." Now, Jesus as God could not tell a lie. If he told one, he was a man and not God. But if he did not lie, then he did not know the day or the hour, and since he said God *did* know, then he himself could not possibly have been God. My opponent, therefore, is on the horns of a dilemma. His contention that Jesus was deity is refuted out of the very mouth of Jesus.

There are other verses which have always bothered those who assert the deity of Jesus—verses which cannot possibly be reconciled with the deity idea. Let us consider some of them: The New Testament is full of them. John, for instance said (John 1:18), "No man hath seen God at any time." And again in I John 4:20 we read: "He that loveth not his brother whom he hath seen, cannot love God whom he hath not seen." Now, if Jesus was God, men had certainly seen him, and these two verses of Scripture are strong evidence against the deity of Jesus.

IF JESUS WAS GOD, how then can my opponent explain the verse (John 14:12) where Jesus said to his disciples:

"The works that I do shall ye do also, and greater things than these shall ye do."

Were his disciples to become not only gods, but greater gods than Jesus?

IF JESUS WAS GOD, how could he say (John 20:17)

"I ascend unto my Father and your Father, and unto my God and your God."

How could God ascend unto himself? Notice, too, that in this phrase, he places his disciples in the same relation to his Father as he was himself. He speaks of God as "my Father and your Father," as "my God and your God."

IF JESUS WAS GOD, how could he "increase in wisdom and stature and in favor with God and man" (Luke 2:52)? Can God increase in wisdom; can he increase in favor with himself?

How could the infinite God be disappointed, as for example, when Jesus came to the fig tree (Mark 11:12–14) expecting to find figs, and found none?

IF PETER THOUGHT JESUS WAS GOD, how could he say in his Pentecostal sermon,

"Jesus of Nazareth, a *man* approved of God among you." (Acts 2:22.)

IF PAUL BELIEVED THAT JESUS WAS GOD, how could he possibly say (I Cor. 8:6)

"There is but *one* God, the *Father*, of whom are all things."

IF JESUS WAS GOD, why did he cry on the cross, as reported in Matthew 27:46 and Mark 15:34,

"My God, my God, why hast Thou forsaken me?"

Can God forsake himself?

I challenge my opponent to produce one direct statement from the sayings of Jesus, as recorded in the New Testament, where Jesus says straight out, "I am God." There are verses which, by clever casuistry, can be twisted so that they seem to mean that Jesus was God, but there is no out-and-out statement, and surely if the doctrine of the deity of Jesus is as important as orthodox Christians maintain, and if Jesus came to earth as deity, he certainly was morally obligated to declare himself in unquestionable, direct terms.

Furthermore, my opponent cannot produce one passage in the whole Bible which affirms the doctrine of the Trinity in unmistakable terms, and we all know the Trinity is the attempted theological explanation of the deity of Jesus.

I want to call your attention now to two passages, either one of which is sufficient to prove my contention this evening:

IF JESUS WAS GOD, how could he say (John 14:28)

"My Father is greater than I."

I can see no possible way in which my worthy opponent can reconcile that verse with the doctrine of the deity of Jesus.

Again,

IF JESUS WAS GOD, how could he say,

"Why callest thou me good? There is none good but one, that is, God."

This verse is absolutely destructive of the doctrine of the deity of Jesus. It is one of the best attested sayings of Jesus. It is found in Mark 10:18, Luke 18:19 and Matthew, 19:17. Here Jesus states directly that God is the only good one, and disclaims even goodness for himself.

THE DEFINITIONS

In the light of these passages let us look at those definitions again. If deity is "the eternal and *infinite* spirit," and if infinite means "without limit in power, capacity, knowledge or excellence," do not Jesus' own confessions of limitations refute the deity doctrine from his own mouth? His *power* was limited for we read that he could do no mighty works in a certain place because of their unbelief. His *knowledge* was limited as the incident of the fig-tree shows, when he expected to find figs and was disappointed, and that his knowledge was limited is shown by his belief that disease was due to demon-possession, a theory which every physician now knows to be false. Furthermore, he confessed to limited knowledge when he said that he did not know the day or hour of the coming of the Son of Man. If then he was obviously and confessedly limited, he could not have been infinite and therefore could not have been deity or God.

The greatest objection I have to the doctrine of the deity of Jesus is that it robs us of Jesus. You can say all you want about his being truly man and truly God. The moment you make him God, the second person of the Trinity, he becomes a theological abstraction. He is put upon a pedestal, nay, upon a throne, a crown upon his head, and he is called King of Kings and Lord of Lords. But Jesus was no monarch. He repudiated monarchy. When they came to him fawning, and tried to call him "Lord, Lord," he said, "Why call ye me Lord? Why don't you just do the things that I say?" When they offered him the crown in Galilee, he quietly disappeared from the throng.

No, Jesus was no King of Kings or Lord of Lords. He was a man, a democratic human individual who lived among common folks and loved them, who tried to get them to see that they, fishermen and carpenters, might live so that they were really children of God. Shall we permit the theologians to take Jesus away from us? When they deify him, they remove him from our midst. They take him from the chain of evolution by which we and our fathers, long ages ago, evolved from still more primitive ancestors. Out of all this struggle, this drama of evolution, this chain of cause and effect, this turmoil of life, they would take him and place him in the skies. I tell you he is not sitting at the right hand of the throne of God. He is in our hearts and will be in our hearts until the end of time. He was tempted as we are. He did feel the urge, and push, and thrust, and drag of our common humanity. He, the carpenter of Nazareth, knew what it was to work until the sweat stood out on his brow. He knew what it was to be tired, hungry, thirsty, far-spent. He knew woe and struggle, and because of that fact, because he is one of us, his triumph is far greater than as if he were some sort of theological being, a sort of super-angel, dwelling with God before the beginning of the world who came down and assumed our flesh and fooled us into believing that he was one of us. If he was a god in disguise, if he was crucified as a god, and went back to Heaven after a short period on earth, then we want nothing to do with him. But if he was one of us, as the records indicate, and as our hearts feel sure, then to him we look with reverence, with admiration, with sympathy, and with love. His triumph becomes our triumph over sin and sorrow. He is the greatest of humans, and he is our own. All down through the centuries, since his life, theologians have attempted to call him God. Great councils have asserted that he was God, but always the common men have protested. When he was alive the common people heard him gladly because he was one of them. He knew what was in man because he was a struggling man himself. There has always been an earnest band of protesting common people insisting upon his humanity and denying that he was a God from Heaven. That band of Jesus' lovers has always been persecuted, but they have insisted upon holding Jesus as one of themselves. Today the protest is growing stronger. All around the world the liberal movement is spreading mightily. The old orthodox theology is tottering upon its foundations. There is not a church which is not feeling the surge and flow of the new recognition of Jesus as a man. Theologians still are striving to take him from us and place him on the throne of deity, but they will never succeed. Slowly, inexorably, finally, mankind will claim Jesus as its own. It is only a matter of time when the truth will be recognized. If the churches refuse to recognize the manhood and non-deity of Jesus, then the people will leave the churches as millions have already left them. Somewhere, inside the church or outside the church, will come the final recognition of the absolute humanity of Jesus, our great leader, teacher, brother, our lover and our friend, not a magical deity, but the supreme triumphant human personality of the ages.

II

FOR THE NEGATIVE[1]

Resolved, That Jesus Christ was Entirely Man Instead of Incarnate Deity

Mr. Chairman, Honorable Judges, Mr. Potter, Ladies and
 Gentlemen:

Dr. Straton: It is a self-evident truth that there can
be no given effect without an adequate cause. This is
just as true in connection with a personality as it is in
the field of material facts.

The unique and extraordinary elements in Jesus Christ
demand a unique and extraordinary Cause to have produced such an Effect as He was. It is simply impossible
to account for Him on any ordinary or naturalistic
grounds!

The very paradoxes of His life forbid it. Though He
is recognized as the most remarkable character of all time,
yet, strange to say, He was not of the great. He was
born among the lowly and the poor. He was a carpenter
by profession, and nearly all His life was spent amid the
humble surroundings of an obscure and despised village
in Galilee. He made no discovery of science; He wrote
no book; He built no city; He effected no military con-
quest; He left behind Him no colossal fortune. He
gathered about Himself a little handful of obscure and,
for the most part, ignorant disciples who, at the time of
His supreme crisis deserted Him and scattered in con-

[1] First speech for the negative, by Rev. John Roach Straton, D.D.,
Pastor Calvary Baptist Church, New York.

25

fusion and despair. His enemies completely triumphed over Him. He was crucified between two thieves. His lifeless body was committed to a tomb that was not His own; and to make sure that He would no longer harass them, His powerful foes had a guard of soldiers stationed at its mouth, and the seal of Rome placed upon the stone.

Measured now by all historic precedent, and by any human standard, what is to become of that man?—of His name and His influence? Under such circumstances who would be so bold as to prophecy anything but that He would be speedily forgotten, even as the thousands of others before Him who had died upon the cross?

But such is not the case. The name of that humble man now shines as the sun in the central dome of history! Though He was not of the great, yet He was supremely great. Without the learning of the schools, He has become the Teacher of the world. Without the aid of fortuitous circumstances, He has become the most vital Force for righteousness ever known to mankind. The mightiest achievements of the race in art, literature, science, and governmental relationships are traceable to His influence. The most majestic temples on earth stand in His honor. The greatest power and enlightenment of the world belong to the nations which follow Him. About His personality, the tides of interest and discussion down the centuries have flowed, and around His name have revolved the most vital events of the past two thousand years. He has literally changed the face of the earth, revolutionized religion, and given a new direction to the history of mankind.[2]

[2] There can no longer be any dispute over the fact of an historic Christ. The myth theory has been exploded, and the idea that Jesus was a literary invention has also been abandoned, even by unbelievers, as impossible. John Stuart Mills in his essay on "Religion." though not an orthodox believer, nevertheless repudiates the view that Christ was not historical, declaring that it is absurd to think that the rude rustics and fishermen of Galilee or the early Christian writers could have created such a character. Renan admits that there must have

In the face, then, of such seeming contradictions and paradoxes, is there any wonder that the human mind, awestruck and puzzled, has adopted the question which He Himself put to His foes, and has asked down the ages: "What think ye of Christ? Whose Son is He?" We have to give some answer to that age-long question. We have to adopt some theory to account for Jesus Christ. What theory, then, best takes in all the facts?— the facts of His parentage, birth, achievements and character?

I reply with absolute confidence, and without a

---

been some basis of fact for the Gospel narratives. He says, "So far from Jesus having been created by his disciples, He appears in everything as superior:" and the French skeptic Rousseau said, "The Gospel has marks of truth so great, so striking, so perfectly inimitable that the inventor of it would be more astonishing than the hero. If the life and death of Socrates, are those of a sage, the life and death of Jesus are those of a God." While another has said, "It would take Jesus to forge a Jesus."

Dr. A. H. Strong has well said:

"No sources can be assigned from which the evangelists could have derived such a conception. The Hindu avatars were only temporary unions of deity with humanity. The Greeks had men half-deified, but no unions of God and man. The monotheism of the Jews found the person of Christ a perpetual stumbling-block. No mere human genius, and much less the genius of Jewish fisherman, could have originated this conception. Bad men invent only such characters as they sympathize with. But Christ's character condemns badness. Such a portrait could not have been drawn without supernatural aid" (Systematic Theology, page 89).

In addition to the well known passages in Josephus, there are a few historical references to Jesus—as many as might be expected when the scorn of the early Romans for such a religion as Christianity is remembered.

Tacitus, in his "Annals" (15:44), says: "The author of this name (i. e., of Christians) was put to death during the procuratorship of Pontius Pilate while Tibererius was emperor." Pliny writes: "and they sing a hymn to Christ as God." Suetonius (Lives of the Cæsars, Claudius, XXV) writes: "The Emperor Claudius drove the Jews from Rome, because, excited by Chrestus, they kept up a continual uproar."

moment's hesitation, only the theory that He was not only the Son of Man but, in a unique sense He was also the Son of God. It is simply impossible to take in all the facts concerning Christ on any ground other than that He was an actual incarnation of deity, coming into our world by a superhuman intervention, from a world higher than any thing which we understand by the term "natural."

NO "COMPLIMENTS" FOR JESUS

Nor can these matters be dismissed by merely complimenting Jesus. I think that I can speak for Him in saying that He does not care for our compliments. Certainly He wants no compliment from those who condescend to Him; who shower upon Him fulsome praise; who say that He was the leading prophet of all time, the noblest example and pattern of virtue, the greatest and best of all the children of men; and yet that He was only a man, at last; that He was merely "a child of His own times," as they express it; that, when rightly viewed, He was really not as great as some of the Modernists, because He did not have our scientific knowledge or understanding of the world; and that, since He lacked our modern "scholarship," He really did not rightly interpret the Hebrew Scriptures. "He that sitteth in the Heavens shall laugh!" And surely the laughter of God must be stirred by the spectacle of puny men, in their pride of "scholarship" and vanity of mind, condescending even to the Almighty, trying to measure an infinite universe with the yard-stick of their finite minds, and patting Jesus Christ complacently on the back as a "Good Fellow" but "really, now, you know, no God"!

Nor does it alter the matter even though the hand that seeks to take the diadem from His brow is a "polite" hand. Jesus Christ simply does not care for our compliments, even though they come from sincere, though self-deluded, minds. Nicodemus—a great man and a Ruler of the Jews—once complimented Him most enthusiastically; but Jesus replied to him bluntly by saying: *"Ye must be born again"*; and, "except a man be born again he cannot see the kingdom of God." He cannot even see it, much less enter into it. And then Jesus pointed him to His own uplifted cross as the way of regeneration and everlasting life. (John 3:3-7.)

Rousseau, Renan, Bolingbroke, Voltaire and many other unbelievers and infidels have complimented Jesus. Robert G. Ingersoll even paid Him glowing compliments. He said of Him:

"His life is worth its example—its moral force, its heroism of benevolence. For that name I have infinite respect and love. To that great and serene man I gladly pay the homage of my admiration and my tears."

And yet Ingersoll lived and died an unbeliever, and wrecked the faith of multitudes.

Jesus wants something better than such condescension. He deserves and demands not our patronage but our obedience and worship. Rather than the empty words of Ingersoll, He wants such faith as was in the heart of Shakespeare, the world's greatest literary genius. Shakespeare said in his will:

"I commend my soul into the hands of God my Creator, hoping and assuredly believing, through the merits of Jesus Christ my Saviour, to be made partaker of life everlasting."

Jesus wants what was in the heart of William E. Gladstone, the noblest statesman of his generation, who said:

"All that I think, all that I hope, all that I write, all that I live for, is based upon the deity of Jesus Christ, the central joy of my poor, wayward life."

That is the attitude of faith which Jesus Christ de-

serves, and He will accept no other! For that faith I
contend in this debate.

THE QUESTION FOR DEBATE

The question for debate is "Resolved, that Jesus Christ
was Entirely Man Instead of Incarnate Deity." Deity
means God, and incarnate means to clothe with flesh, to
embody in flesh.

In championing the affirmative of this subject, my
opponent has undertaken the task of disproving the deity
of Jesus Christ by showing that He was entirely—that is
exclusively and altogether—man, and not incarnate deity,
not God embodied in the flesh.

To accomplish this, my opponent must be thorough-
going and exhaustive. If Jesus went beyond mere manhood at any point and to any degree, then He was not
entirely and exclusively man, but must have been in part
God. He must have been incarnate deity; or, as stated
usually, He must have been divine.

Now the faith on which the Christian church is built is
faith in the deity of Jesus Christ. To worship a mere
man is idolatry, and the uncounted millions of Christians
down the centuries have not been idolaters. They have
worshipped Jesus Christ as the only divine Son of God.

Because, therefore, he seeks to overthrow that faith,
the burden of proof is upon my opponent. He must
prove, by sound reasoning and facts that are understandable to our minds and hearts, that the faith in the deity
of Jesus Christ which has rejuvenated mankind, redeemed
sinners, built schools, hospitals, orphanages and asylums
the world over, erected unnumbered churches, sent missionaries to all heathen countries, and given humanity its
only touch of true brotherhood and its only rational hope
of heaven, is without foundation and is a false faith. I
submit that he has by no means done this in his opening
speech, and I shall reply in my rebuttal to what he has said.

THE TASK OF THE NEGATIVE

My task in the debate, therefore, is simple. It is to meet my opponent's efforts to prove that Jesus Christ was a mere man—for that is what it all comes down to—with the facts which prove (until they are disproved and overthrown) that He was more than man—that He was an absolutely unique personality. We both agree that He was a real man, a man of like passions with ourselves; and yet I contend that He was different from all other men, in that He had both a human and divine nature in the one Personality.

I will go just as far as my opponent in glorifying the manhood of the Master and in recognizing the value of His human influence and example. He was a true man. He had a human mother, a material body like all other men, a body which wearied and suffered and which in every sense was wonderfully human. Jesus had the affections, the mentality, the emotions, the spirit of a true man. Jesus had a human soul as well as a human body. He was a true and perfect man in every sense of the word "man."

I recognize, too, that it is difficult for our finite minds to comprehend the combination of God and man. It seems strange to us that these two aspects of Jesus could abide united in one person. We are not to think of God becoming a man, nor indwelling a man, nor deifying a man, but we are to think of a God-Man. He is God manifest in Flesh. God did not unite Himself to a human being, but became a human, while still remaining God.

It is said that "the Christ of Scripture is not reasonable." But even if this were granted, it would only prove the genuineness of Christ. We do not have to understand Jesus before we can accept and follow Him. We do not have to reason Christ out. Indeed, we cannot reason Christ out. The God-Man is a Miracle, and a

miracle is not bound or answerable to human laws and
rules.   Faith must be brought into operation in thinking
and dealing with this God-Man, the Redeemer.   Indeed,
we are surrounded on every side by mysteries that we
cannot understand, and yet that we constantly use, even
in the most practical affairs of life.   We have to walk
by faith not sight."

But even though we cannot fully understand it, nevertheless, the facts prove that He was and is the God-Man—
an actual incarnation of deity, and the second person in a
divine trinity.   I deny, therefore, the affirmation that
Jesus was only a man—however great and good He is
admitted to have been—and I assert that He was incarnate
deity.   And with the issue thus clearly defined, I feel that
my task is comparatively easy, for the proofs of the
uniqueness and deity of Jesus Christ are overwhelming!

These proofs are found in the Bible.   The Bible is our
source of knowledge about these things.   If its teachings
are accepted as true, then the way is clearly opened for a
sane solution of this problem as to whose son Jesus is.   If
the Bible teaching is rejected, then we can only continue
to flounder in the quagmire of doubt and unbelief.

My argument, therefore, will be as follows: First, that
the general teachings of the Bible set Christ forth as a
divine being.   Second, that its specific teachings picture
Him as having all the attributes of God, and therefore
that He is God.   Third, that He Himself explicitly claimed
to be divine, and unless this claim was true, then He was
either a fool or a knave; and fourth, I shall show from
His after influence that Jesus of Nazareth was more than
man, that He was the divine Son of God—incarnate deity.

I. THE GENERAL TEACHINGS OF THE BIBLE

My first argument is that the general teachings of the
Bible prove that Jesus Christ was incarnate deity.

To begin with, the Bible sets forth Christ as Creator.
The very first verse of Genesis has a reference to Him

where it is written: "In the beginning God created the heavens and the earth." That this creation of our world was by and through the Christ who finally walked the earth in the person of Jesus of Nazareth, other Scriptures make amply clear. The Apostle John, for example, says:

"In the beginning was the Word, and the Word was God. All things were made by Him. And the Word was made flesh and dwelt among us (and we beheld His glory, the glory as of the only begotten of the Father) full of grace and truth." (John 1:1-4.)

Here John states that the Word—Christ—was in the beginning,—was the God who made all things, and that the Word became flesh and dwelt among us.

The Apostle Paul, in all his writings, recognizes the same great truth of the creative power of Christ. He says:

"For by Him were all things created that are in heaven, and that are in earth, visible and invisible, whether they be thrones or dominions, or principalities or powers: all things were by Him and for Him and He is before all things, and by Him all things consist." (Col. 1:16.)

And in Hebrews 1:10 it is specifically said:

"And Thou Lord, in the beginning hast laid the foundation of the earth: and the heavens are the work of thy hands."

The context here clearly shows that the Lord addressed in this passage is the Lord Jesus. Thus it becomes perfectly clear that the God of the first verse of Genesis was none other than the Christ of the New Testament.

The Bible not only teaches that Christ was Creator, however; it also teaches that He is the only Re-Creator—the only Saviour. The very first prophecy in the Bible—that the "seed of the woman" would bruise the serpent's head—had to do with Christ, because the other prophecies that followed after, and that avowedly were fulfilled in the coming of Christ, clearly so state. Isaiah, with prophetic prevision, said "A virgin shall conceive and bear a son and shall call His name Immanuel" (Isaiah 7:14).

And Isaiah further identified this coming virgin-born
Saviour as God by giving Him divine names. He called
Him "The Mighty God," the "Everlasting Father," "The
Prince of Peace." (Isaiah 9:6.)

Now the New Testament specifically identifies Jesus
Christ as this One who was to be born of a virgin and
who was described in advance as God. Luke tells us that
the angel Gabriel was sent from God to Nazareth, and
that there he appeared to the Virgin Mary and told her
that the Holy Ghost would come upon her, that the power
of the Highest would overshadow her, and that a holy
Being, thus conceived by divine power, would come from
her womb. The angel told Mary that she would "call
His name Jesus," but that He would be the "Son of God"
(Luke 1:26–35). Then Mary, as reported further by
Luke, declared to her cousin Elizabeth that what the angel
promised had actually come to pass. Mary said: "He that
is mighty hath done to me great things, and holy is His
name" (Luke 1:49); and because of the One who was
thus to be born of her womb, Mary said that all generations would call her "blessed."

Matthew also takes up the story. He starts his narrative, by saying: "Now the birth of Jesus Christ was on
this wise." Then he tells us that Joseph, to whom the
Virgin Mary was espoused, or "engaged" as we would
say, found, *before they came together,* that Mary was with
child. Then Joseph planned to put Mary away privily,
to hide her shame, but he was told in a dream by the
angel of the Lord not to be afraid to take Mary as his
wife, because that which was conceived in her was conceived by the Holy Ghost. And Matthew says that
Joseph, when he awakened from his dream, did as the
angel told him and took unto him his wife, *but did not
know her in the relation of husband and wife "until she
had brought forth her first born son"* whom they called
Jesus.

Then Matthew says:

"Now all this was done that it might be fulfilled which was spoken of the Lord by the prophet [Isaiah] saying: behold, a virgin shall be with child, and shall bring forth a son, and they shall call His name Immanuel, which being interpreted, is *God* with us" (Matthew 1:18–25).

Now, this absolutely identifies Jesus Christ as the one who was to be "the mighty God, the everlasting Father, and the Prince of Peace."

The matter is further confirmed by Luke, who tells us how Mary brought forth Jesus, and how the angels told the shepherds that the One thus born in the City of David was the "Saviour—Christ the Lord" (Luke 2:10–11).

Now that this One, thus *conceived by God Himself* and born of the Virgin, was really Jehovah—God manifested in the flesh—is confirmed and explicitly declared.

In Matthew 3:1–3 it is written:

"In those days came John the Baptist, saying repent ye, for *this is he* that was spoken of by the prophet Esaias, saying, the voice of one crying in the wilderness, prepare ye the way of the *Lord,* make his paths straight."

The word for Lord used by Isaiah, and as quoted by John, is Jehovah (Yaveh) which means Very God (Isaiah 40:3). So that the One whom John the Baptist thus proclaimed—Jesus Christ—was the Lord Jehovah, Very God. The Greek word "Kurios," translated "Lord" in the New Testament, is the equivalent of the Hebrew designation of Deity. The Septuagint uses "Kurios" when rendering Adonay, Eloah, and Elohim into Greek.[3]

---

[3] The "Messiah," though in some sense different from Jehovah, is nevertheless recognized, even in the Old Testament, as One with Jehovah.

The following passages will illustrate this: "Unto us a child is born, unto us a Son is given . . . and His name shall be called Wonderful Counsellor, Mighty God, Everlasting Father, Prince of Peace" (Isaiah. 9:6); "thou Bethlehem . . . which art little . . . out of thee shall come forth unto me that is to be Ruler in Israel;

The Bible plainly teaches, then, that the *conception and birth* of Jesus Christ were different from those of all other men. The Bible plainly teaches that Joseph was not the natural but only the *legal* father of Jesus, because it tells us that when Joseph learned that Mary was with child before their marriage he was so shocked that he planned to put her away, until the angel told him that the Holy Ghost was the child's father. The angel told Mary that the Holy thing thus conceived in her was to be the "Son of God," and after His birth He was so recognized. As, then, He was not the Son of Joseph but was conceived by God the Holy Ghost, He was God's "only begotten Son," just as declared by the Bible; and, therefore, He was more than man, He was incarnate deity. That is to say, He was God manifested in human flesh.

The Bible makes this plain in many other places.

In the acts of the Apostles it is written:

"The Church of God, which He hath purchased with His own blood" (Acts 20:28).

It was Christ who shed His blood upon the cross to purchase the church, and since it is called the church of God, therefore, it was God who made the sacrifice upon the cross.

In the correct translation of Titus 2:13, the translation given in the English revision, our Lord Jesus is spoken of as "our great God and Saviour Jesus Christ." In Romans

---

whose goings forth have been from old. from everlasting" (Micha, 5:12); "Thy throne, O, God, is for ever and ever. . . . Therefore, God, thy God, hath anointed thee" (Psalms. 45:6, 7); "I send my messenger and he shall prepare the way before me: and the Lord, whom ye seek, shall suddenly come to his temple; and the messenger of the covenant whom ye delight in" (Malaciah, 3:1). Henderson, in his commentary on this passage, points out that the Messiah is here called "the Lord" or "the sovereign"—a title nowhere given in this form (with the article) to any but Jehovah; that he is predicted as coming to the temple as its proprietor; and that he is identified with the angel of the covenant, elsewhere shown to be one with Jehovah himself.

9:5, Paul tells us that "Christ is over all, God blessed forever." The Unitarians have made desperate efforts to overcome the force of these words, but the only fair translation and interpretation of the words that Paul wrote in Greek are the translation and interpretation found in both our Authorized and Revised Versions. There can be no honest doubt to one who goes to the Bible to find out what it actually teaches, and not to read his own thought into it, that Jesus is spoken of by various names and titles that beyond a question imply Deity and that He is called God. In Hebrews 1:8 it is said in so many words, of the Son:

"But unto the *Son* he saith, thy throne, O *God* is forever and ever; a sceptre of righteousness is the sceptre of thy kingdom."

Here "the Son" is called "God." If we go no further it is evidently the clear and often repeated teaching of the Bible that Jesus Christ was really God.

A DIVINE TRINITY

To sum up, then, at this point, I will say that the Bible clearly teaches that God is a Trinity—three persons: God the Father, God the Son and God the Holy Spirit—in one divine nature.[4]

[4] Merely because we cannot understand the trinity is no proof that it is not true. Man himself is a trinity. We have body, mind and spirit, and yet the three make one personality.

The Godhead is a tripersonal unity, and the light is a trinity. Being immaterial and homogenous, and thus essentially one in its nature, the light includes a plurality of constituents, or in other words is essentially three in its constitution, its constituent principles being the actinic, the luminiferous, and the calorific, yet in glorious manifestation the light is one, and is the created, constituted, and ordained emblem of the tripersonal God—of whom it is said that "God is light, and in Him is no darkness at all" (I John, 1:5). The actinic rays are in themselves invisible; only as the luminiferous manifest them, are they seen: only as the calorific accompany them, are they felt.

Dr. A. H. Strong well says: "The doctrine of the Trinity is not self-contradictory. This it would be, only if it declared God to be

I will not take the time to quote many passages that might be quoted showing this, but will refer to one or two that are typical, comprehensive and emphatic. It is written in First John 5 :7 :

"For there are three that bear record in heaven, the Father, the Word [Son] and the Holy Ghost; and these three are one."

While there is some criticism of this verse on textual grounds, nevertheless it states the matter concisely, and its statement is confirmed in many other places in the Bible. In connection with the Baptism of our Lord, for example, there was a physical manifestation of the entire deity, with the Son in the water beneath, the Holy Spirit, in the form of a Dove, descending upon Him, and the Voice of the Father, above, saying "This is My beloved Son, in whom I am well pleased" (Mat. 3 :13–17).

Again, in Colossians 2 :9 it is said of Christ:

"In Him dwelleth all the fulness of the Godhead bodily."

It is here declared that in the body of Jesus Christ dwelleth all the fullness of the Godhead, or deity. Now as before remarked, the Bible teaches that fullness of deity is manifested in Father, Son, and Holy Spirit. It is therefore asserted in this passage in Colossians that Father, Son, and Holy Spirit—the fullness of deity—dwelleth in

three in the same numerical sense in which he is said to be one. This we do not assert. We assert simply that the same God who is one with respect to his essence is three with respect to the internal distinctions of that essence. or with respect to the modes of his being. The possibility of this cannot be denied except by assuming that the human mind is in all respects the measure of the divine. Neither God's independence nor God's blessedness can be maintained upon grounds of absolute unity. Anti-trinitarianism almost necessarily makes creation indispensable to God's perfection, tends to a belief in the eternity of matter, and ultimately leads, as in Mohammedanism, and in modern Judaism and Unitarianism, to Pantheism. 'Love is an impossible exercise to a solitary being.' Without trinity we cannot hold a living Unity in the Godhead." (Systematic Theology, pp. 167–168.)

the body of Jesus Christ. So Jesus Himself said, "The Father dwelleth in Me" (John 14:10); and again it is written in Second Corinthians 3:1-17: "The Spirit giveth light . . . now the Lord is that Spirit."

We have, then, a clear Biblical foundation for a logical and undeniable conclusion. It is this: Since the Father is in Jesus Christ, and since the Spirit is in Jesus Christ, and since Jesus Christ Himself is the Son, therefore, the fullness of the Father, Son and Holy Spirit is in the body of Jesus Christ. That is to say all there is of God in His eternal state is in Jesus Christ, and there is no God apart from Him. These are perfectly clear statements in which there is no shadow of doubt about words.

The Bible, therefore, in its general teaching,—culminating in this specific teaching of a Holy Trinity,—affirms that while Jesus Christ during His earthly life, was a real man, He was and is also Very God.

And the climax of it all is reached in that sublime passage where the Bible not only declares that Jesus was equal with God before He came to this earth, but that He is to be finally recognized as God by the entire universe. In speaking of Jesus, therefore, it is written:

"Who, being in the form of God thought it not robbery to be equal with God: but made Himself of no reputation, and took upon Him the form of a servant, and was made in the likeness of men: and being found in fashion as a man, He humbled Himself, and became obedient unto death, even the death of the cross. Wherefore God also hath highly exalted Him, and given Him a name which is above every name: that at the name of Jesus every knee should bow, of things in heaven, and things in earth and things under the earth; and that every tongue should confess that Jesus Christ is *Lord*, to the glory of God the Father." (Phil. 2:5-11.)

These are tremendous words, and they cannot possibly be applicable to a mere man. They clearly teach the full deity of Jesus Christ, and indicate for Him a future universal sovereignty.

II. The Specific Teaching of the Bible

With this foundation, then, in the general teaching of the Bible upon this question, and in order that we may view the matter from another angle, I pass on now to my second argument, namely: that the Bible specifically teaches that Christ had and has all the attributes of God, and consequently that He was and is God.

1. CHRIST'S WISDOM AS A PROOF OF HIS DEITY

Take, for example, His wisdom. It is universally recognized that perfect wisdom is a necessary attribute of the divine nature. It is self evident that the Creator and Preserver of this vast universe must be a supremely wise Being.

Now in Jesus Christ, as pictured in the Bible, we find a wisdom higher than that of earth. Therefore, the conclusion is inevitable that Christ's wisdom must have been divine. We are told explicitly in John 16:30 that Jesus knew "all things," and in Colossians 2:3 we are told that in Him "are hid all the treasures of wisdom and knowledge."

We are given very little about the boyhood of Jesus, but in the midst of the few references made to His youth, Luke is careful to say that as the child grew He was "filled with wisdom: and the grace of God was upon Him" (Luke 2:40). We find Christ when a boy of only twelve disputing with the learned doctors in the Jewish Temple. They were evidently so amazed at the extraordinary wisdom of this mere boy that they were willing to devote days of their valuable time to answering His questions and asking Him questions. It is evident that these—the most learned and wisest men of the age—recognized in Him a uniqueness and a wisdom entirely out of the ordinary.

Later in His life, men were sent to place Him under arrest, and when they came back without Him, they gave as a reason for their failure to bring Him this statement: "Never *man* spake as this man."   There was something in His speech so absolutely unearthly and heavenly in its wisdom that soldiers found themselves powerless to lay their hands upon Him.

Take, for example, His forms of expression.   They are faultless.   The greatest literary genius that the world has ever known cannot improve upon His parables.   They are perfect, both as to their matter and their form.   His speech was neither Oriental nor Western.   It was universal and authoritative.   The record of it appeals to the mind and changes the heart of the Chinaman or Indian in the same way that it does the American.   And the manner in which He met His adversaries and confounded them, again and again, gives proof of a wisdom and an understanding higher than that of man.

Again and again His astute foes endeavored to trap Him—learned lawyers and skilfull priests and scribes—but each time He outwitted and refuted them with a simplicity, and yet a profoundness of wisdom, to which they could find no answer.   On one occasion they tried to impale Him on one or the other horn of a dilemma.   They asked Him the simple question: "Is it right to pay tribute to Caesar?"   If He had replied that it was right, then that would have prejudiced the Jews against Him. If He had answered that it was not right, that would have left Him liable to the charge of treason under the Roman law.   When the question was put to Him, therefore, with a wisdom that was nothing short of divine, He gave that immortal answer which has passed into the wisdom literature of the world: "Render unto Caesar the things that are Caesar's, and unto God the things that are God's."

The principles He laid down without argument, but with the assumption of undisputed authority, so appeal to us as to be accepted as elemental truths.   They are self evident, and forceful as axioms in mathematics.

As, for example, when He said, "A good tree cannot bring forth evil fruit, neither can a corrupt tree bring forth good fruit. Wherefore, by their fruits ye shall know them."

His sermon on the mount is recognized as embodying a wisdom beyond the present reach of men. It is so divine in its wisdom and beauty that many thoughtful minds have declared that its precepts and principles can only be put into full and active practice when Jesus Himself has come back to guide and enforce them as a ruling King.

May I call your attention to one other illustration? In a model prayer of only 65 words, He gives the very essence of every utterance possible to a man in the act of prayer. The germ of it all is there. The Fatherhood of God—"Our Father"; the transcendence of God as a living personality—"Which art in Heaven"; the unapproachable holiness of God—"Hallowed be thy name"; the sovereign rulership of God—"Thy kingdom come, thy will be done"; and then the needs and aspirations of man —"Give us this day our daily bread"; and a right relationship between us and our fellow men—"Forgive us our trespasses as we forgive those who trespass against us"; protection from evil—"lead us not into temptation but deliver us from the evil one"; and all of it climaxed with a reemphasis upon the eternal power and greatness of God—"for thine is the kingdom and the power and the glory forever and ever." Yes, the very essence of all true prayer is there. We may expand and enlarge the parts of this prayer, but, at last, it will be found that it is all inclusive.

I submit that it surpasses human wisdom and understanding thus to comprehend all the possible aspirations and needs of the human heart for all time, and to condense it all into five printed lines!

As we contemplate the wisdom that Christ manifested

in His teaching and His conduct, do we not find ourselves unconsciously looking up to Him as to God Himself? Perfect wisdom is an attribute of deity only, and
this wisdom that was in Christ proves that He was more
than even the greatest and best of men—that He was
incarnate deity.

CHRIST'S SINLESSNESS.

Holiness is another attribute of God. The human
mind intuitively recognizes that "the Judge of all the
earth must do right." Now in Christ, we find holiness
in its perfection. He was more than merely a good man.
He was a sinless man, and since sin is recognized as a
universal characteristic of humanity, when we find One
who was without sin, we know that He was more than
a man. The absolutely holy nature of Jesus Christ proves
Him divine, for only God is holy.

The incident to which doubters sometimes refer in
which Christ said to the rich young ruler: "Why callest
thou me good? There is none good but God," was not a
disclaimer either of His deity or His righteousness. It
was no more than a rebuke to a young man's hastiness in
reaching conclusions about strangers. This rich young
ruler had just met Christ, and when he immediately addressed Him as "good," the Master's reply to him, manifestly was intended to correct a fault in his nature. His
thought was: "Why do you call me good—you who know
nothing about me? God is the only One whom all men
know to be good, and you do not yet know that I am
God." And the fact that immediately after that incident with the rich young ruler Christ assumed the position of God, passing judgment upon the young man, even
though He had loved Him, and declared to His followers
that he was a lost soul, and the further fact that He
then passed on and spoke of His resurrection from the
dead—a divine miracle—proves in this very connection

that He was God.   In other places He explicitly announced Himself as a perfect model and called people to follow Him.   Therefore, there is no force to the contention that this remark of Jesus's to the rich young ruler was a disclaimer either of sinlessness or of deity.

Doubters say, that the fact that Jesus prayed proves that He understood that He was not equal with God. But this contention merely shows a lack of understanding of the true nature of prayer.   The very essence of prayer is communion, and not mere petition; and the prayers of Jesus were always primarily characterized by this element.

There is also, in this connection, a most significant fact, and that is that never in one of His prayers have we any record of a single confession of sin.   Now, the very first impulse of the human heart in the act of prayer is toward confession.   When we bow in the presence of the holy God, we are smitten as at no other time with the sense of our own sinfulness and unholiness, but here was One who prayed constantly and fervently, yet the confession of sin was never upon His lips.   He addressed God always with that perfect assurance and confidence which was born of the consciousness of innocence, sinlessness and oneness with God.

So strong was this conviction within His heart that He dared even to challenge His deadliest enemies by saying: "Which one of you convicteth me of sin?"   They could not convict Him!   Even those who were not His friends were forced to concede His moral rectitude. Pilate, His judge, declared repeatedly, "I find no fault in Him."   Pilate's heathen wife, also, warned in a dream, and with a woman's deep intuition, advised her husband: "Have nothing to do with that just man."   Even the iron hearted Roman centurion stationed at the cross exclaimed: "Certainly this was a righteous man."   And sceptics, worldlians and unbelievers in all the after ages have followed the example of Pilate and recognized the moral beauty of Jesus, even if they did not accept Him as God and Saviour.

David Strauss called Christ "the highest model of religion."

John Stuart Mills said that He was "the guide of humanity."

Leckey declared that he was "the highest pattern of virtue."

Martineau referred to Him as "the divine flower of humanity."

Robert Owen called Him "the irreproachable."

Benjamin Disraeli, the Jew, while Prime Minister of Great Britain, also extolled Christ's moral supremacy. He said:

"The pupil of Moses may ask Himself whether all the princes of the House of David have done so much for Jews as that Prince who was crucified. . . . Had it not been for Him the Jews would have been comparatively unknown, or known only as an Oriental Caste which had lost its country. Has not He made their history the most famous history in the world? The wildest dreams of their Rabbis have been far exceeded. Has not Jesus conquered Europe and changed its name to Christendom? All countries that refuse the Cross wilt, and the time will come when the countless myriads of America and Australia will find music in the songs of Zion, and solace in the parables of Galilee."

What a touching, beautiful tribute to come from the heart of a Jew!

And time fails us to speak of the raptures of song and the exquisite paeans of poetry which the sinlessness of Jesus of Nazareth have called forth. Take but one, that lovely verse of Sidney Lanier:

"But thee, but thee, O sovereign seer of time,
    But thee, O poet's Poet, wisdom's tongue,
    But thee, O man's best Man, O love's best Love,
    O perfect life in perfect labour writ,

> O all men's Comrade, Servant, King or Priest,
> What if or yet, what mole, what flaw, what lapse,
> What least defect or shadow of defect,
> What rumor tattled by an enemy,
> Of inference loose, what lack of grace
> Even in torture's grasp, or sleep's or death's—
> O, what amiss may I forgive in Thee,
> Jesus, good Paragon, thou Crystal Christ?"

There is nothing amiss that we can forgive. The Bible says that Christ "was in all points tempted like as we are, yet without sin" (Heb. 4:15). There is no place in the record of His life where we can put our finger and say: "Here He did that which was wrong!" No spot of sin ever fell upon the stainless soul of Jesus of Nazareth. No thought of impurity ever found lodgment in the temple of His radiant mind. No impulse of selfishness ever enthralled His faultless heart. The pride of the mind, the lust of the flesh, and the vainglory of life were utterly subordinated and kept under in Him, by a holiness that was higher than any that the children of men have ever had. In the light of the universal sense of sin in every man, does not this sinlessness of Christ prove that He was more than human, that He was divine—even as Gabriel said "A Holy Thing?"

THE LOVE OF CHRIST AS PROOF OF HIS DEITY

Closely akin to this, I will point out the love of Christ as a proof of His deity. The supreme attribute of God is love. God is not an arbitrary tyrant. God is not a heartless despot. God is not a mere king, ruling in majesty and ruthless might. Our hearts respond to the glorious truth that God is our heavenly Father; and we know that the highest summary of the very essence of the divine Being is given when the Bible says "God is love."

And I ask you if it is not true that we find in Jesus Christ the manifestation of a love so pure and holy and

perfect that it proves in itself that He was God. Paul
says in speaking of it "herein is love"—just as though
real love had never been known until God's love was
manifested in Jesus Christ. There was a day when the
little children came running to Him, but men even as
high as the Apostles, because they were only human,
sought to drive them away. But see Christ yonder as He
takes the little children into His arms and presses them
to His heart and pillows their curly heads in the hollow
of His shoulder and says:

"Suffer little children to come unto Me, and forbid them
not, for of such is the Kingdom of Heaven."

Human compassion at its best demands an antiseptic
when disease is touched, and even the kindliest doctors
put rubber gloves on their hands when they are in contact
with contagion. But see Jesus again as He touches the
leper to heal him of his loathsome disease. See Him
again as He stood at the tomb of Lazarus and wept in
divine sympathy with the heart-broken sisters of the dead.
See Him again rebuking the men who, though equally
guilty, would have stoned the fallen woman. See Jesus
as with infinite tenderness and delicacy He reaches down
His hand to her and lifts her up and sends her forth,
with a new hope in her heart, and says to her with divine
tenderness and authority: "Go, and sin no more."

See Him again as He stands and refuses to defend
Himself before Pilate because He knows that He must
fulfill His mission of salvation to a lost race. See Him
suffering as His white flesh quivers beneath the lash.
See Him staggering beneath the weight of His Cross, and
at last nailed to its remorseless arms. Hear Him, even
in the midst of mortal agony, providing for His widowed
mother, and saying to Mary, "Woman, behold thy son,"
and to John the Beloved, "Son, behold thy mother." See
Him again, when with a love greater than earth had ever

known before, He prayed to the Father and said, referring even to those who were putting Him to such a death,
"Father, forgive them; they know not what they do."
No mere man could ever so pray. See Him again in the
supreme anguish of that moment when the sin of a lost
race fell upon His stainless soul, in the agony of vicarious
suffering, when God, for a season, withdrew from Him,
and He exclaimed, "My God, My God, why hast thou
forsaken me?" See Him in those ways, and you must
see Him exemplifying a love purer and sweeter and
higher than any that our poor earth has ever known—a
love that was divine, yea, the holy and perfect redemption love of God Himself. See Him thus, and then you
will understand what the Bible means when it says that
"God *so* loved the world that He gave His only begotten
Son that whosoever believeth on Him should not perish
but have everlasting life" (John 3:16); and that "God
was in Christ reconciling the world unto Himself."

In Christ there was a love higher than the love of man
because Christ was willing to die for His enemies. The
Bible says peradventure for a good man some would be
even willing to die—"But God commendeth His love toward us in that while we were yet sinners (and enemies)
Christ died for us" (Romans 5:8). Here was a love
beyond the love of men. It was a divine love that was in
Christ.

THE POWER OF CHRIST AS A PROOF OF HIS DEITY

The deity of Jesus Christ is attested also by the power
which He manifested. He performed wonders during
His walk upon this earth, if the records of His life are
to be believed at all, which proved that He possessed
omnipotence, which is an attribute of God alone.

In appealing, now, to the miracles which Christ
wrought as a proof of His deity, I would say that unless
we do accept and believe the miracles, then we have to

reject the Bible entirely as the greatest tissue of lies which has ever deluded the children of men.

Hume took the position that miracles are incredible and, therefore, that no amount of testimony can prove them. But that is mere scepticism and *a priori* dogmatism, which assumes that we know all the laws of nature and what an infinite God could or would do.

The miracles recorded in the Bible cannot be dismissed by mere doubt or subjective scepticism. Since the Bible teaches that the universe is primarily a spiritual order and not a mere material machine, and that it is ruled by a living God, miracles are inevitable and to be expected. As a father, I do every day things that are miracles to my little boys, because they are utterly beyond their comprehension and powers, so we must expect that our heavenly Father and our Divine Saviour would do things that to us are supernatural and beyond our present understanding. While miracles are beyond our understanding, however, they are not beyond the understanding of God. The Bible says "with God all things are possible," and this is true because He is an Almighty Being. The miracles are not violations of natural law, but are events which occur according to higher laws which are fully known to God though entirely unknown to us.

And we must believe the miracles recorded in the Bible because while they are beyond our limited experience and are above our understanding, nevertheless they are attested by witnesses as competent, disinterested and trustworthy as any which history knows. If we reject the Bible miracles, therefore, we can do so only on the ground that there are certain alleged occurrences which we will not believe even though the testimony to them may be overwhelming. In other words, we put our own subjective scepticism against any testimony that may be adduced, and we thereby assert that we will not believe anything outside of the limits of our own experience and understanding.

Now this is not only a very narrow and egotistical position to take, but it is really absurd, because if accepted it would prevent any more new truth ever coming into the world.

We must, therefore, accept the Biblical miracles because of the testimony to them.

LEGAL TESTIMONY

Simon Greenleaf, author of "The Law of Evidence," one of the great standard authorities on evidence in the courts of the English-speaking world, wrote also another remarkable book entitled "The Testimony of the Evangelists Examined by the Rules of Evidence Demonstrated in Courts of Justice." I have that book here. With his trained legal mind, and in the same judicial style in which his "Law of Evidence" was written, Greenleaf carefully reviews and weighs the Bible evidence, and considers the character of these Bible witnesses. Having done this with great care, he reaches the conclusion that, from a strictly legal and rational standpoint, the Bible narratives are proved, and the witnesses are absolutely trustworthy. Listen then to his own statement giving these conclusions. He says (pages 30, 31) in speaking of the Bible writers:

"Their writings show them to have been men of vigorous understanding. If then, their testimony was not true, there was no possible motive for this fabrication. It would also have been irreconcilable with the fact that they were good men. But it is impossible to read their writings and not feel that we are conversing with men eminently holy, and of tender conscience, with men acting under an abiding sense of the presence and omniscience of God, and of their accountability to him, living in his fear and walking in his ways. Now, though in a single instance a good man may fall, when under strong temptations, yet he is not found persisting for years, in deliberate falsehood, asserted with the most solemn appeals to God, without the slightest temptation or motive, and against all opposing interests which reign in the human breast. If, on the contrary, they are supposed to have been bad men, it is incredible that such men should have chosen this form of imposture; enjoining, as it does unfeigned repentance, the utter forsaking and abhorrence of all falsehood and of every other sin, the practice of daily self-denial, self-abasement and self-sacrifice, the crucifixion of the flesh with all its earthly appetites and desires, indifference to the honors, and hearty contempt of the vanities of the world; and inculcating perfect purity of heart and life and intercourse of the soul with heaven. It is incredible that bad men should invent falsehoods to promote the religion of the God of truth. The supposition is suicidal. If they did believe in a future state of retribution, a heaven and a hell hereafter, they took the most certain course—of false witness—to secure the latter for their portion. And if, still being bad men, they did not believe in future punishment, how came they to invent falsehoods, the direct and certain tendency of which was to destroy all their prospects of worldly honor and happiness, and to insure their misery in this life? From these absurdities there is no escape, but in the perfect conviction and admission that they were good men, testifying to that which they had carefully observed and considered, and well knew to be true."

What possible escape, my friends, short of mere stubborn doubt and superficial scepticism, is there from such logic? This great legal authority has here given us a judicial decision on the reliability of these records and the trustworthiness of these witnesses who tell us of the miracles that Christ performed. I submit, therefore, that unless some contrary and more reliable documents and more trustworthy witnesses can be introduced to overthrow them, then the miracles, which it is here declared Christ performed, are established as facts. And we must inevitably conclude, therefore, since such miracles are above the powers of man, that Christ was more than a mere man.

His miracles went beyond those performed even by

men to whom God had given miracle working power. They swept the whole gamut of heavenly power, and were specially intended to manifest Christ's glory and to prove his deity.   In connection with his first miracle it is written: "This beginning of miracles did Jesus in Cana of Galilee, and manifested forth his Glory; and His disciples believed on Him" (John 2:11).   And later in appealing to his enemies Jesus called upon them to "Believe me for the work's sake."   Because, therefore, of the absolute and all inclusive power manifested in these miracles, and because of their object, which was to produce faith in His deity, we must believe that he was Incarnate God.

WHAT POWER WAS IT

The teaching of the Modernists, therefore, that Jesus was a good man and a great prophet and a high example or model, but that he did not have the power of God, cannot be true.   Jesus Himself said:

"All power is given unto me in heaven and on earth" (Matt. 28:18); and in Hebrews 1:3, Christ is referred to as "upholding all things by the word of His power."

The Modernists, therefore, flatly contradict the Bible, including Christ's own explicit statements, when they say that He did not have the power of God.

If it was not the power of God that was in Jesus of Nazareth, then I ask what power was it that converted the billows of Galilee into a marble pavement for His majestic foot-steps?   What power was it by which He clothed Himself in the glories of uncreated light on the Mount of Transfiguration?   What power was it by which he spoke into life the corrupting tenant of Lazarus' sepulchre; by which He reinstated the deposed and distracted reason upon the throne of the demoniac's mind; by which He opened the blind eyes and unstopped the deaf ears and caused the "lame man to leap as a hart and the tongue of the dumb to sing?"   Yea, what power

was it that shattered the iron bands of death itself, and on
the resurrection morning brought Christ forth as victor
over death and the grave? The entire Christian world
has just celebrated once more in its beautiful Easter
ceremonies, the actual resurrection of Jesus Christ from
the grave.

In speaking of His death and His resurrection, Christ
said:

"I lay down my life that I might take it again. No man
taketh it from me, but I lay it down of myself, I have power
to lay it down, and I have power to take it again." (John
10:17, 18.)

The power within the dead to overcome death is surely
the supreme power. Man does not have it. Only God
has it. Therefore, the supreme miracle of the resurrection of Christ is a proof that He had divine power and
that He was more than mere man, that He was incarnate
deity.

I wish at this point to ask my opponent two pertinent
questions:

First, if you do not believe in these miracles as recorded
in the Bible, then must you not say that these seemingly
sensible and good people who wrote the Bible were really
either self-deluded fanatics or else they were liars and
deceivers?

Second, if you do believe in the miracles, then do they
not *prove* that Jesus Christ had divine and superhuman
powers, and, therefore, that He was more than man, that
He was incarnate God?

III. CHRIST'S CLAIM FOR HIMSELF.

I come, now, to the climax of the Bible's teachings
about Jesus Christ, namely, what He Himself had to say
about the question of His deity. Some who are given
to questioning the teachings of the Bible in some of its
parts nevertheless say that Jesus taught the truth, and,

therefore, that *He* can certainly be believed and followed. In other words, His teachings are recognized as the very *heart* of the Bible. If they are rejected, then the entire Bible must simply be thrown away.

Now when we come to the question of Christ's claims for His teaching about Himself, we find that doubters and critics are left in a dilemma.

All reputable critics now admit two things concerning Jesus of Nazareth. First, as I have already proved, that He was a Wise man, and secondly, as I also showed, that He was a good man. But if this much is admitted, then His deity must also be admitted, for He claimed to be divine. Now if He was a wise man, He would not have been so foolish as to make such an absurd and egotistical claim unless He was divine; and if, on the other hand, He was a good man, He would not have sought to mislead and delude His fellows by a claim so monstrous and blasphemous, unless it was true.

DID JESUS CLAIM TO BE DIVINE?

The issue at this point turns, therefore, upon the question of whether Jesus did claim deity; and that He did must be conceded by any impartial mind who will study the record.

Notice, for one thing, that this claim was involved in the beautiful similes which he applied to Himself. He said, "I am the light of the world," "I am the way," "I am the truth," "I am the vine," "Ask in my name and your prayers shall be granted," "Eat my body, drink my blood," "I am the resurrection." And these expressions were used not with the egotistical vanity of even the highest of men, which would have called forth only ridicule and scorn from those who heard them; but they were spoken with such unruffled calmness, such sublime selfpossession, and such poise of authority that those who heard them fell down and worshipped Him.

His claim to deity is involved also in His teaching concerning His relationship to the most vital interests of life. For example, He presumed to forgive sins, and only God can claim that power. It is written here: "That ye may know that the Son of man hath power on earth to forgive. sins, He saith to the sick of the palsy, I say unto thee 'Arise, and take up thy bed, and go thy way into thine house.' " (Mark 2.)

He proclaimed Himself as a lawgiver. He said, "It hath been said by them of old time, thou shalt do no murder," etc., etc., but I say unto you," etc. . . . He claimed the right to promulgate a higher moral law even than that which had come from the divine hands at Sinai; and to show His full supremacy, He said, "The Son of man is Lord even of the Sabbath."

He had a great deal to say in regard to the Kingdom of God, and He announced Himself as the Ruler in that Kingdom. In Luke 19:12 and in other places He used such expressions as this: "That ye may eat and drink in my Kingdom."

Jesus declared that He would be the Judge of all mankind, and emphasized the fact of the Divine character of the office. In John 5:22, 23, He said:

"For neither doth the Father judge any man, but He hath given all judgment unto the Son, that all men may honor the Son, even as they honor the father."

He claimed the right to direct events as an overruling Providence. In Matthew 24 and 25, we have the wonderful picture which He drew of the time when He shall return, attended by His holy angels, to direct the closing events in the history of this present age, and to judge all nations in righteousness.

The future raising of the dead is claimed by Him in John 6:39, 44:

"And this is the Father's will which hath sent me, that of all which He hath given me I should lose nothing, but should raise it up at the last day.   No man can come to me, except the Father which hath sent me draw Him: And I will raise Him up at the last day.

The bestowal of eternal life is claimed by Him.   In John 10:28, He says:

"And I give unto them eternal life, and they shall never perish, neither shall any man pluck them out of my hand."

And in John 17:1, 2, He says:

"Father, the Hour is Come; glorify thy Son, that the Son may Glorify thee; even as Thou gavest him authority over all flesh that to all whom thou hast given Him, He would give eternal life."

He claimed even to have full control of natural forces. He said to the storm-tossed waves, "Be still" and to the howling tempest, "Be muzzled," and they obeyed His voice.   In each of these great and important relationships He put Himself in the place of God.

Indeed, He accepted worship, as illustrated in such passages as this:

"Thomas answered and said unto Him: 'My Lord and My God.' "

"Jesus saith unto Him, Thomas because thou hast seen me, thou hast believed; blessed are they that have not seen and yet have believed."   (John 20:28.)

Here He accepted Thomas' worship.

In connection with the establishment of the Lord's Supper Jesus Himself said, "This do in remembrance of Me."   And Paul said, "As often as ye eat this bread and drink this cup, ye do show the Lord's death till he comes" (1 Cor. 11:26).   Our worship, therefore, in connection with the holy rite of the Christian church—the Lord's Supper—is an act of worship instituted by Christ Himself.

When the devil tempted Him on the Mount, He replied, "Thou shalt not tempt the Lord thy God." (Luke 4:12).

When He asked His disciples, "Whom say ye that I am?" Simon Peter answered "Thou art the Christ, the Son of the living God." And instead of rebuking him, greatly rejoiced by this flash of insight into His true character, Christ exclaimed, "Blessed art thou, Simon Barjona, for flesh and blood hath not revealed it unto thee, but my Father, which is in Heaven." Peter had had a direct revelation from the Heavenly land concerning Christ's true divine nature, and so He said: "I say unto thee that thou art Peter and upon this rock (the rock of faith in His divinity) I will build my church; and the gates of hell shall not prevail against it" (Matthew 13: 13-18).

SPECIFIC CLAIMS

In even more striking and specific ways, and again and again, Jesus deliberately claimed that He was God. In His question to the Pharisees 'What think ye of Christ? Whose Son is He?" He was arguing for His own full deity, for He pointed out to them that while Christ was of the seed of David, according to the flesh, nevertheless David with prophetic prevision called Him "Lord."

In the midst of a beautiful prayer, Christ claimed that He had sat on the throne of the universe with God the Father before the world was. He said, "And now, O Father, glorify thou me with thine own self with the glory which I had with thee before the world was." (John 17:5). And referring again to this matter, He said, "I am from above." (John 8:23). And once more, He said, "What and if ye shall see the Son of Man ascend up where He was before?" (John 6:62).

Furthermore, He put Himself on an absolute equality

with the other members of the Godhead, in giving the great commission, when He said: "Go, ye therefore, and teach all nations, baptising them in the name of the Father, and of the Son and of the Holy Ghost." (Matt. 28:19). And speaking to John, in Revelation, He said explicitly: "I am Alpha and Omega, the beginning and the ending, saith the Lord, which is and which was and which is to come, the *Almighty*." (Rev. 1:8.)

In the case of the man who had been blind from his birth, and whose eyes Jesus opened, after this man had been put out of the synagogue by the hostile Jews, because he would not give false testimony against Jesus, it is recorded here:

"Jesus heard that they had cast him out; and when He had found him, He said unto him, Dost thou believe on the Son of God? He answered and said, Who is He, Lord, that I might believe on Him? and Jesus said unto him, 'Thou hast both seen Him and it is He that talketh with thee.' And he said, 'Lord, I believe' and he worshipped Him." (John 9:35-38.)

It is here stated that Jesus specifically declared that He was the Son of God, and that He meant *this in the sense of full deity* is *proved absolutely by the fact that He accepted this man's worship!* I challenge my opponent to account for this.

Again, when his enemies declared that he had a devil, Jesus answered them by remarking:

"If a man keep my sayings he shall never see death."

His enemies retorted: "Art thou greater than our father Abraham, which is dead? . . . Whom maketh thou thyself?" Jesus answered:

"Your father Abraham rejoiced to see my day and he saw it and was glad."

Then His enemies said unto Him,

"Thou art not yet fifty years old, and hast thou seen Abraham?"

Then it is written:

"Jesus said unto them, Verily, verily, I say unto you, before Abraham was, I AM" (John 8:48–59).

Then it is recorded they took up stones to stone Him, but that Jesus hid Himself and went out of the Temple, thus escaping death at their hands.

They thus sought to stone Him to death because in the Expression, "I AM" He not only claimed eternity of existence, but He used the holy name which God gave to Himself when He spoke to Moses at the burning bush. In that incident of the burning bush Moses asked God to tell Him His name so that he could give answer when the Jews, to whom he was being sent as deliverer, should demand of him who commanded him to do this work and who sent Him, and God answered Moses from the burning bush and told him to say, "I AM hath sent thee." "I AM that I AM" is the great all-comprehending name of the eternal God, given by God Himself, and when the Jews heard Jesus claiming that name for Himself they regarded it as blasphemy and sought to stone Him to death. The literal rendering here is "Jesus said to them, Amen, Amen, I say to you, before Abraham was I Am." The "Amen, Amen" is practically an oath. Jesus, therefore, took oath before them that He was God—the eternal "I AM." They immediately understood what He meant and therefore sought to stone Him to death. (John 8:48-59).

These Jewish enemies would not forget the claim that Jesus made for Himself, nor would they forget their charge of blasphemy against Him.

Therefore, in the tenth chapter of John's gospel it is recorded that some time later Jesus was walking in the Temple in Solomon's porch, and the Jews once more crowded around Him and said unto Him specifically,

"How long dost thou make us to doubt? If thou be the Christ, tell us plainly."

In reply to that Jesus answered them with that tremendous statement:

"I and My Father are one."   (John 10:30.)

Then it is written again that "the Jews took up stones again to stone Him."   But this time Jesus expostulated with them.   He said:

"Many good works have I showed you from my Father; for which of these works do you stone me?"

They answered, "For a good work we stone thee not, but for blasphemy and because that thou being a man *maketh thyself God*."   (John 10:33.)   Thus His enemies clearly understood His distinct and unmistakable claim to deity, and they sought to put Him to death for that claim, which they regarded as blasphemy.   After they had arrested Jesus and haled Him before Pilate, they exclaimed to the governor: "By our law He ought to die, because He made Himself the Son of God."   (John 19:7.)

There is a yet more solemn affirmation of His own deity, which was made by Jesus on the very night before He died.   In the 26th chapter of Matthew's Gospel it is recorded that He was brought before the high priest and put under oath and commanded to say once more if He claimed to be God.   Caiaphas, the high priest, said to Him, "I adjure thee by the living God that thou tell us whether thou be the Christ, the Son of God."   Jesus answered with the most positive and solemn form of the Jewish affirmation: *"Thou hast said it."*   Whereupon, it is written here, "The high priest rent his garments, saying, He hath spoken blasphemy; what further need have we of witnesses?   Behold, now ye have heard His blasphemy.   What think ye?   They answered and said. He is guilty of death."   (Matt. 26:63-68.)

It was for the answer that He made there, to the high priest, that they condemned Jesus and put Him to death. "Blasphemy" was the word used against Him in His death warrant, because He had claimed to be the Son of God. Pilate would not write the inscription for Him on the cross the way the Jews wanted it. They wanted as the death warrant, "He called Himself God's equal." And the Lord admitted the impeachment. He would not retract, because he could not and be truthful. He stretched out His hands on the arms of the cross, and through those quivering palms they drove the cruel nails, and lifted Him up and crucified Him. The last testimony to His deity was the outpouring of His blood, and as that blood ran over the cross and down the slope of Calvary, even the hard hearted Roman centurian cried out:

"Verily, this was the Son of God."

Undeniably, Christ did believe and did declare that He was the Son of God, and if this claim was not true, then He was the greatest fraud and humbug who ever walked the earth. Unless He was fully God, as He claimed to be, then He was either a fool or a knave. We know that the author of the sermon on the mount was not a fool, and that the unselfish Christ of Calvary was not a knave.

I wish to ask my opponent which horn of the dilemma he will take. I wish to ask him this question:

If you admit that Jesus Christ was both a wise and good man, then must you not also admit that He was what He claimed to be—the divine Son of God—incarnate deity?

IV. CHRIST'S AFTER INFLUENCE

My final argument is that Christ's after influence proves that He is divine. I first showed from both the Old and New Testaments the general Bible teaching that Christ was God—the second person in a divine Trinity; I next showed that He had the great outstanding attributes of God, namely, divine wisdom, holiness, love and power, and, therefore, that He was and is God. I then quoted the clear and overwhelming claims and teachings of Christ Himself that He was the Son of God in a unique sense. I pointed out that to overcome these claims of Christ, sceptics and critics have to impale themselves on one or other horn of a dilemma—they have to say either that Christ was not a good man or else that He was not a wise man, unless He spoke the truth when He said that He was divine.

I now submit, in closing, that His after life has confirmed His claims to deity, and that His influence and transforming power for the past two thousand years prove that He is still alive—a divine personality. The effects that Christ is still bringing to pass in the world, especially His soul changing, life giving, regenerating power—are the effects of one personality influencing another, which prove that Jesus Christ is at present a divine living Personality at work in the world. The regeneration of such men as Saul of Tarsus, Augustine, Moody, Jerry McCauley, and just recently the brilliant literary genius Pappini, proves that Jesus Christ has lived and now lives as a real, divine miracle working Being.

And, my friends, it is a most significant fact that those branches of the Christian church which most sincerely believe in the deity of Jesus Christ are the ones which grow most rapidly, and seemingly do the most good in the world. I pass by the great Roman and Greek churches, with their teeming millions of faithful believers in the divine Son of God, and with their good works the world over, and point out certain significant facts among Protestant Christians.

To avoid any possible semblance even of personalities, I wish, rather than giving direct statements of my own, to quote some words from Dr. Charles R. Brown, Dean of the School of Religion of Yale University. Dr. Brown is recognized not only as a great scholar, but as a pre-eminently fair and just man; and the fact that he is a Congregationalist,—the denomination out of which the Unitarians originally largely came—in this country—

makes his words all the more weighty and convincing. In his little book on "Who is Jesus Christ," Dr. Brown says:

"I am a Congregationalist myself. A little over a hundred years ago we had a split in our denomination. There were those who held the lower view of Christ's person [that is that he was not incarnate deity]. They insisted upon that view and they brought about a division of the Congregational Church. We have no strongly centralized authority in our body, and this radical difference in belief divided the denomination almost equally. These men who held the lower view of the person of Christ withdrew, taking with them a large amount of property and a large number who belonged to the Congregational Church. That was a little over a hundred years ago. At that time the Unitarian leaders were saying that within twenty-five years all the Christians in the country would come over to their side. They now number something like 80,000 or 90,000, while the other branch of the Congregational Church holding the other view of Christ's person [that is that He is incarnate deity] numbers 800,000. And we are a very small denomination as compared with the Methodists with their 7,000,000, or the Baptists who have as many more, or the Presbyterians with their three or four millions, or the Lutherans with several millions or the Episcopalians with a million more. Somehow these branches of the Christian Church which have held strongly and steadily to the higher view of Christ have had the wind and tide with them. That branch of the Christian church which has held the lower view has not been able to show in its gospel that regenerating power which will take hold of a bad man and make him good. Show me among them a single work like that being done by the Jerry McAuley Mission in New York, the McCall Mission in Paris, the Pacific Garden Mission in Chicago, or the work of our own Bill Ellis in the Yale Mission in New Haven. Can you name a single place of that kind where they are making saints of men, who were wrecked by their sins through the preaching of this lower idea of Christ's person? If you want to get the spirit of evil out of a man and the spirit of God into him, it seems that the higher view of Christ's person is needed to do the business. . . . When we observe that in seventeen centuries of Christian activity somehow the larger measure of success comes with the higher view; it surely must mean something."

Dr. Brown is right. It does mean something. It means that Jesus Christ is alive now and is still at work in the world through His Holy Spirit. It means that He is still performing miracles among men where they will believe on Him as God. He will convert and transform the lives of all who will accept Him as Savior and live in obedience to His holy will.

In the beautiful city of Baltimore, at the entrance of the great Johns Hopkins Hospital, there stands an exquisite white marble statue of Christ. It is in the hallway just inside the entrance door. Many times during my pastorate in that city, in going to visit the sick in the hospital, I stood and looked upon the statue, and never once did I see it, that my heart was not deeply stirred. It is a majestic and yet most compassionate figure. The arms are outstretched, the nail wounds are seen in the hands, and the genius of the sculptor has put upon the face an expression of benignant longing, and yearning compassion. Inscribed upon the base of the statue are those words that fell from His own gracious lips, "Come unto Me all ye that labour and are heavy laden, and I will give you rest. Take my yoke upon you and learn of me, for I am meek and lowly in heart and ye shall find rest unto your souls." It is an appropriate monument for the entrance to a hospital, and many a troubled spirit and pain-racked body has been blessed in looking upon it. But it is said that once there came a cynic and a doubter, and he looked long and attentively at the figure. He viewed it from right and left, and then walked once more in front, but turned away at last with cynicism still written upon his face. But there was standing also near a little girl, and with childish eagerness and curiosity she watched his face, and then, with a girl's deep intuition of spiritual things, when she saw him turn away without having read the deep message of that beautiful figure, she ran up to him and said: "Oh, sir, you cannot see Him that way. To see Him you must come up very close, and fall on your knees, and look up!"

That is what we all need to do today. We need to turn from the self-sufficiency and the intellectual pride which looks at Jesus Christ in a condescending way. We all need to come very close to him in Faith, to fall upon our knees in humility, and to look up with unfeigned gratitude to Him, who loved us and gave Himself for us!

III

REBUTTAL FOR AFFIRMATIVE[1]

Mr: Potter: I am informed that inasmuch as my opponent took five minutes more than the allotted hour in his speech, I am allotted five minutes more in my second speech: Inasmuch as I took only forty-five in my first speech I suppose I might claim more, but, really, all I want is twenty minutes.

My opponent began by saying that there is no effect without an adequate cause, and somehow he managed by clever casuistry to deduce that that proved the fact of the Deity of Jesus! But the fact that the life of Jesus has had a most remarkable effect upon the world doesn't prove him Deity. It only proves him a most unusual man, the supreme man, as I have already stated.

As for mere compliment not being wanted by Jesus, I gave no mere compliment; I gave the tribute from the depth of my heart to the greatest man that I ever heard about.

As I prophesied in my first speech, there was on the part of my opponent that usual orthodox attempt to conjure up a holy mystery that we mustn't try to understand. For my opponent stated that it is difficult (and these are his exact words) for our finite minds to comprehend the Deity of Jesus. But these are the only minds we have brought with us tonight!

I could not get at all the logic of his opening statement regarding the general teaching of the Bible prov-

[1] By Rev. Charles Francis Potter.

ing that Jesus was the Creator. He quoted the first verse of the first chapter of Genesis, which says that in the beginning God created the Heavens and the earth, and then went on to say that this says that Jesus created the world. How he got the deduction, I cannot see; can you?

To be sure he linked with that the first verse of the first chapter of the fourth Gospel where it says, "In the beginning was created the word," and which goes on to say that the word was made flesh, but here is where John is adding to the Gospels an imported Logos doctrine from Alexandria, Egypt, which was a very popular doctrine at the time. You will notice that Jesus, Himself, had nothing to say about the Logos doctrine.

In Hebrews 1-10 my opponent quoted the statement that "Thou, Lord, in the beginning has made the Heavens and the earth." But Hebrews is a very questionable book to deduce as authority, because nobody knows who wrote it.

I thought for a while that my opponent was going to have his earnest wish granted, namely, the redebating of the third debate. I refuse the challenge because it has no proper part in this debate. I will only say that for him to quote the prophecy in Isaiah that referred to the name "Immanuel—God with us" as a proof of the Deity of Jesus was rather bad judgment, because, while Immanuel (which, by the way, Jesus was never called during his lifetime) does mean "God with us," the word Timothy means "the Glory of God" and the word Elijah means "God, the Lord." Does that prove that Elijah was Deity?

I hope you won't be deceived by the statement made by my opponent that the word "Lord" from the Greek "Kurios" means God. You had better take Paul. Paul, I think, is safer in that regard. First Corinthians, 8 ÷ 6, read it carefully. "There is one God, the Father, and one Lord Jesus Christ." They are very carefully distinguished. They are not coincident or identical.

We can not accept his statement that the Trinity is taught in the Bible. I challenged him, you remember, to produce one verse or one section in which the Trinity was proved.* He took Colossians 2:9, John 14:10 and First Corinthians 3:1-17, from scattered parts of the New Testament, and molded them into a beautiful mosaic and said, "See, the Bible proves the doctrine of the Trinity." That is a trick that used to be worked a long while ago, but it doesn't go any more. You can prove anything by that method. He said that the Bible's general teaching proved the Deity of Jesus, and then by dexterously skipping back and forth from passage to passage he produced in your minds the impression that the Bible did, but you will notice that he was very careful not to give direct verses. His strong point was Philippians 2:5–11, which he quoted with great rhetoric and at some length. But then you will notice that he inserted an interpolation there, "Confess that Jesus Christ is Lord"; and then he added *that is Kurios; that is God.* But that is not in the text, "Confess that Jesus Christ is Lord, to the glory of God, the Father," but that doesn't say that Jesus is God, or was God, or will be God. It uses that word "Lord" which means master or teacher or leader.

In implying that Christ had all the attributes of God, he imputed to him perfect wisdom, but the very passage in Mark that I quoted, Mark 11, 12–14, where Jesus came to the fig tree expecting to find figs and was disappointed, proves that he did not have perfect wisdom.

I was interested when he brought in the statement that Jesus was sinless, and his very agile dodge in trying to get around the verse which I introduced where the young man asked him, and he said that there was none good but

* The verse in First John 5:7, which he mentions has been proved a forgery and is rejected in all recent translations.

one; that is God. It was clever, but it didn't answer the point at all. He said that it was a rebuke to a young man's hastiness in forming opinions about a stranger. Well, maybe, but that is an interpolation and an interpretation, and it is not stated that way in the Gospel.

He anticipated a possible argument of mine that Jesus' praying to God would indicate that he, himself, was not God, and he answered my anticipated remark by saying that the prayers of Jesus were all communion and therefore not petition and therefore could not be adduced as proving that he was not God.

Let me get that clear in your mind. He said that when Jesus prayed he wasn't petitioning; he was simply communing with God, a sort of celestial conversation. Very well. How then does he explain that agonized petition which was not a communion idea, but a real petition, which indicates a separation from God, that petition on the Cross, "My God, My God, why hast Thou forsaken me?" Is that communion? It is the very opposite of communion.

He said that none of Jesus' prayers were a confession of sin. But when you pray and confess sins, you don't get an audience around to listen, and during the prayers which Jesus made, which may have been confessions of sin, of course there were no disciples around to listen. He went alone to the mountains, we are told, and what happened there between that man and his God you and I do not know and it is not for us to inquire.

When the Judge, Pilate, said, "I find no fault in this man," how possibly could we deduce Deity from that? When a judge sitting on a bench says, respecting a certain case brought before him, "Not guilty; excused; dismissed," does that mean that he thinks that the person who is excused is perfect, is a Deity? When Pilate said, "I find no fault in this man," he did not mean that he was perfect Deity. He merely meant that the charges brought against him did not seem to him to be justified.

And as for Pilate's wife, she gave him good advice, but then that is no proof of Jesus' sinlessness, nor of his Deity.

How can you call Jesus sinless when you have a record of only a few days of his life? Buddha was regarded by his followers as sinless centuries before Christ was born and just as good proofs were adduced for that. Only we do not happen to be Buddhists and so, of course, we don't believe it! And I cannot in my mind reconcile, nor can you in your heart of hearts, the idea of a sinless Jesus with that statement, "Why callest thou me good? There is none good but one; that is God."

"The supreme attribute of God is love," said my opponent and Jesus was a lover of men, but you can't go on and say, therefore Jesus is Deity, for there are many men and women who love, who love honestly, purely and sincerely and do not claim to be Deity.

He said that no man will die for his enemy. How about in the World War, when many of our boys died for their enemies?[2]

As for Jesus performing miracles when he healed the leper, that power over disease which he had, disease which he thought was due to demon possession but which none of us think is due to demon possession now, that power he did not himself think made him Deity, for he recognized that others had that power. You have his own words for it, Matthew 12, 27—"And if I by Beelzebub cast out devils, by whom do your children cast them out? Therefore they shall be your judges." And that statement in itself shows that he did not consider his power over disease an attribute of Deity.

And as for the miracles? "How can we refuse to accept them?" says my worthy opponent. I do not re-

[2] Many instances are recorded where American boys pulled wounded German boys from No Man's Land to safety at the risk of and even loss of their own lives.

fuse to accept them. I simply say that the miracles are not a proof of the Deity of Jesus. For instance, you will find when you come to examine the Bible that there are just as good records of other miracles. If miracles are a proof of Deity, then we ought to worship Elijah and Elisha, for the Bible reports them to have worked miracles even to the raising of the dead, Second Kings 8, I and First Kings 17, 22. If miracles are a proof of the Deity of Jesus, then shall we say that we too are Gods for Jesus, himself, said, "The works that I do shall ye do also and greater things than these shall ye do." Is this any argument for the Deity of those who perform wonderful things? And so I answer that pointed question put to me by my opponent. He said, "If you do not believe in these miracles, then you must say that the people were deluded; if you believe in the miracles, do they not prove him to be more than God?" I answer, "No, they do not." If it be granted that Jesus did work miracles, it is reported equally well in the Bible of a great many other people that they worked miracles, and we do not worship them or claim them to be God. If you begin by expanding the Trinity to include the miracle-workers, you will have a big Trinity.

My opponent pointed out that Jesus was wise and good and claimed to be divine, and therefore if he was wise he wouldn't have claimed to be divine unless he was. But he did *not* claim to be Deity and as I pointed out, and as my opponent very carelessly dismissed, there is a distinction between Deity and divinity.

If you want to get down to the very Latin of it, Deity comes from Deus, "God"; and divinity comes from divinitas, divus, "like God"; and there is a great deal of difference between being God and having the attributes of God or being like God, pertaining to God, related to God. Why, there is divinity within each one of us,

sometimes concealed, sometimes expanding, but still a
spark of divinity within every human breast.

I hope you noticed the verses which my worthy opponent quoted as proving Jesus' claim to Deity. They
did not prove his claim to Deity. He quoted these verses:
"I am the light. I am the way. I am the truth. I am
divine." But did he quote any other saying, "I am Deity"
or "I am God?" He quoted some which in connection
with others might be interpreted so to mean, but, as I
said before, there is no direct statement of Deity claimed
by Jesus.

When Thomas said, "My Lord and My God," that was
no proof of the Deity of Jesus, since we have on record
the very words of the Secretary of the Emperor Domitian
who adoringly called his employer, in this letter which we
still have, "Dominus et Deus meus." "My Lord and My
God" was a common phrase at that time, and did not
imply Deity. Certainly the subjects of the Emperor Domitian knew him well enough not to imply that he was
Deity! When Jesus at the last supper said, "This do in
remembrance of me," is that a proof of his Deity or is it
simply that he wanted them to remember him? "Thou
art the Christ, the Son of the living God," yes; that was
said; but it doesn't prove the Deity of Jesus. It does
not say, "Thou art the living God." It says, "Thou
art the Christ, the "Christos," the anointed one, the *son*
of the living God." Simon did not call him God; he
called him the *Son* of God and you will find another
verse of the New Testament which says, "Now are we
all sons of God."

The other verse brought up by my opponent, "Before
Abraham was, I am" does not prove Jesus Deity. "If
Thou be Christ, tell us plainly," and Christ answered
(John 10, 30), "I and My Father are one." Yes, but in
John 17, 11, he prayed, "Holy Father, keep through thine
own name those whom thou hast given me, that *they*

may be one, as we are." He was speaking of his disciples, and certainly did not mean to convey that all his disciples were Deity. This "I and My Father are one" was his simple statement of his feeling of communion with his Father. He felt so close to God that he felt almost one with Him, and every mystic that has ever written—read James' "Varieties of Religious Experience" and you will find a dozen souls, great mystics who have said, "I felt as if I were caught up and as if I were with God, that I was one with God." The whole Oriental doctrine of absorption into Nirvana means I am one with God, but that doesn't prove that the devotee is Deity. Keep to the point. And how the outpouring of Jesus' blood upon Calvary proved his Deity my opponent neglected to state, although he said that it did prove his Deity. Simply the fact that his blood was poured out and that theologians have since connected that with the old legend that without the shedding of blood there is no remission of sins, does not prove anything. It only affords a basis for a certain type of orthodox theology.

My opponent made the statement that Jesus was either a fool or a knave, if his statements were not true. But he went on the assumption that Jesus has claimed to be Incarnate Deity and I maintain that Jesus never claimed to be Incarnate Deity. And that is the thing that we are discussing tonight; not Son of God; not "Lord"; not any of these attributes or subordinate beings, but Incarnate Deity, itself. Jesus knew better than to claim that. Never, never did he attempt to.

My opponent went on to state that the after-influence of the life of Jesus in the lives of Moody and Jerry Mc-Cauley and Papini was proof of the Deity of Jesus. Have you read Papini's book? Papini's book has in it a great many things that are beautiful, but it has a great many other things which are hardly complimentary to the character of the man who wrote the book, and if the virulent, hateful spirit which Papini manifested in his book is an evidence of the Deity of Jesus, I fail to see it.

I would like to quote you some other names of people who have not believed in the Deity of Jesus and yet who have lived the life inspired by the man Jesus. I would give you Ralph Waldo Emerson, Theodore Parker, Henry Wadsworth Longfellow, the whole series of American poets. I might go on here half the night telling of the great, noble souls who have rejected the doctrine of the Deity of Jesus and yet who have been inspired by His life.

I fail to get the argument that those churches which believe in the Deity of Jesus have grown most rapidly and then the inference that therefore the Deity of Jesus is true. Numbers is no argument. I tried to tell my opponent that before. If the denseness of population in any auditorium is a tribute to the correctness of belief of the people there, I would like to ask my opponent how he accounts for the great number of people attending certain shows on Broadway tonight. If numbers is an argument, how about the fact that although there are 800,000 Congregationalists and seven or eight million Baptists and seven or eight million Methodists, there are on the other hand over 200 million Buddhists?

And now although it is somewhat beside the argument, the fact that my opponent brought it in makes it necessary for me in closing to answer something of a slur on the denomination from which I come. The statement was quoted from Rev. Charles R. Brown that Unitarianism and Congregationalism 100 years ago divided evenly and that now the Congregationalists have 800,000 to the Unitarians 80,000—those numbers are manipulated a little bit, not intentionally, I know. It happens that the Unitarians have nearly twice as many as that and I suppose the Congregationalists have a few more than that, but the point is this: that although the numbers of Unitarians have not increased as rapidly as the numbers of the Congregationalists, nevertheless, the Congregationalists have gradually accepted the Unitarian doctrine, and you will find in almost all Congregationalist pulpits today a teaching that would have caused these ministers to have been expelled from their denomination one hundred years ago.

Let me tell you, for instance, that Congregationalism and Unitarianism have come together; that in a certain town in Massachusetts the son of a Congregationalist has married the daughter of Samuel A. Eliot, President of the American Unitarian Association. The son is the son of Dr. MacGiffert, the President of Union Theological Seminary. The son of a Congregationalist has married the daughter of a Unitarian and they are minister and minister's wife in a United Unitarian Congregational Church in Massachusetts. That is typical. The 800,000 Congregationalists have increased so rapidly because you can be a Unitarian in a Congregationalist Church, without the opprobrium of the name "Unitarian." You can be a Unitarian in almost any church nowadays, and the fact that there are only 80,000 or 150,000 or whatever it is, Unitarians recognized in the Unitarian denomination, is no measure of the Unitarians that there are throughout the United States at large.

Let me say what I have said before, namely, that in the Hall of Fame there were 65 names chosen of eminent service-rendering Americans. Twenty-two of the 65 are Unitarians.

My opponent asked me to show one good work done by Unitarians to compare with the Jerry McCauley Mission and other similar missions. I point to two or three little facts in closing, namely, that Dorothea Dix, who did the pioneer work for the insane in the United States; that Horace Mann, Charles W. Eliot and Arthur E. Morgan of Antioch College, the three greatest educators that America has had; that the Red Cross, which was started in All Souls Unitarian Church of this city as the Sanitary Commission by Henry W. Bellows; that Civil Service and practically every other great social reform was started by Unitarians.

That, however, is an aside merely to answer my opponent's remark. It really doesn't prove anything one way or the other. My main contention stands, namely, that my opponent has not yet produced any verse in which Jesus directly states that he is God. He has not answered the many verses which I produced in which Jesus admitted that He was not God and since our resolution is "Resolved, that Jesus Christ was entirely man instead of Incarnate Deity," I maintain that the many points which I have produced and which have not been answered, and that the points which my opponent has produced but which I have answered, prove the affirmative of this debate.

IV

REBUTTAL FOR THE NEGATIVE[1]

Dr. Straton: I will take up first the rebuttal of my opponent's opening speech, and then pass on to some good-natured remarks about the Unitarians, and then about some other things that he brought in in his rebuttal.

He made the point in the beginning that Jesus was deified by the after-thought of the people. My friends, when that argument is analyzed, it comes down to this that within less than two generations those early Christians had turned into idolaters. One historian, in speaking of the degeneration of pagan Rome, says that those pagans finally reached what he calls the "incredible baseness of deifying the Emperor"; and we are asked to believe that within a few short years after Jesus' death those early Christians had turned into idolaters and were guilty of the "incredible baseness of deifying" a man. A little common sense is often better than a mass of critical speculation and labored learning, and such a view of the development of early Christianity as this modernism offers is simply impossible on the face of it.

[1] By Rev. John Roach Straton, D.D.

The modernists usually point to John's Gospel in their effort to bolster up this idea. They argue that the early Christians allowed their imaginations to come into play and, through that, that the process of the deification of the Lord went forward, was completed, and finally expressed itself explicitly in John's Gospel. Now Jesus was put to death about the year 33. The Fourth Gospel was written as many of the most radical critics even, admit, between the years 95 and 100. According to this idea, therefore, in 60 years Christianity had become idolatry. It started as the purest and loftiest religion ever preached, and yet in that short time it had become radically

77

vitiated. The heroic efforts of "the noblest of prophets," had resulted in swift decay, and Christianity had become a corrupt religion setting forth an enormous lie, namely, the Deity of Jesus Christ. Now the worship of man is idolatry. Therefore, according to this idea Christianity had degenerated into a system of idolatry within two generations after the death of Christ.

My opponent made the point that Jesus was only a man because he was tempted. But he was the God-man, and, therefore, in his humanity, he could be tempted.

Of course, the argument from John's Gospel means but little at last, as Matthew, Mark, Luke and the Epistles are all full of the doctrine of the deity of Jesus.

ADVANTAGES OF CHRIST'S DEITY

It is not true, as my opponent argued again and again, that to accept Jesus as divine removes Him from us. No! It makes Him nearer and dearer than ever. When we hear the God-Man say: "I will no longer call you servants, but I will call you friends," our hearts thrill with the wonder and glory of it. Jesus as divine is a personal present friend to the believer every day and hour.

So far from it being a disadvantage, the Deity of Christ is the greatest possible advantage. It does not take the man Jesus Christ from us, and it does bring God down to us. The human heart has ever longed to know God. When Philip said: "Show us the Father and it sufficeth us," he expressed a universal longing of man's heart to know God. And in the face of Jesus Christ, we see and know God. He is the express image of the Father's glory, and when we look upon Him in His sympathy and His love and His power, we can say, "God is like Jesus." We have, therefore, in the God-Man all the advantages of human fellowship and inspiration, plus the immeasurable advantages also of God brought near to us.

My opponent endeavored to draw some fine distinctions in defining the difference between "deity" and "divinity," but, as I remarked in my opening speech, I will use the word divine in the popular and commonly understood sense that it is thought to carry with it. Also, I will not be drawn into a fog-bank of fine definitions and metaphysical speculations.

My opponent also split some hairs over the finite and the infinite. We may not be able to understand the relationship between the finite and the infinite, but when we see the glories of Jesus Christ, we can accept the blessings which come from such a combination of the two, even though we do not understand it.

My opponent had a good deal to say also on reason versus faith. But this is a purely imaginary conflict. This debate is on a religious question; therefore, it involves faith because faith is recognized as the fundamental element in real religion. The Bible says, "without faith it is impossible to please God." We need to remember that man has a heart as well as a head, and scripture declares truly: "Out of the heart are the issues of life." Reason goes just as far as it can, and is a good servant as far as it goes, but when Reason has reached the utmost limit of her journey then Faith spreads her white wings and bears us on to the shining goal of spiritual truth!

MISINTERPRETED SCRIPTURES

My opponent quoted a number of Scripture passages alleging that they were evidence proving that Jesus was not God. He quoted Matthew 24:36 where Jesus, in speaking of His second coming, said: "But of that day and hour knoweth no man, no, not the angels of heaven, but my Father only." This does not prove that Jesus was filled with ignorance like other men. The simple answer to that argument, and all other arguments which my opponent founded upon different Scripture verses that seem to show a limitation in Jesus, is that there was a *self limitation* in Him. When the divine took on human- ity, there was of necessity a certain temporary subjection on the part of the divine to the conditions of the human. It is expressly stated in the Bible that when Jesus became man He "emptied Himself" of certain things in connec- tion with the form of God. It is freely admitted, there- fore, that the divine nature submitted to certain self limitations and in a sense was humbled during our Sav- ior's earthly life. Therefore, these passages which set forth Christ's human weakness, and limitations as to some matters, are entirely consistent with the fact of His eternal deity. They apply to His earthly state of humil- iation rather than to His original and present glory.

The Bible also makes plain that there is an order of office and operation in the Godhead, which, while it is consistent with essential oneness and equality, neverthe- less permits the Father to be spoken of as first, the Son as second, and the Holy Spirit as third. In the light of this obvious Bible truth, such passages as first Corinth- ians 15:28, therefore, need to be interpreted consistently with other passages such as John 17:5, etc.

But, in His state of humiliation, Christ was the essen- tial truth, and any limitations, therefore, in connection with His human nature never led to error or false teach- ing. This understanding of the plain facts removes all difficulty from such statements from Jesus as "My Father is greater than I," and other such passages as my oppo- nent quoted, like that of the fig tree, etc.

My opponent quoted John 1:18 that "no man hath seen God at any time." It is true that men have never seen the divine essence, or the entire triune personality of God, but they have seen the manifestations of God. In the old dispensation, God manifested Himself in an- gelic forms many times, and in Jesus Christ God was manifested in the Flesh so that He could say "He that hath seen me hath seen the Father."

"As to my opponent's quotation of John 14:12. "He that believeth on me, the works that I do shall he do also; and greater works than these shall he do; because I go unto my Father," it is sufficient to say that these greater works were to be done not in human strength but through the guidance of the Holy Spirit whom Jesus promised to send into the world after He went to the Father. As to Jesus's statement that He ascended to the Father, certainly the resurrected, glorified God-Man could ascend to the throne of God, which He did, and now rules there!

My opponent quoted Luke 2:52 as an argument against the deity of Christ because it declares the boy Jesus "increased in wisdom and stature." Well, what else could He do? Since the divine became incarnate in human flesh, how else could the boy Jesus become the man Jesus except through growth?

He quoted Acts 2:22 "A man approved of God." Certainly He was that. The God-Man was approved on His manward as well as His divine side by God the Father.

He quoted first Corinthians 8:6 "To us there is but one God, the Father," etc. The real contrast, however, which Paul makes here is not between God the Father and the Lord Jesus Christ, but between the one God and the many gods of the idolaters, about whom and their meat eating, Paul was speaking. So far as any contrast between God the Father and the Lord Jesus Christ is concerned, it is merely a contrast between the Father as the ultimate source of all being and the Son as the immediate agent. Paul's acceptance of the full deity of Jesus, as expressed again and again elsewhere, makes the thought entirely untenable, therefore, that in this verse he is denying the very thing which elsewhere he explicitly accepts. After his meeting with the divine Christ on the road to Damascus, Paul could only refer to Him as "The Lord of Glory."

THE RICH YOUNG RULER AGAIN

Though I anticipated my opponent in my first speech, and gave an exposition of the passage where Jesus asked the rich young ruler: "Why calleth thou me good," my opponent tried further to play upon that passage. To show just what an extreme twisting and straining of Scripture it is to try to make that passage a disclaimer on the part of Jesus either of His sinlessness or His deity, let me quote to you the actual words which Jesus employed just after the young man had gone away. Jesus not only clearly asserted His divine authority by teaching the disciples in that connection that, because of the young man's lack of faith and his failure to follow Him, he was a lost soul, but He began immediately talking about His eternal and divine glory. He said:

"Verily I say unto you, that ye which have followed me, in the regeneration when the Son of man shall sit in the throne of glory, ye also shall sit upon twelve thrones, judging the twelve tribes of Israel." (Matt. 19:28.)

He not only asserts, right in connection with this incident of the rich young ruler, His own righteousness as the Judge of all the earth and His own divine glory, but He tells His human followers that they are to be exalted to positions of power and rulership under Him. Scripture must be interpreted in the light of Scripture, and when this entire incident is taken, instead of a garbled part of it, there is absolutely no difficulty with it. To offset my opponent's twisted, incomplete, and one-sided exposition of this passage, let me again point out that Jesus undoubtedly set himself up as a perfect model, and challenged even his foes by asking "which one of you convicteth Me of sin?" I quoted a dozen passages showing his absolute sinlessness, and my opponent did not even refer to them at all. Why?

So, also, of my opponent's quotation of the statement that Jesus could do "no mighty works," etc. The fact was not a proof of a lack of ability on His part but merely of a lack of faith on the part of the self-sufficient and unbelieving people. Faith is the condition which God the Father and Christ the Son have both laid down as prerequisite to success in spiritual works. It is a condition chosen in divine sovereign wisdom, and Christ could not do mighty works under those wrong conditions because He would not. He would not violate His own spiritual law of faith.

THE TROUBLE OVER THE TRINITY

My opponent several times questioned the doctrine of the Trinity. I would point out, however, that neither in his first speech nor in the rebuttal did he even touch the tremendous array of Scripture truth which I presented in that connection. It is not true, as my opponent asserted, that I did not give a single verse setting forth the doctrine of the trinity and that I did not give chapter and verse for my other citations. I gave enough quotations —and if time permitted could have given scores of others —showing that the truth of the trinity lies like a bedrock beneath the entire scripture. My opponent not only did not shake that truth—he did not even scratch the surface of it.

There is no force, either, to the argument that because in heathen religions there was an effort to find God, and even some gropings after the idea of a trinity, therefore, the Bible teaching of a trinity is not true. The gropings of the heathen religions after a trinity, and their inability to construct a consistent scheme of that view of the Godhead, are only evidences of a rational need and desire in human nature, which only the true Christian doctrine is able to supply; and the fact that Christianity is able to satisfy the inmost need of the believer is in itself proof of this truth. Dr. Shedd has well said, "the construction of the doctrine of the trinity started not from the consideration of the three persons, but from belief in the deity of one of them,"—namely Christ. Old Jeremy Taylor strikingly said:

"He who goes about to speak of the mystery of the trinity and does it by words and names of man's invention, talking of essence and existances, hypostacies and personalities, priority and coequality, and unity in pluralities, may amuse himself and build a tabernacle in his head, and talk something— he knows not what; but the renewed man that feels the power of the Father, to whom the Son is become wisdom, sanctification, and redemption, in whose heart the Spirit of God is shed abroad—this man, though he understands nothing of what is unintelligible, yet he alone truly understands the Christian doctrine of the Trinity."

JESUS NOT A PRODUCT OF EVOLUTION

In asserting again the idea that the Deity of the Lord robs us of the Human Jesus, my opponent referred to evolution. He asserted that Jesus came from "the chain of evolution by which we and our fathers, long ages ago, evolved from still more primitive ancestors"—that is, the beasts! This makes Jesus Christ a half-brother to the apes! In fact, his entire argument was that Jesus came by purely naturalistic means; as my opponent put it, "out of all this struggle, this drama of evolution, this chain of cause and effect." Like other Modernists, therefore, my opponent claims that Jesus Christ was merely a product of evolution. The Modernists call Him the "fairest flower of evolution." They say that He was divine, in the sense that all men have in them a spark of divinity, but that He had it in an unusual degree. But can this claim that Christ was a product of evolution stand in the face of known facts? I answer emphatically that it cannot. If He was a product of "evolution," then he came simply as the result of the combined influences of

His heredity and His environment. We cannot believe that such was the case. As to His environment, He was born in one of the most sin-cursed and degraded days in the world's history, and in the sordid, sensuous Roman Empire; and as to His heredity, if He was not what the Bible clearly claims for Him, then He was the illegitimate son of an impure woman. And from such an environment and such an heredity, we are told, sprung the profoundest wisdom, the greatest love and the most beautiful holiness that our earth has ever known! We can not accept such a contradiction!

If Jesus came by evolution, then why are we not now evolving other and higher Christs? The fundamental dogma of its devotees is that evolution is a continuous process. Then why doesn't it continue by producing higher Christs? No! Jesus Christ was not only not a product of evolution, but His life, and especially His resurrection from the dead, utterly disprove the theories of evolution. His resurrection broke the "law of death," and that miracle negatives the entire idea of evolution. How could a dead man "evolve" back into life? It is absurd!

GORILLAS AT CHURCH

We notice from the papers this morning that my opponent celebrated "Evolution Day" in his church yesterday, and that he unveiled there Mr. Carl Akeley's statue called "The Chrysalis"—a statue of a man emerging from a gorilla. This statue, though it was rejected by the Academy of Design, is supposed to give an artistic expression of man's alleged emergence from the brute.

What we need in our churches today, however, are statues of the divine Christ and not statues of men coming out of gorillas! I take this opportunity, though in perfect good humor, to rebuke my opponent for such a desecration of the sanctuary!

I noticed that both Mr. Akeley and my opponent, as reported in this morning's papers, said at the unveiling of that statue that animals are not "bestial"—that "only man is bestial," etc. What becomes, then, of the theory of evolution? We thought that we were coming up all the while! We thought that "every day in every way we are getting better and better!" But if men are more "bestial" than the animals from which they are supposed to have come, then doesn't that, in itself, prove that we are a fallen race and that we need a divine Savior? All history confirms that fact. The Bible teaches it explicitly and tells us that the God-Man, Jesus Christ, is the Savior —not a product of evolution, but "the only begotten Son of the Father."

REBUTTAL OF THE REBUTTAL

Now a few words of rebuttal of the rebuttal, and I will try to make all this "butting" just as gentle as possible, because my opponent has simply not established the affirmative of this debate at all!

My opponent, appealing still to mere rationalism, remarked that our finite minds are the "only minds we have brought with us tonight." Yes, but some of us, at least, have also brought our hearts, and once more the Bible says: "Guard thy heart with all diligence, for out of it are the issues of life."

His remarks on the Logos doctrine were entirely beside the mark. The Greek word Logos is simply one of the terms used in the Bible in connection with the eternal Son of God; and the significant fact is not how the word came to be used by the writers of the New Testament, but that it is employed to express the thought that Christ was God's Son; and, contrary to my opponent's assertions, John did specifically declare that it was the Logos, the Christ, who made the world.

My opponent had something to say about old fashioned Bible exposition, and he remarked that it "doesn't go any more." He thus endeavored skilfully to glide around an entire group of Scripture quotations, which I gave, and my argument founded upon them; but I merely point out that this clever evasion did not answer either the Bible facts or my arguments. I retort, therefore, by saying that that sort of dodging by the Modernists does not "go" either! Bible exposition and matching of verse with verse is entirely legitimate. We are commanded to "rightly divide the word of truth." That is only what Jesus did when "beginning at Moses and all the prophets, He expounded unto them in all the Scriptures the things concerning Himself" (Luke 24:27).

THE CRY FROM THE CROSS

My opponent asks again how Jesus could have been divine when He cried from the cross "My God, My God, why hast thou forsaken me?" I will tell him. In His suffering on the cross Christ, as our vicarious atonement, took the place of sinful men. The tragic and terrible result of sin is separation from God, which means spiritual death; and on the cross, as our substitute, Jesus Christ tasted death for every man. When that agonized cry was wrung from His parched lips, "My God, My God, why hast thou forsaken me?" it meant that Jesus, in that crucial hour of the atonement, was separated from God the Father, and thus He endured for all mankind that supreme penalty for human sin! Instead of being an occasion for doubt and almost for ridicule, that solemn and heart-piercing cry ought to bring us all to our knees in penitence at the foot of the cross!

That was surely a strange remark my opponent made when, in his effort to answer my argument that it was a divine and not a human love that was in Christ because He died for His enemies, he said that that was nothing— that many during the World War died for their enemies. Well, I for one, did not hear of any one, even soldiers, during the war dying for their enemies. I thought that our American soldiers crossed the seas, and endured the privations of muddy trenches, and suffered pain and even laid down their lives, in defense of human liberty and eternal righteousness, and for the sake of the loved ones at home. I did not hear of any American soldiers who died for the Germans. Only Christ, the divine Son of God, could do such a thing as that.

SUPERIORITY TO JESUS CHRIST

My opponent, commenting on "demon possession" in Christ's day, gave himself away, and nullified all of his tributes to Christ's greatness, by remarking: "But we now know better than that, and none of us believe in demon possession." There we have it! We of today are wiser than the eternal Christ! Think of the absurdity of having as an object of religious leadership one whom we know to have been more foolish than we ourselves! And like other modernists, my opponent even insinuated that Jesus was a sinner like the rest of us. This is shocking, and I very definitely rebuke it. Let no mortal man cast that reproach upon the Stainless Son of God!

I sufficiently covered the subject of miracles in my main speech. I will only remark here, therefore, that while some men have worked miracles, their miracles were performed only through the direct power of God, which was given them specifically for the working of those miracles. My opponent said that Elijah raised the dead, and gave us the scripture, (First Kings 17:22); but it does not say Elijah raised the dead; it says, "And the Lord heard the voice of Elijah, and the soul of the child came into him again, and he revived." 1st Kings 17:21 says that Elijah stretched himself upon the child three times and cried unto the Lord. And in Acts 3:12, Peter, after a miracle, asked: "Why look ye so earnestly at us, as if we made this man to walk?" But this miracle-working power was native and permanent in Jesus Christ, as was proved by the fact that He worked all sorts of miracles and was constantly performing miracles. With the will of divine authority and not calling upon God at all, He cried with a loud voice: "Lazarus come forth," and he came forth! (John 11:45). The further fact that it was through His own power that He Himself was raised from the dead proves that nothing short of the power of God Himself was in Him.

UNITARIAN "GROWTH"

And now as to the matter of the rapid growth of the great Protestant denominations and the slow growth of the Unitarians in comparison, I wish to say that I was particular not to violate the courtesies of this debate. I did not cast any "slur" on Unitarians, as my opponent alleged. I have no unkindness in my heart toward any one, but this debate is really over the issues that divide Trinitarianism from Unitarianism and, therefore, what I said was entirely legitimate in the discussion.

I wish to point out, in this connection, that during this series of four debates, I have not once mentioned my own great and glorious Baptist denomination,—eight millions strong, in this country. I have carefully avoided that, as we are discussing great and dignified religious issues, and I did not care to capitalize the debates for the profit of my own denomination.

On the other hand, in every debate, my opponent has seemingly endeavored to make capital for the Unitarians. He had the right, of course to do this, if he so desired, and I will not criticize him for getting any possible credit he can for his struggling denomination.

We have endeavored to keep these debates on a high plane, and there is nothing of unfriendliness or unkindness in what I have said. It is simply a question of facts, and as my opponent has referred repeatedly to the Unitarians in the course of the debates, it is entirely proper that I should give the real facts in the case. When in the first debate (that on the Bible), I mentioned Daniel Webster, my opponent (always very alert and very agile) in his rebuttal speech immediately claimed Webster for the Unitarians. In the second debate (that on Evolution) when the name of Charles Darwin came up, my opponent seized upon that name at once and announced Charles Darwin as a Unitarian. In the third debate (that on the Virgin Birth), my opponent took occasion to bring in the name of Dr. Elliot, and proudly paraded him as a Unitarian; and again and again, in all the debates, my opponent has referred to the proportion of Unitarians in the Hall of Fame. Well, if they have done a worthy service, I am glad they are in the Hall of Fame, but the Hall of Fame is not a religious institution. We are talking about what is being done in the realm of religion, and the facts that I gave are entirely germane to this debate. I was entirely within my rights when I referred to the undeniable fact that, just as Dr. Brown said, the body which conspicuously holds the lower view of Christ's person does not grow and increase, nor show the missionary zeal and soul winning power that characterize the denominations that hold to His deity and worship Him as God. That is what I said, and I was careful, instead of giving direct statements of my own, to quote Dr. Brown, who is not a member of my own denomination, and who is recognized as one of the fairest men in the country, and one who is certainly not given to prejudice.

POISONING THE TRUTH

It is not a question simply of "social service," or starting this reform agency, or the other, as my opponent seems to think, judging by the names of Unitarians which he mentioned, and the different social service and relief organizations with which they are connected. It is primarily a question of real religious power and of soul-winning enthusiasm and zeal; and Dr. Brown is entirely right in pointing out that only those who hold to the higher view of Christ's person have this miraculous, spiritual soul-saving power. He says further in his little book "Who is Jesus Christ":

"The denomination which holds the lower view of Christ's person [that is the Unitarians] once had a piece of property in Boston where they had been using their own humane methods to help people, and they had been doing it with unstinted generosity. But they discovered that their preaching did not lay hold of the people in that section. It was in one of the poorer parts of Boston, not far from the red light district, a place where men and women were overcome by the coarsest sins. By and by they took what was a very large-minded action. They went to the Methodists and said that they were willing to let them take the property for a nominal rental and see what they could do with it. The Methodists took the work over. Today it has become the great Morgan Memorial work in Boston. It was a very handsome action on the part of the owners of the property, but it was practically a recognition of the fact that the gospel containing the higher view of Christ's person has a power over men that their gospel has not."

This is a concrete illustration of what I mean when I say that there is a regenerating power through faith in Jesus Christ as divine. Nor does the number of Buddhists have anything to do with it. The idea of comparing the ignorant hordes of Buddhists with the enlightened hosts of Christianity! And certainly there would be fewer Christians in the world, and even more Buddhists in proportion, if we had depended on those who deny Christ's deity to send out missionaries and make converts in the heathen lands, for it is notorious that there is no real missionary zeal among those who thus deny the Lord.

My opponent boasted that many Congregationalists and others today are being won over to Unitarian views, even though they do not become Unitarians in name. This doubtless is in some part true, but only in part. Modernism did not come out of Unitarianism, but Unitarianism came out of Modernism. These forces, however, at the present time are undoubtedly working hand in hand, and if my opponent gets any satisfaction out of the fact that the Unitarians and the other Modernists are poisoning the springs of religious truth in the Protestant denominations and endeavoring to paralyze their soul-winning zeal and power, then he is welcome to that sort of glory.

ADROIT SIDE STEPPING

My opponent said that I quoted from Jesus such statements as "I am the Light," "I am the Resurrection," "Eat my Body," etc., and that I claimed, therefore, because of these passages, that Jesus was divine. You will remember, however, that I only claimed that these particular passages to which my opponent refers *implied* the deity of Jesus, and I passed then from such passages to a whole array of other passages, in which the teaching was very specific that He was more than man. Why did not my opponent reply to these other great and striking passages? He challenged me to give one scripture in which Jesus explicitly claimed that He was God, and I gave not only one but several. Why did not my opponent reply to that tremendous passage which I quoted from Revelation (1:8), in which Jesus specifically said *"I am . . . the Almighty"?*

Why did he not reply to the passage I quoted where Jesus said to the blind man that He was the Son of God and accepted the man's worship? When Jesus said that He was "the Son of God," that meant just what the Bible means elsewhere where it refers to Him as "the only begotten Son of God." It means that He was God's Son,—begotten by God only and born of the Virgin Mary. It means that through that incarnation he was God-incarnate—deity in human flesh. Such statements from Jesus claim just that, and they cannot mean anything else at all.

My opponent made no reply, in fact did not even attempt to reply, to that great passage in Romans 9:5, where it is said "And of whom concerning the flesh Christ came, who is over all God Blessed forever." Nor did he answer that other great passage from Titus (2:13), the authorized version translating it, "looking for that blessed hope and the glorious appearing of our great God and Savior, Jesus Christ,"—both God and Savior! And so with other like passages.

WHY NOT FAITH?

When it comes to Thomas, he just adroitly got around that and referred to a Roman Emperor. But we are not debating a Roman Emperor here tonight; we are debating Jesus Christ here tonight! And Thomas said to Jesus, "My Lord and my God!" and Jesus did not rebuke him and say: "I am only a man; do not worship me; that is idolatry; that would be blasphemous, Thomas." No. When Thomas said *directly to Jesus*, "My Lord and my God," Jesus, delighted by it, went on and spoke of his faith and commended it and accepted his worship, even as he accepted the worship of the blind man whose eyes he had opened! Why try to discount this clear and overwhelming passage by the assertion, that some Modernists make, that the words of Thomas were a mere exclamation—a sort of oath born of his surprise—when it is known that the Jews were not given to any such blasphemous oaths? Or, again, why try, as my opponent did, to dismiss this tremendous passage by a mere quibble over what some servile sycophant said to a rotten old Roman emperor?

I take this opportunity to enter an earnest protest against this wrong dealing with God's word. I humbly, but most emphatically, rebuke these methods as unwarranted; and I express the hope that my opponent, with his naturally noble mind, will throw off the influences which have come to him from his modernistic schooling and forego further effort to discredit scripture by such means.

Every author has a right to be allowed to say what he is trying to say, and that applies to the Holy Spirit, the Author of the Bible, as much as to any other author. Why torture and twist and distort the Old Book? Why snatch at every imaginary straw of scepticism and dust of doubt, even, in the frantic effort to discredit it? Why try to pick its every alleged flaw? Why not a little faith and trust? Why not a little appreciation for its glorious truth and beauty? Why not the acceptance of the Bible, and a word of praise for its noble fruitage of righteousness and truth down the ages? And at least why not fair treatment and square dealing with it? Why not bow with Thomas in reverence and love before Jesus Christ, instead of straining every point to explain the incident away and minimize His glory?

SUMMARY OF ARGUMENT

I will not go into further detail, therefore, in answer to the efforts of my opponent to dispose of these tremendous Bible passages which, beyond any question, teach that Jesus Christ was more than a man, that He was incarnate deity.

I have shown the overwhelming sweep of Scripture teaching, though I have by no means used all of the great passages that I might have used, and his effort to establish the mere humanity of Jesus, as against this great array of Scripture teaching, I submit has been entirely futile. I have shown in specific instances where my opponent made errors in interpretation even, when he did take up certain passages, and I have shown how he has failed to reply to the overwhelming array of scripture passages showing the fact that Jesus Christ was more than a mere man.

My opponent has given absolutely no satisfactory explanation of the tremendous paradoxes in the life of Jesus Christ, which I pointed out in the beginning, which must be satisfactorily explained if he is to be classified as only man. I presented a great array of passages showing that the general teaching of the Bible sets forth the fact that God is a Trinity and that Jesus Christ is a member of that Trinity. In the next place I then cited many Bible passages which ascribed to Jesus Christ all the attributes of God—such as wisdom, sinlessness, love and miracle working power—which prove, therefore, that he was God incarnate. I next brought to your attention the overwhelming claims which Jesus Christ made for Himself, and then I pointed out His world changing, soul-saving after-influence as a proof of His past and present deity.

To establish the affirmative of this debate, and win the decision, it was necessary not merely for my opponent to answer these specific teachings of the Bible in adequate fashion, but it was necessary for him to bring a stronger array of proof to substantiate his contention that Jesus Christ was nothing more than man.

I submit that he has not done this at all. Not only this, but I submit that he has not replied in any adequate or comprehensive way to any one of the main divisions of my arguments, much less all of them taken together.

My opponent has not only not proved the affirmative, thereby disproving the deity of Jesus, but at the really vital points he scarcely touched the true issue, and step by step I have answered what he did have to say. I therefore ask for a decision at the hands of the judges.

NOT ACADEMIC ISSUES

I wish to say, in closing, that we are not dealing with mere academic issues in these debates. These religious issues are of vital and tremendous moment. Listen: Roger Babson, one of the greatest business men of this nation, has said recently that the one hope of the world is a revival of real religion. He is right in that. He said that, my friends, as a business man.   Richard Edmonds, the editor of the Manufacturers' Record, has given utterance again and again through his great commercial paper, to the same vital truth.   What we do need today, above everything else, is a revival of faith in the divine Christ, such as laid the foundations of this nation in purity, erected family altars in our homes, made the marriage vow a sacred thing, protected us from the divorce evil, and produced a race of pure women and noble men.   Yes, what we need today is a revival of faith and love and hope—a revival of belief in Jesus Christ, the world's only Savior!

And with great solemnity of soul, and yet a deep sense of responsibility, I wish to point out the Bible teaching that there is no other name given under heaven among men whereby we must be saved except the name of Jesus. If he is not a divine Savior, then the world is still lost and without a Savior.   It is idle to speak of the unity and beauty of God apart from Jesus Christ.   The Bible clearly teaches that we cannot find and truly know God the Father without faith in Christ the Son.

Jesus Himself said, in John 14:6 "No man cometh to the Father except by me."   And John, the beloved disciple, in the fifth chapter of his first epistle says:

"Whosoever believeth that Jesus is the Christ is born of God, and every one that loveth Him that begat (that is the Father) loveth Him also that is begotten of Him" (that is the Son) (1st John 5:1).

The Bible makes very clear also the further fact that only those who are thus born again through faith in Christ the Son of God can overcome the world and live as God would have them live.   So it is written here again in I John (5:4)

"Whatsoever is born of God overcometh the world; and this is the victory that overcometh the world, even our faith."

Then John makes it clearer still, and reinforces it by asking again:

"Who is he that overcometh the world, but he that believeth that Jesus Christ is the Son of God?" (John 5:5.)

Yes, the divine Christ is the Light of the World and the only hope of lost men. And He Himself taught that unbelief in Him is the supreme sin. He said that when the Holy Spirit was come, He would reprove the world "of sin, because they believed not on me" (John 16:9). And again He said:

"For God so loved the world that he gave his only begotten Son, that whosoever believeth on him should not perish but have everlasting life. He that believeth on Him is not condemned, but he that believeth not is condemned already, because he hath not believed in the name of the only begotten Son of God. And this is the condemnation, that light is come into the world and men loved darkness rather than light because their deeds were evil." (John 3:16–19.)

A PERSONAL RELIGIOUS EXPERIENCE

I wish here to take the witness stand, if I may. In the first debate of this series my opponent quoted an experience that he had, and gave his testimony in connection with some of his doubts about prayer and about the Bible, etc., when he was a lad. I therefore accept this opportunity to give my experience. Yes, I will take the witness stand, if you please, for my Lord and Savior Jesus Christ. I was reared in a good home by godly parents, but at the age of eighteen, under the temptations of a great city, had drifted into sin. Through scepticism about these very old truths of God's Word, I had turned from my moral ideals, and was loving sin and following it. But I happened one day into the First Baptist Church of Atlanta, Ga. I heard there an old-fashioned gospel sermon. It was taken right out of the Bible, and it held up Christ on the Cross as the only hope of sinful men. The voice of

God spoke to my conscience through that sermon, and the Power of Christ changed my heart and altered the whole direction of my life. I was truly born again, I was literally made "a new creature." The sins I had loved, I hated and turned away from, and the righteousness I had despised I grew again to love and follow. What power was it that thus gave this poor man a new heart and a transformed life, if it was not the power of the divine Christ? Nothing can ever take that experience away from me. As well let an infidel tell a man who had been cured of the smallpox, that he was mistaken, that there is no such thing as smallpox and that he had not been cured, as to tell me that Jesus Christ is not the Son of God, when I know by my own experience that he worked a miracle, and by His divine Power changed my heart and redeemed my life from sin and spiritual death! I can stand, therefore, in the presence of all who doubt the deity of Jesus and say with that blind man whose eyes He opened: "One thing I know, that whereas I was blind, now I see"; and I can say also with that same man, in answer to the sceptics who doubt Jesus:

"Herein is a marvelous thing that ye know not from whence He is, and yet He hath opened mine eyes."

AGE-LONG POWER

And it is through this transforming power on individuals that Jesus Christ has wrought His miraculous changes in social customs and human institutions. Into that fierce and strenuous Roman World, surrendered to sensualism and steeped in selfishness, He sent a transforming power that softened and elevated it. That power has continued to work in all the after ages.

As we are debating here tonight, men and women and little children the world over are giving their lives in the service of Jesus Christ, because they believe Him to be divine and because they worship Him as God. Down in the slums of our great cities, out upon the frontiers of the far West, on the ships plowing distant seas, among the snows of the frozen North, in the burning heat of the tropics, in the midst of the superstitions and the sordid shame of heathenism everywhere, the ambassadors of Christ are working to carry his message and to redeem sinful men by the power of His divine love. Yes, and the round world over, they are still writing and singing in His worship the most glorious hymns that have ever sprung from the human heart—"Jesus, Lover of My Soul," "Look, Ye Saints, the Sight Is Glorious," "Nearer My God to Thee," "Love Divine All Love Excelling," "In the Cross of Christ I Glory," and hundreds of others that pour out the love of grateful souls to the divine Son of God! Instead of seeking to lessen His stature, all the children of men should strive to enlarge it and to add greater glory to His name.

It is said that when Victoria was crowned Queen of the British Empire a touching and inspiring incident occurred. Those in charge of the ceremonies in Westminster Abbey had instructed the young Queen to remain seated at the close of the exercises. When the choir reached the climax of Handel's oratorio, "The Messiah," all the people, commoners and nobility alike, were expected to stand, except the Queen, in order that royalty might be given distinction. But when the great choir reached that sublime passage, "He shall reign forever and ever," the young Queen was seen to tremble upon the throne; and then when a great rush of melody swelled out in that supremely glorious line, "Lord of Lords and King of Kings," it is said that Victoria could stand it no longer, but that she also rose from her seat upon the throne and, with tears on her cheeks and trembling hands, removed the crown from her head and bowed in humility before Him who alone has the right to expect the veneration of our minds and the homage of our hearts.

May we of today so bow before Him!

If the diadem is snatched from His brow, then the glory of our race has faded! If the scepter is taken from His hand, then our last hope is dead! Instead of carping criticism and pale-lipped doubt, as we stand in that sublime Presence, every heart should exultingly sing:

"All hail the power of Jesus' name!
Let angels prostrate fall;
Bring forth the royal diadem,
And crown Him Lord of all!

Let every kindred, every tribe
On this terrestrial ball,
To Him all majesty ascribe
And crown Him Lord of All!"

V

THE JUDGES' REPORT

Upon the return of the judges, Judge Almet F. Jenks delivered the opinion of the Judges as follows:

JUDGE JENKS: Mr. Chairman, ladies and gentlemen: My associates have honored me by asking that I should announce the unanimous decision of the judges. It seems germane that I should read the question debated tonight, although you have heard it before: "Resolved, that Jesus Christ was Entirely Man Instead of Incarnate Deity." This was qualified by the statement which represents the concensus of the debaters: "It is understood between us that the issue of this debate is on the Deity of Jesus Christ. It is admitted by both sides that He was truly man, but Dr. Straton takes the position that He was more than man, that He was also incarnate deity—the God-Man. This Mr. Potter denies, and that is the issue of the debate."

The Judges unanimously agree that the negative, as presented by Dr. Straton, has prevailed in the debate, and our judgment is based upon the relative merits of the presentation or argument.

TITLES IN THIS SERIES

The Evangelical Matrix
1875-1900

■ 1.William R. Moody
D. L. Moody,
New York, 1930

■ 2. Joel A. Carpenter, ed.
The Premillennial Second Coming:
Two Early Champions
New York, 1988

■ 3. - 6. Donald W. Dayton, ed.
The Prophecy Conference Movement
New York, 1988

■ 7. Delavan Leonard Pierson
Arthur T. Pierson
New York, 1912

■ 8. Helen Cadbury Alexander Dixon
A. C. Dixon, A Romance of Preaching
New York, 1931

■ 9. Amzi C. Dixon
The Person and Ministry of the Holy Spirit
Baltimore, 1890

■ 10. Arthur T. Pierson, ed.
The Inspired Word: A Series of Papers and
Addresses Delivered at the Bible Inspiration Conference,
Philadelphia, 1887
London, 1888

■ 11. Moody Bible Institute Correspondence
Dept. *First Course — Bible Doctrines, Instructor—*
R. A. Torrey; Eight Sections with Questions,
Chicago, 1901

The Formation of
A Fundamentalist Agenda
1900-1920

■ 12. Amzi C. Dixon,
Evangelism Old and New,
New York, 1905

■ 13. William Bell Riley
The Finality of the Higher Criticism;
or, The Theory of Evolution and False Theology
Minneapolis, 1909

■ 14.-17 George M. Marsden, ed.
The Fundamentals: A Testimony to the Truth
New York, 1988

Fundamentalism Versus Modernism
1920-1935

■ 24. Joel A. Carpentar, ed.
Modernism and Foreign Missions:
Two Fundamentalist Protests
New York, 1988

■ 25. John Horsch
Modern Religious Liberalism: The Destructiveness
and Irrationality of Modernist Theology
Scottsdale, Pa., 1921

■ 26. Joel A. Carpenter,ed.
Fundamentalist vesus Modernist
The Debates Between
John Roach Stratton and Charles Francis Potter
New York, 1988

■ 27. Joel A. Carpenter, ed.
William Jennings Bryan on
Orthodoxy, Modernism, and Evolution
New York, 1988

■ 28. Edwin H. Rian
The Presbyterian Conflict
Grand Rapids, 1940

Sectarian Fundamentalism
1930-1950

■ 29. Arno C. Gaebelein
Half a Century: The Autobiography of a Servant
New York, 1930

■ 30. Charles G. Trumball
Prophecy's Light on Today
New York, 1937

■ 31. Joel A. Carpenter, ed.
Biblical Prophecy in an Apocalyptic Age:
Selected Writings of Louis S. Bauman
New York, 1988

■ 32. Joel A. Carpenter, ed.
Fighting Fundamentalism:
Polemical Thrusts of the 1930s and 1940s
New York, 1988

■ 33. *Inside History of First Baptist Church, Fort*
Worth, and Temple Baptist Church, Detroit:
Life Story of Dr. J. Frank Norris
Fort Worth, 1938

■ 34. John R. Rice
The Home — Courtship, Marriage, and Children: A
Biblical Manual of Twenty -Two Chapters
on the Christian Home.
Wheaton, 1945

■ 35. Joel A. Carpenter, ed.
Good Books and the Good Book: Reading Lists by
Wilbur M. Smith, Fundamentalist Bibliophile
New York, 1988

■ 36. H. A. Ironside
Random Reminiscences from Fifty Years of Ministry
New York, 1939

■ 37 Joel A. Carpenter,ed.
*Sacrificial Lives: Young Martyrs
and Fundamentalist Idealism*
New York, 1988.

Rebuilding, Regrouping, & Revival
1930-1950

■ 38. J. Elwin Wright
*The Old Fashioned Revival Hour
and the Broadcasters*
Boston, 1940

■ 39. Joel A. Carpenter, ed.
*Enterprising Fundamentalism:
Two Second-Generation Leaders*
New York, 1988

■ 40. Joel A. Carpenter, ed.
Missionary Innovation and Expansion
New York, 1988

■ 41. Joel A. Carpenter, ed.
*A New Evangelical Coalition: Early Documents
of the National Association of Evangelicals*
New York, 1988

■ 42. Carl McIntire
Twentieth Century Reformation
Collingswood, N. J., 1944